Know-So Religion

The Witness of the Spirit
With Special Emphasis Upon John
Wesley's Perspective

by
Robert E. England, D. Min.
President, Allegheny Wesleyan College

Schmul Publishing Company
Salem, Ohio

Published by Schmul Publishing Co.
PO Box 716
Salem, Ohio USA

Printed in the United States of America

Permission to quote from the following copyrighted versions of the Bible is acknowledged with appreciation:

The *New American Standard Bible* (NASB), © the Lockman Foundation, 1960, 1962, 1968, 1971, 1972, 1973, 1975.

The Holy Bible, New International Version (NIV), copyright © 1978 by the New York International Bible Society.

The *New King James Version* (NKJ), copyright © 1982 by Thomas Nelson, Inc.

All Biblical citations are from the King James Version unless otherwise indicated.

ISBN 0-88019-451-0

10 9 8 7 6 5 4 3 2 1

Contents

Dedication

To my wife Marilyn,
>   who has been a loving companion
>   and gracious helpmeet throughout our marriage;

To our children,
>   Joanna and Brent, Becky and Dan, Danny and Ronda,
>   Robbie and Rachel, and Kristin,
>   who have brought much joy to our home;

To my mother,
>   Mrs. Maxine D. England,
>   who has taught me the value of selflessness and hard work;

To my father-in-law,
>   Mr. Frank Hofacker,
>   who has led a quiet, Christian life with constant cheerfulness;

And to all seekers after God
>   who desire to know Him
>   and enjoy an abiding witness of His Spirit.

Acknowledgements

Grateful acknowledgement is given to the faculty and library personnel of Nazarene Theological Seminary. Special recognition is due to Dr. Wesley Tracy who inspired me to make John Wesley's life and teaching an integral part of my research and writing for this project. Appreciation is also extended to Dr. Ed Robinson, Director of the Doctor of Ministry Program at NTS, for helpful guidance in both content and design. Gratitude is also due to Dr. Richard Neiderhiser, Associate Director of the project. Thanks is also due to my friend, Rev. Edsel Trouten, for his repeated encouragement and also for his suggestion that the Puritan influence upon Wesley be incorporated into the study. Appreciation is also due to my former student, Rev. Wallace Thornton, Jr., for providing various materials to facilitate my research, as well as other assistance. Thanks should be given to my friend, Rev. Larry Smith, for his helpful dialogue concerning early Methodism. Gratitude must also be expressed for my In-Parish Committee, comprised of Rev. Kenneth Manning, Professor Garen Wolf, Mrs. Beverly Rhoades, Mr. Ron Shew, and Mr. James Orndorff, who met with me several times and gave me several insightful suggestions. Special thanks to Mr. James Kunselman for his computer assistance.

Special thanks is due to several friends who have taken time to read the manuscript and to write in its behalf. Thanks to Dr. Richard S. Taylor for writing the Foreword; to Dr. William Kostlevy, the Preface; to Dr. Leonard Sankey, the Introduction; to Rev. Wallace Thornton, Jr., the Historian's Prologue; and to Dr. Noel Scott and Dr. Ed Robinson, endorsements.

Finally, and perhaps most of all, acknowledgment is due my wife Marilyn, who has been my best critic and encourager. Without her support the project would not have been completed. Her numerous suggestions and assistance have been invaluable. She has typed all of the rough drafts and the final copy as well.

Foreword

"I want that faith which none can have without knowing that he hath it," is an early plaint of the young Wesley (pg. 84). His quest would culminate at Aldersgate (May 24, 1738) when his heart was "strangely warmed," and he *knew* his sins were forgiven, "even his." In that moment he experienced what he had long searched for, the faith of assurance. And thus was born one of Methodism's surest hallmarks, the privilege and normality of the witness of the Spirit—called by common folks throughout many generations, a "know-so religion."

But in Wesley's phrasing of his search was also a hint of the tendency to identify faith with the witness of the Spirit, making them two aspects of the same thing. At that early stage of his thinking he came to agree with Böhler's position that faith was "an instantaneous work," ..."given in a moment" and evidenced by instant turning "from darkness to light, from sin and misery to righteousness and joy in the Holy Ghost" (pg. 85).

In thus seeing faith as a gift instead of a voluntary action as a condition for the witness, a shade of Calvinism is betrayed, since Calvinism sees conversion as a unilateral action of the Spirit in infusing faith and spiritual life concomitantly upon the elect.

Yet the doctrine Wesley learned from Böhler was hedged against antinomianism by its perception of saving faith as "inseparable from a pardon for all past, and freedom from all present sins" (pg. 88).

With great skill England traces Wesley's spiritual struggles even after Aldersgate, as he gradually acquires an understanding of the principles which govern the maintenance of assurance and of its place in a victorious Christian life. And, as England explains, "Wesley came to the conclusion that justifying faith is not necessarily connected with assurance" (pg. 91). In other words, while normative it is not absolutely indispensable to salvation. Susannah Wesley did not receive the witness of the Spirit until about four years before her death, but it is doubtful if the mature Wesley would have considered her lost had she died before that event.

Wesley's own experience also illustrates the counter peril of an over-emphasis on assurance, by his own excessive dependence on feeling, as evidenced by his strange denial January 4, 1739, that he was even a Christian, because he was not conscious of "possessing the love of God, the peace of God, or the joy of the Holy Ghost in his heart" (pg. 92).

Yet in spite of such occasional waverings, Wesley continued to teach that sinners could not only be forgiven but know it. This certainty was the normal privilege not only of justifying grace but sanctifying grace as well.

While England finds that Wesley's Journals provide consistent support for his convictions respecting the witness of the Spirit, he does not find obsessive attention given therein to the subject. It is to Wesley's Sermons that England turns for doctrinal emphasis and clarification. Speaking of the sermon titles of Volume I, England observes: "One can readily see that Wesley's great emphasis is upon helping people enter into experiential, heart-religion" (pg. 106).

England attaches considerable importance—and correctly so—to the fact that the two major sermons specifically on the subject of the Witness do not alter substantively though they are twenty years apart. However, England notices a shift in Wesley's placement of the doctrine. In 1745 (in a letter) he calls assurance "the *main* doctrine of the Methodists," whereas in 1767 he calls it "one grand part of the testimony which God has given (the Methodists)."

Perhaps also England makes a distinct contribution to the doctrine by raising the issue respecting Wesley's use of the preposition *to* instead of *with* as translation of *sum* in *summartureo*, when he translates Romans 8:16 by "the Spirit of God directly witnesses *to my spirit*" instead of "*with my spirit*," since in doing so he was going against standard usage, and thereby laying the ground for an unnecessarily sharp cleavage between the immediate witness of the Spirit and the indirect witness of the believer's spirit (see Ftn. 95, pg. 126). In other words, the dual witness should be viewed as a joint witness, not two tandem witnesses. The evidence of life change will be confirmatory of the one witness.

The support which England finds for the doctrine of assurance in the voluminous correspondence is both fascinating and illuminating. Wesley's letters highlight his warmth of affection, his great counseling wisdom, but also the consistency of his pressing his correspondents not to rest until they knew for sure their sins were forgiven, or that they were sanctified entirely.

It is difficult to do justice to this work in a Foreword or exaggerate the measure of its importance for the contemporary evangelical world (not just Wesleyan). It is comprehensive in covering the controversies concerning the doctrine of the witness of the Spirit in Wesley's time and also in demonstrating beyond any doubt that Wesley never slackened in his exhortations to seek this assurance. This passion was undiminished even at the very end of his life.

Our debt to England for this competent and comprehensive work is underscored by the fact that it is the first major systematic treatment of the subject since Arthur Yates' doctoral dissertation in 1952, and *that* was the first—as far as is known—for two hundred years.

—RICHARD S. TAYLOR, TH.D.
Professor Emeritus
Nazarene Theological Seminary
Author, *A Right Conception of Sin*;
Understanding Ourselves; et al.

Preface

Given its central role in the history of Pietism and Methodism, it is ironic that the experience of the "witness of the Spirit" has received so little attention from serious students of the Evangelical revival and Methodism. As Wesley himself insisted, it "is one grand part of the testimony given them [the Methodists] to bear to all humanity." Nevertheless the emphasis upon experience implicit in Wesley's understanding of the "witness of the Spirit" led to repeated charges that Wesley's movement encouraged rank fanaticism. In spite of Wesley's denial and the denials of his spiritual heirs the charge has plagued Wesleyanism throughout its history. As recently as the early twentieth century, Borden Parker Bowne, perhaps the father of theological liberalism in Methodism, would dismiss evangelical emphasis upon a subjective sense of acceptance with God as unworthy of the rationality of modern society.

At the same time, it is clear that Wesley's own experience of assurance or the "witness of the Spirit" at Aldersgate transformed his ministry from one of self-absorbed legalism into a dynamic movement whose impact continues to be felt around the world. In the movement he led and inspired, the experience of assurance of acceptance with God has continued to be a common reality in the lives of believers. In his thoughtful *The Story of God*, theologian Michael Lodahl asked the question, why did Wesley believe that such an experience was possible? In response, Lodahl noted that Wesley found the experience in the Bible, most notably in Romans 8. "The Spirit himself bears witness with our spirit that we are children of God."

Fittingly, Robert England begins his thorough study of this neglected Christian experience with the exposition of Scripture. Drawing from the principle New Testament passages, Romans 8:15-16; Galatians 4:4-7; I John 3: 24; 4:13; and 5:10, England's careful exegetical study sets a solid foundation for the historical analysis that follows. Turning to Wesley, England locates the roots to Wesley's views in Puritan-Anglican authorities he read and edited for inclusion in the *Christian Library*. After a careful study of Wesley's own experience, England explores his journals, sermons and letters. I am especially impressed with his use of Wesley's letters of spiritual advice. England skillfully draws on Wesley's insightful commentary on spiritual experience in the Christian life. These letters of encouragement provide Wesley's heirs with a very valuable resource for Christian nurture.

As England concludes, "Wesleyan theology…is a theology of hope."

As with any substantial work of scholarship, England has invested years in serious research. The fruits of his labor will enrich future generations of Christians. Although scholars will appreciate his thorough analysis, the work will also greatly aid pastors as a resource in their counseling of sensitive souls. This is a book to be read prayerfully and carefully. I cannot recommend it too highly.

—WILLIAM KOSTLEVY
Archivist, B.L. Fisher Library
Asbury Theological Seminary

Introduction

The publication of Robert England's book on the Witness of the Spirit is a matter of vast importance to the evangelical world. The Witness of the Spirit is an essential doctrine and yet, often, it has been surrounded with confusion and mired in sectarian debate. I believe that Dr. England's treatise will be a positive contribution to illuminating this glorious scriptural truth.

An extensive bibliography demonstrates the wide spectrum of sources from which Dr. England draws his conclusions and delineates his position. His careful study into the writings and preaching material of John Wesley provides the reader with an enormous wealth of material on this important theme from this pivotal figure in church history. Dr. England's New Testament word studies help to clarify the teaching of scripture.

Robert England is a careful student of the Word, an unwearying researcher, and is superbly qualified to bring us a clear, cogent, scriptural, and theologically sound discussion regarding the Witness of the Spirit. It is a theme which is invested with the eternal well-being of those who apprehend its truth.

I warmly commend Dr. England for his decision to publish his efforts for the benefit of all, and I strongly recommend the book to all who want to assure themselves of the biblical teaching of the Witness of the Spirit.

—LEONARD SANKEY
General Secretary,
Interchurch Holiness Convention

Historian's Prologue

Late nineteenth-century Methodism experienced a climactic theological and cultural shift that was marked by loss of the traditional emphasis on Scriptural holiness among its chief educational and hierarchical architects. This rejection of entire sanctification as an instantaneous, definite work of grace subsequent to conversion fueled the formation of a Holiness Movement that, although maintaining many members among Methodism, the Holiness Movement has thus sought to perpetuate the original theological and spiritual distinctives of the great revival that God set in motion through such instruments as John and Charles Wesley.

The conflict over entire sanctification within Methodism, and the subsequent efforts of the Holiness Movement to champion this doctrine and experience, has been vigorously examined by scholars for over fifty years. However, another essential component of early Methodism has been largely ignored by historians and theologians (and perhaps even more seriously, pastors and evangelists)—the Wesleyan emphasis on the witness of the Spirit. In actuality, this foundational Biblical tenet has been, as G. W. Wilson thus observed over a century ago in the *Christian Witness,* that "there is great danger to-day that this glorious doctrine, like that of entire sanctification, is being eclipsed... If this truth is misrepresented or denied, a vital religion must be supplanted by a nominal one. This condition exists already in many churches" (June 21, 1900, p. 2).

This warning seems as timely now as when originally published. It ought especially to resonate among those who seek to herald the Wesleyan message of holiness of heart and life. Ultimately, will the doctrine and experience of entire sanctification prosper if the doctrine of the witness of the Spirit languishes? Perhaps this lies at the core of much spiritual lethargy today. This doctrine thus demands renewed appreciation among all Christians, particularly the heirs of Wesley in the Holiness Movement, who seek to declare faithfully the whole counsel of God.

Dr. Robert England provides in this book a wonderful instrument to facilitate such renewed appreciation for the Wesleyan doctrine of assurance. His thorough examination of the primary Biblical passages treating the witness of the Spirit underscores Wesley's commitment to the authority of Scripture. These chapters provide an excellent introduction to Paul's writings in Romans and Galatians, extensive insight into the Person and work of the Holy Spirit, and lucid delineation of progress in the Christian walk. The place of tradition, reason, and experience in illuminating Wesley's understanding of Biblical Christianity is apparent through the book. The discussion of Puritan contributions, modified by the early church fathers and Anglican theologians, proves especially enlightening, showing the breadth and depth of Wesley's reading and dependence on (as well as differences with) other divines. The examination of Wesley's Journals, Sermons, and Letters reflects his preoccupation with practical theology.

Dr. England's interpretation of Wesley and his sources reflects the author's many years of teaching, evangelizing, and pastoring. Those who have sat under his teaching or preaching will recognize here the same spiritual vitality linked with vigorous logic that has characterized his ministry in pulpit and classroom. While employing the scholarly analysis requisite for in-depth theological study, including insights based on his mastery of New Testament Greek, Brother England keeps pastoral concern and evangelistic application foremost. Ultimately, he, like Wesley, seeks to help his readers and those they influence to have assurance of their heavenly citizenship. This remarkable balance between the academic and the pastoral, mirroring qualities that the author has discovered in Wesley, commends this book to both scholars and laypersons. All who are interested in having a meaningful relationship with God should read it with profit; especially pastors, evangelists, teachers, and all others entrusted with the ministry of soul care. I highly recommend it to seekers after God, believing that, like its author, it can serve as a tool for revival of assurance in an age of uncertainty.

—WALLACE THORNTON, JR.
Author, *Radical Righteousness;*
From Glory to Glory; et al.

Pastor's Prologue

As a young teenager I had a dynamic conversion experience. The witness of the Spirit was "bright and clear." The Kingdom of God had indeed been set up in my heart, being manifested by "righteousness, peace, and joy in the Holy Ghost" (Rom. 14:17b).

It seemed like I was on "Cloud Nine," in the spiritual heavenlies, as it were, for many, many days. Finally, my feet touched the earth. Oh, how I loved the Lord! Often I had wonderful seasons of prayer when an hour would pass so quickly.

When my heart was flooded with love, joy, and peace, it was so easy to be on top of all my circumstances. But when those wonderful feelings were withdrawn and heaviness pressed down my spirit, it was easy to question why I was in such a state and to listen to subtle temptations of our great Adversary without realizing the implication to my spiritual well-being.

On two different occasions in my early journey with God, after passing through severe testing when I could not sense the witness of His Spirit nor joy in my soul, I cast away my confidence because I thought I could not have such feelings and be right with God. If only I had had a soul friend who could have guided me past the "hiding rocks and treacherous shoal" of unbelief. For when I cast away my confidence in a pardoning God, my soul was then plunged into deep darkness. Little did I know that "without faith it is impossible to please Him…" (Heb. 11:6). I did not realize that walking by faith is not synonymous with walking by inward feelings.

Having been involved in evangelism for many years, I sometimes see earnest seekers who pray and pray and never seem to find inward rest, peace, and the Spirit's witness. There may be numerous reasons why assurance is not obtained, but clearly one is that of unbelief.

I remember a dear man who sought to be saved in one of my revival meetings. I think he was at the altar every time an altar call was given. He prayed earnestly but could never seem to find victory. But the tragic thing is this, he had been seeking for months and months, perhaps for a couple of years.

When one is struggling to find assurance, he needs the skillful guidance of a pastoral theologian, a soul friend, whose work has been wrought in the crucible of life and faith. Such a man was John Wesley.

Mr. Wesley knew what it was to search earnestly for spiritual assurance. When he was nearly thirty-two years of age, he heard his father say, "The inward witness, son, the inward witness, ...that is the proof, the strongest proof, of Christianity."[1] These pungent words of Rev. Samuel Wesley uttered on his deathbed to his son John, succinctly express the basic thrust of this dissertation.

John Wesley admitted that he did not understand at the time what his father was saying, although he had used the expression more than once.[2] John had been an earnest seeker after God for nearly ten years by the time his father died on April 25, 1735. His father's words would become much more meaningful in approximately three years, when John would find "the inward witness" at Aldersgate on May 24, 1738.

From Aldersgate until his death on March 2, 1791, the doctrine of the witness of the Holy Spirit with man's spirit was one of Wesley's strongest emphases. In a letter to John Smith dated December 30, 1745, Wesley calls the witness of the Spirit "the main doctrine of the Methodists."[3] About twenty-two years later, in his second sermon entitled "The Witness of the Spirit," Wesley modifies his statement by calling the witness "one grand part of the testimony which God has given them"[4] (i.e., the Methodists). As Wesley saw it, one of the tasks of the Methodists was "to understand, explain, and defend this doctrine" of the witness, "which had been for many years wellnigh lost and forgotten."[5]

Among all evangelical scholars in the Christian church no name is more synonymous with the doctrine of the witness of the Spirit (in the sense of certifying one's acceptance with God) than that of John Wesley.

A resurgence of interest in Wesley and his theology has taken place during the past century, particularly during the last fifty years. Special interest has often centered on Wesley's conversion experience, which can hardly be separated from the doctrine of the witness.[6] With the three-hundredth anniversary of Wesley's birth near at hand, interest will doubtless increase.

The main purpose of the dissertation is to explore the biblical doctrine of the witness of the Spirit/assurance with special emphasis upon John Wesley's understanding and teaching of the doctrine.

Since Scripture is Wesley's final authority for doctrine and duty, the first two chapters deal with the biblical basis. In order to determine the validity of the texts Wesley used to support his position on the witness, five different Greek texts were analyzed to see if there is a strong uniform foundation in the original text for the doctrine of the witness.

Chapter One treats Wesley's key text for the witness, namely, Romans 8:15-16. Fortunately, the various Greek texts are in substantial agreement one with another, differing only in accenting and spelling.

In order to better understand Romans 8:15-16, an examination is made of the context, both broad and immediate. Keywords are dealt with, including sin, law, grace, righteousness, justification, faith, spirit, flesh, and adoption. Of particular interest is the distinction between the direct and the indirect witness of the Spirit.

Chapter Two is a continuation of the first chapter. The major discussion centers around Wesley's second important text, Galatians 4:4-7. Brief attention is also given to a few Johannine texts which deal with assurance. The same pattern is followed, examining the broad and immediate contexts before the text itself. The evidence is conclusive that God has provided a joint-witness, whereby one is assured of being in a justified/regenerated relationship with God.

Although each of Wesley's parents chose to leave the ranks of the Puritans and join the Anglican Church, the influence of Puritanism was bound to impact them and their children. When John Wesley compiled a fifty-volume set called *A Christian Library*, he chose more authors from the Puritans than from the Anglicans. Chapter Three deals with the Puritan influence on Wesley regarding the witness. The Puritans wrote profusely on the doctrine, and while they differed one from another, it is quite obvious that he learned from them and could agree in many ways.

If one wants to know the chronology of events in Wesley's life, he must read his *Journals*. If one wants to understand Wesley's theology, he must study his *Sermons*. If one wants to see Wesley as a pastoral theologian with the tender heart of a shepherd, he must read his *Letters*.

Chapter Four focuses on Wesley's *Journal* entries. The objective is to trace his experiences prior to, at, and after Aldersgate . His spiritual pursuits, struggles, insights, and victories are disclosed in his own language. Aldersgate is a crucial point in Wesley's search for assurance. Subsequent to this crisis experience, his ministry will be seen to bear much fruit (in contrast to little or no fruit prior to Aldersgate) and also will be a great factor in the outbreak and continuation of the Evangelical Revival during the next fifty years.

Sermons are very important in early Methodism. Wesley chose the sermon form to be the main medium to express and teach his theology. Above all else, Wesley was a preacher, so some attention is given to him as a preacher in Chapter Five; but the major interest lies in examining his two sermons on the witness, published more than twenty years apart (1746, 1767), noting similarities, dissimilarities, and new or added insights.

Chapters Six and Seven explore Wesley's letters which depict him as a spiritual director, a soul friend to some sixteen hundred correspondents over a period spanning more than a half century.

The witness of the Spirit/assurance is a topic Wesley mentions frequently in his letters (often using language other than "the witness of the Spirit" or "assurance"). How patient and kind is Wesley, the letter-writer, as he encourages serious seekers after God to pray for and expect, even now, the witness of God's Spirit with one's own spirit that he is a child of God.

The entire church world is indebted to John Wesley for emphasizing the fact that God's plan of salvation is attested to by God's Spirit bearing witness with one's spirit, resulting in "righteousness, and peace, and joy in the Holy Spirit" (Rom. 14:17b NKJ).

What a glorious message of heartfelt, knowable salvation that delivers from all sin. Every true Christian is privileged to proclaim such good news, especially those of us who are engaged in pastoral and evangelistic ministries.
—ROBERT E. ENGLAND

Endnotes

1. John Wesley, *The Works of John Wesley;* begun as "The Oxford Edition of the Works of John Wesley" (Oxford: Clarendon Press, 1975-1983); continued as "The Bicentennial Edition of the Works of John Wesley" (Nashville: Abingdon Press, 1984) 26:288-89 (hereafter cited as *Works).* Since this edition is not yet completed, it will sometimes be necessary to use the edition by Thomas Jackson.

2. Ibid.

3. Ibid., 26:182.

4. Ibid., 1:285.

5. Ibid., 1:285-86.

6. A cursory check on titles in the *Wesleyan Theological Journal* during the past few years reveals an increased interest in Wesley, and especially in regard to his conversion and the doctrine of assurance. For example, see Rob L. Staples, "John Wesley's Doctrine of the Holy Spirit," *Wesleyan Theological Journal* 21, nos. 1 and 2 (spring-fall, 1986): 91ff; see also Kenneth J. Collins, "Twentieth-Century Interpretations of John Wesley's Aldersgate Experience: Coherence or Confusion?" *Wesleyan Theological Journal* 24 (1989): 18ff; also see David L. Cubie, "Placing Aldersgate in John Wesley's Order of Salvation," *Wesleyan Theological Journal* 24 (1989): 32ff; see also W. Stephen Gunter, "Personal and Spiritual Knowledge: Kindred Spirits in Polanyian and Wesleyan Epistemology," *Wesleyan Theological Journal* 35, No. 1 (spring, 2000): 130ff.

The number of scholarly books on Wesley of recent publication also point to an obviously heightened interest. One example is Randy L. Madox, ed. *Aldersgate Reconsidered* (Nashville: Kingswood Books, 1990); also see Kenneth J. Collins and John H. Tyson, eds. *Conversion in the Wesleyan Tradition* (Nashville: Abingdon Press, 2001).

Chapter One

A Biblical Basis for the Witness
of the Spirit: Part I

In the Preface to his first volume of sermons John Wesley revealed the inmost thoughts of his heart. Possessing a keen awareness that he would soon pass through this life and then face an "unchangeable eternity," Wesley expressed one supreme desire: he wanted to know "the way to heaven; how to land safe on that happy shore."[1]

Wesley then noted that God had descended from heaven to teach the way one must journey in order to reach the heavenly land. Furthermore, God had written about the way to heaven in a book, namely the Bible, concerning which Wesley cried out: "O give me that book! At any price give me the book of God! I have it. Here is knowledge enough for me. Let me be homo unius libri."[2]

Few of Wesley's contemporaries were more avid readers from more diverse sources than he. Nevertheless, Mr. Wesley could boldly, yet sincerely, say, "Let me be a man of one book." From the context in which he made this statement it is clear that he believed the sacred Scriptures alone can teach us the way to heaven. For Wesley, the Bible was the only authoritative source for both doctrine and life.

The greatest issue facing any mortal being is that of preparation for an eternal world. In light of the serious consequences connected with eternity one must not follow "cunningly devised fables" manufactured by human beings, but rather the "more sure word of prophecy" inspired by God Himself (2 Pet. 1:16, 19; 2 Tim. 3:16).

God has provided this "more sure word" in the sixty-six books of the Bible. If one desires to formulate correct theological positions on the subject of salvation or other doctrinal issues, he must begin with the written word of God. Only as one's beliefs and teachings are in alignment with Scripture can a Christian theology be developed.

The purpose of this chapter and the following one is to analyze key biblical passages which either assert or suggest that there is such a phenomenon as a witness of the Holy Spirit with the spirit of one who has come to God through Christ in order to be justified/regenerated. The thesis of this dissertation is that such a witness provides the seeker with an assurance that God's grace has been conferred upon him.

Romans 8:15-16

These are the classic verses of Scripture upon which the doctrine of the witness of the Holy Spirit to one's conversion is based. This passage, along with those which will follow in the next chapter, will be examined under a three-fold division.

Greek Texts

A comparison of several Greek texts reveals remarkable agreement in Romans 8:15, 16.[3] In fact, the only differences relate to spelling and accenting. In three of the texts ἀλλά (v. 15) retains the final vowel, whereas in two others it is elided. In accenting the word Ἀββά, four of the texts cited accent the ultima; but only two of them agree in using a grave, while one text uses the acute and another, the circumflex. One text uses no accent.

Verse sixteen is exactly the same in each of the Greek texts cited, except for a minor difference in the spelling of one word. The verb which means "to bear witness with" is spelled συμμαρτυρεῖ in each text except that of Westcott and Hort, where it is spelled συνμαρτυρεῖ Liddell and Scott point out that σύν, when used in composition before β, μ, π, φ, or ψ becomes συμ.[4]

Apparently Wesley used a Greek text which was slightly different for verse sixteen from the ones cited above, since he translated the opening words as "the same Spirit, whereas most translators render it as "the Spirit Himself."[5] In all the texts mentioned above the term αὐτό is used in the predicate position; thus αὐτὸ τὸ πνεῦμα, which gives an intensive meaning: "the Spirit Himself." To translate as Wesley did would indicate that αὐτό was placed in the attributive position; hence τὸ αὐτὸ πνεῦμα, which would be rendered as "the same Spirit."[6]

In examining all of the variations cited above, one fact is most obvious: none of them affects the basic meaning of the passage. It is the Holy Spirit Himself Who bears witness with one's human spirit, and He is the same Spirit as the Spirit of adoption mentioned in verse fifteen.

Context

Romans 8:16 is the most explicit verse in all Scripture for identifying the witness of the Spirit to one's conversion. This text cannot be properly treated nor understood apart from its context. Before an examination is made of the immediate context, brief attention needs to be given to the larger context, particularly the chapters which precede the text. Since the doctrine of the witness

of the Spirit entails much subjectivity, it will be necessary to give careful attention to the more objective components that are treated in the context of this and
other Scripture passages in order to sharpen the focus on the meaning of the
Spirit's witness.

Broad Context

Unlike the other churches to whom Paul had written, he had not visited the
saints at Rome when he penned the epistle to them. One would therefore expect
Romans to be a full and well-balanced epistle which would clearly explain the
good news of salvation and related doctrines, as well. J. A. Beet considers
Romans to be the "most general and complete" of all the Pauline epistles and
"the Gospel according to Paul."[7] George Allen Turner believes Romans was
the "first systematic theology of the Christian Church."[8]

In order to understand Romans 8:15, 16, one must first be acquainted with
Paul's teachings in chapters one through seven. In these chapters he has much
to say regarding sin, law, grace, righteousness, justification, and faith.

Sin. Paul's treatment of sin (1:18-3:20) is doubtless the most intensive discussion of any single passage in either Testament of Scripture. In this lengthy
passage Paul proposes and proves that all people, Jews and Gentiles, are sinners before God. God's wrath is revealed against all ungodliness and
unrighteousness (1:18). Even the heathen who have never seen a Bible or heard
a Gospel message will be held accountable to God because He has revealed
Himself in nature (1:20) and through laws written upon human hearts as well as
through the conscience (2:15). The Jews have been the recipients of God's law
in the Holy Scriptures (3:2; 9:4) and therefore will be judged by the law (2:12b).
The law of God, whether it was the written law given to the Jews or that which
was written upon the hearts of heathen, has been transgressed by everyone, for
"all have sinned and come short of the glory of God" (3:23).

Law. The Apostle Paul also discusses the significance of the law. He notes that
"the Law is holy, and the commandment is holy and righteous and good" (7:12
NASB). Paul asserts that transgression cannot take place except where there is
law (4:15b). In describing his own personal experience Paul said: "I would not
have known sin except through the law. For I would not have known covetous-
ness unless the law had said, "You shall not covet" (7:7 NKJ).

While the law is used by God to bring a sinner to an awareness of sin, the
law does not have power to save from sin, for "no one will be declared righteous in his sight by observing the law" (3:20a NIV).

Grace. A third important doctrine for Paul is grace. This term expresses God's
favor and goodness toward undeserving sinners. In his epistle to the Ephesians

Paul describes grace as "the gift of God" (Eph. 2:8c). Unlike one who keeps the law and boasts of doing so, no one can boast in himself concerning grace, for it is not of one's own self but wholly of God. Therefore Paul declares that sinners are "justified freely by His grace through the redemption that is in Christ Jesus" (Rom. 3:24 NKJ). Whatever has been lost through the fall of the first Adam has been more than offset by the free gift of the second Adam (5:12-21). What a blessed fact is exclaimed in Romans 5:20b: "...where sin abounded, grace did much more abound."

Righteousness. Another significant term in Romans is that of righteousness. After describing the gospel of Christ as "the power of God to salvation for everyone who believes," Paul then adds these informative words: "...for in it the righteousness of God is revealed from faith to faith; as it is written, 'The just shall live by faith'" (1:16, 17 NKJ).

The phrase "righteousness of God" has been the subject of much discussion among Bible scholars.[9] Does it denote one of God's attributes, or does it express the work God performs in a sinner when he is regenerated by the grace and power of God? As in many areas of theological study, it is not a matter of *either/or*, but rather *both/and*. God is both righteous in His essential being, and He makes sinners righteous when they come to Him in faith.

In discussing God's righteousness Paul asserts that it is "apart from the law" (3:21 NKJ), "through faith in Jesus Christ" (3:22 NKJ), imputed to one who believes God (4:3, 5, 9, 11), a gift (5:17), related to grace (5:21), and connected to obedience (6:16).

Paul sums up the predicament of the Israelites in Romans 10:3 thus: "For not knowing about God's righteousness, and seeking to establish their own, they did not subject themselves to the righteousness of God" (NASB). The Apostle then contrasts "the righteousness which is based on law" with "the righteousness based on faith" (10:5, 6 NASB). By and large the Jews did not obtain this righteousness of God because they rejected Christ, Whom Paul declared to be "the end of the law for righteousness to everyone who believes" (10:4 NKJ). This righteousness is obtained when "with the heart one believes" (10:10a NKJ).

Justification. Another important doctrine in Romans is that of justification. For Paul, justification is closely connected with grace and faith. "Being justified freely by His grace through the redemption that is in Christ Jesus" (3:24 NKJ). God "justifies the ungodly" when he believes on Him" (4:5 NKJ).

Since God set Christ forth to be a propitiation for us, the Just for the unjust, God is able "to demonstrate ... His righteousness, that He might be just and the justifier of the one who has faith in Jesus" (3:26 NKJ). Through Christ's death and resurrection provision was made for the justification of sinners, for "He was delivered over to death for our sins and was raised to life for our justification" (4:25 NIV). The result of "being justified by faith" is this: "We have peace with God through our Lord Jesus Christ" (5:1).

Faith. A sixth and final Pauline doctrine which is crucial for understanding Romans is that of faith. The fact is, faith is at the very heart of Paul's message to the saints at Rome.

In Romans 1:16 Paul claims that the Gospel is "...the power of God unto salvation to everyone that believeth..." Verse seventeen relates faith to the righteousness of God: "For in the gospel a righteousness from God is revealed, a righteousness that is by faith from first to last" (NIV). Paul then borrows a quote from Habakkuk 2:4c, "The just shall live by faith" (NKJ).

God's righteousness and justification are obtained by faith (3:23, 26; 5:1). Since God has given His own Son to be a propitiation, He has satisfied His justice, which required sin to be punished. Consequently, salvation is a gift from God, which means recipients of salvation have no reason for boasting in themselves, since salvation is not founded on a law of works, but rather on "a law of faith" (3:27), i.e., upon the principle of faith.

Unfortunately, many of the children of Israel did not attain "the law of righteousness. Why? Because they did not seek it by faith, but, as it were, by the works of the law. For they stumbled at that stumbling stone" (9:31, 32 NKJ).

One must not think of faith as a pious exercise of the soul in isolation to God's Word, for "faith comes by hearing, and hearing by the Word of God" (10:17 NKJ).

Immediate Context

Even a cursory reading of Romans will impress one with the sudden change of content in chapter eight. In chapters one through seven the word *spirit* (πνεῦμα) appears just five times,[10] and only one or perhaps two of these occurrences refer to the Holy Spirit. By way of contrast πνεῦμα is found twenty times[11] in Romans chapter eight, and nearly all of them identify the Holy Spirit.

Those who have received Christ walk or follow after the Spirit (8:1, 4, 5). The Spirit is life and is the One Who raised up Jesus from the dead (8:10, 11). God's children are indwelt by the Spirit (8:9). They are also led by the Spirit (8:14). The Holy Spirit makes intercession for the saints of God with "groans that words cannot express," with intercession that is "in accordance with God's will" (8:26, 27 NIV).

The term "flesh" (σάρξ) appears in numerous phrases in the first thirteen verses of Romans chapter eight: "according to the flesh" (8:1, 4, 5, 12, 13 NKJ); "through the flesh" (8:3 NKJ); "likeness of sinful flesh" (8:3 NKJ); and "in the flesh" (8:3, 8, 9 NKJ). Although Paul sometimes uses the word σάρξ to describe a physical body, he is also fond of using it to denote inbred sin or the carnal mind.[12] It is interesting to note that the translators of the New International Version often render the term σάρξ (especially with the definite article) as "the sinful nature" in Romans 8:1-13.

In these first thirteen verses of Romans chapter eight there are twelve references to God's Spirit (πνεῦμα) and thirteen references to the flesh (σάρξ) or sinful nature.[13] The Apostle Paul repeatedly contrasts those who follow after and are controlled by the flesh with those who follow after and are controlled by the Spirit.

Particularly noticeable are the radical transformations enumerated in Romans chapter eight in contrast to the state of the unconverted, which is revealed in earlier chapters. Without Christ and a life controlled by the Holy Spirit, there is guilt before God (3:19); but with Christ and the Spirit in one's life, condemnation is removed (8:1). Sin is depicted as a cruel tyrant who deceives, slays, and brings into captivity (7:11, 13, 23); but through Christ and the "Spirit of life" there is freedom "from the law of sin and death" (8:2).

In his discussion of sin Paul has been careful to note its two-fold nature. He sometimes speaks about acts of sin (1:23, 25, 27, 29-32; 2:21-22; 3:13-15; 6:1, 12, 15-16; 7:15; 8:13). Paul also talks about the nature of sin which lies behind the deeds of sin, out of which these sinful acts flow (6:6; 7:17, 24; 8:7). The Apostle uses a variety of terms to describe the nature or disposition of sin, such as "our old man" (6:6), "sin that dwells in me" (7:17 NKJ), "the body of this death" (7:24), "the carnal mind" ("the sinful mind" in the NIV 8:7), and "the flesh" ("the sinful nature" in the NIV 8:5, 8).[14]

The message of Romans eight, as well as that of other chapters, is expressed repeatedly: There is deliverance from all sin. From the acts of sin which bring guilt and condemnation there is forgiveness through Christ (8:1). From the carnal mind or sinful nature there is a life of peace in which the Holy Spirit indwells the believer (8:6, 9). It involves a crucifixion of the sinful nature and destruction of the body of sin (6:6) which is brought about by the grace of the ord Jesus (7:25).[15]

Text

Considerable space has been given to Paul's teaching in Romans, particularly in chapters one through seven and the first thirteen verses of chapter eight, in order to better understand and explain the doctrine of the witness of the Spirit to one's conversion. Special attention will now be focused on Romans chapter eight, verses fifteen and sixteen. John Wesley developed one sermon on Romans 8:15 and two sermons on Romans 8:16.[16] Although the union of both verses is deemed necessary for laying a biblical foundation for the doctrine of the witness of the Spirit in this study, each verse will be given separate treatment at this junction.

Romans 8:15

There are two main clauses in verse fifteen. The first clause identifies something which the Christian reader has not received, while the second clause reveals something which he has received. In both cases that which has not been received and that which has been received are said to be πνεῦμα or spirit. In the first reference most translations spell *spirit* with a small "s," whereas, in the second most versions use a capital "S." A striking contrast is seen in the two kinds of πνεῦμα: "the spirit of bondage" and "the Spirit of adoption." The reception of "the spirit of bondage" brings "fear," but "the Spirit of adoption" brings filial confidence, through which "we cry out, 'Abba, Father'" (NKJ).

As noted earlier, the term πνεῦμα is used repeatedly in Romans chapter eight, especially in verses one through sixteen. In most of the references the term clearly points to the Holy Spirit. In one or more of the occurrences the spirit of man is addressed. Scholars are not in perfect agreement concerning the one to whom the πνεῦμα applies in each case. For example, in Romans 8:9 (NKJ) these words appear: "But you are not in the flesh but in the Spirit, if indeed the Spirit of God dwells in you." Does the first usage of πνεῦμα in this verse refer to God's Spirit or man's spirit? Many scholars see it as a reference to God's Spirit, but Sanday and Headlam think it points to man's spirit, which has been affected by God's Spirit.[17] This interpretation makes sense, since the contrast is between flesh and spirit, and, without question, the flesh belongs to man; even so the spirit also would appear to belong to man. In any case, man's spirit must be impacted by God's Spirit in order for one to be in right relationship with God.

The next verse reads thus: "And if Christ is in you, the body is dead because of sin, but the Spirit is life because of righteousness" (Rom. 8:10 NKJ). Is the πνεῦμα here identifying the Spirit of God or the spirit of man? Several translators, as well as commentators, see the term as relating to God's Spirit. The New International Version opts for another interpretation, as noted in its translation of verse ten: "But if Christ is in you, your body is dead because of sin, yet your spirit is alive because of righteousness." J. A. Beet likewise treats the verse as dealing with man's spirit.[18] The contrast is more pronounced in this verse since Paul places the σῶμα (body) against the πνεῦμα, whereas in verse nine the σάρξ (flesh) is placed over against the πνεῦμα. On the basis of the grammatical structures of these two verses, one may argue that the term πνεῦμα could stand for man's spirit, especially in verse ten. However, the entire context of this passage stresses the ministry of the Holy Spirit in meeting the needs of sinners. It is only when the Spirit of God imparts life to the human spirit that one is spiritually made alive or regenerated.

Spirit of Bondage. In verse fifteen the term pnema is again used two times. The second usage clearly refers to the Holy Spirit, for He is called "the Spirit of adoption." But what about Paul's reference to "the spirit of bondage?" Whose spirit is he trying to depict in this instance? The full statement in verse fifteen is as follows: "For you did not receive the spirit of bondage again to fear" (NKJ).

Perhaps the key to understanding Romans 8:15 is bound up in the word "received." In order for someone to be a receiver there must be someone else who is a giver. Surely no sane person would give himself the kind of gift Paul mentions in Romans 8:15a. In commenting upon this verse W. H. Griffith Thomas penned these words: "Anything that involves a believer in fear cannot possibly be the work of the Holy Spirit of God, and must come either from his own heart of unbelief or as a temptation of the Evil One."[19]

Few would dispute the accuracy of Thomas' comments. But one must ask this question: To whom is Paul speaking when he talks about those who have received the spirit of bondage? Is he referring to believers? Most assuredly he is identifying believers in the latter part of verse fifteen when he states: "You received the Spirit of adoption by whom we cry out, 'Abba, Father'" (NKJ). However, the inclusion of the word "again" in the previous statement suggests that those who are now addressed as recipients of "the Spirit of adoption" were not believers when they had "received the spirit of bondage ...to fear," for in their present condition Paul said: "You did not receive the spirit of bondage *again* to fear" (NKJ—emphasis mine).

This much, then, is plainly revealed: the Christians at Rome had once "received the spirit of bondage ...to fear," but now that they have come to Christ, they have received, not that same spirit of bondage again, but rather "the Spirit of adoption." From whom, then, did they receive "the spirit of bondage ...to fear" when they were without Christ? From Satan? From themselves? Or from God?

Scripture does not indicate that Satan gives a spirit of bondage to fear unto his followers. To the contrary, his purpose is to keep their minds blinded "lest the light of the gospel ...should shine on them" (2 Cor. 4:4 NKJ). Sinners are also said to be in some sense asleep and dead (Eph. 5:14). If sleepy, blind sinners receive "the spirit of bondage ...to fear, they will doubtless be aroused and awakened out of their slumber. Perhaps they will then be made to see the folly of living in sin and thus be inclined to turn to God. Hence, Satan cannot be expected to be a giver of "the spirit of bondage ...to fear" unto sinners, unless he intends to destroy his own kingdom.

If a sinner had the ability and power to do so, would he bring upon or give himself "the spirit of bondage ...to fear?" According to Scripture, sinners are "lovers of their own selves, covetous, boasters, proud ...lovers of pleasures more than lovers of God" (2 Tim. 3:2, 4). Jeremiah 17:9 paints a vivid portrait of a sinner's inward being: "The heart is deceitful above all things, and desperately wicked: who can know it?" In light of these facts it is quite obvious that a sinner will not initiate his own awakening. There is far too much comfort for one to remain in sin prior to receiving an experience of awakening.

In searching for an answer one must also ask this question: Could it be that God Himself is the giver of "the spirit of bondage ...to fear?" The answer is a resounding YES. From Genesis through Revelation the triune Godhead is seen to be actively involved in providing a perfect salvation for the sinner and in seeking and calling the transgressor back to Himself. In discussing this part of Romans 8:15 Wesley wrote:

> The spirit of bondage here seems directly to mean those operations of the Holy Spirit, by which the soul, on its first conviction, feels itself in bondage to sin, to the world, to Satan, and obnoxious to the wrath of God. This therefore and the Spirit of adoption are one and the same Spirit, only manifesting itself in various operations, according to the various circumstances of the persons.[20]

Some translators, such as W. J. Conybeare, would agree with Wesley in seeing the Holy Spirit to be "the spirit of bondage" in Romans 8:15. Conybeare gives "spirit" a capital "S" and therefore renders this part of verse fifteen as follows: "For you have not received a Spirit of bondage, that you should go back again to the state of slavish fear..." Matthew Henry, the distinguished Calvinistic commentator, identifies "the Spirit of bondage" with the Holy Spirit when He brings conviction upon a sinner.[21]

In attempting, then, to answer the question, "To whom does 'the spirit of bondage ...to fear' refer?" one must conclude that it directly identifies the Spirit of God. Nevertheless, there is a close interworking between God's Spirit and man's spirit, as noted by Sanday and Headlam.[22]

John Wesley's sermon, *The Spirit of Bondage and of Adoption*, is based on Romans 8:15. In giving introductory comments to this sermon Albert C. Outler noted that it is "...Wesley's interpretation of the contrast delineated in Romans 7 and 8, with Romans 7 taken as a description of despair in the 'legal state' and Romans 8 as St. Paul's celebration of 'evangelical grace.'"[23] The fact is, Wesley actually treats a person under three possible states in which he may appear. The first he calls "a natural man;" the second, a person "under the law," and the third, one who is "under grace."[24] Only the last two states are depicted by Paul in Romans 8:15. Thus Wesley has gone back to one's condition prior to this verse in order to describe his first state, that of the natural man, prior to an awakening.

Wesley's rendition of Romans 8:15 is both sensible and scriptural. How numerous are the biblical verses which he quotes, paraphrases, or alludes to in this and other sermons. His skillful use of logic is carefully woven into the fabric of the sermon to bolster his arguments and propositions.

The natural person is described as one who is a total stranger to God, His Law, and spiritual things. Therefore he is asleep and blind and has no fear, since he is not aware of any danger. This person sins daily but senses no condemnation or "bondage." He may even find pleasure in sin and some sense of peace and rest.[25] This is the state of one who has not yet experienced Romans 8:15.

How then is one brought into the state where he receives "the spirit of bondage ...to fear?" As Wesley sees it, this transpires when God touches the heart of the natural person and greatly awakens him out of spiritual sleep to an awareness of present danger.[26] God does this by applying His Word through the power of the Spirit or by means of some terrible providence. The sinner's spiritual eyes are now opened to see the reality of sin, judgment, and damnation. At this point in time God is seen to not only be kind and merciful, but also a "consuming fire." All false peace, joy, and rest now flee away, and an awful fear grips the mind and heart of the sinner: fear of death and hell. The sinner tries to break away from his sins, but the harder the struggle, the greater the bondage. For Wesley, Romans chapter seven describes this awakened person, this one who has received "the spirit of bondage ...to fear." Such fear leads one to cry out in agony of soul: "O wretched man that I am! Who will deliver me from this body of death?" (Rom. 7:24). This desperate cry is for deliverance from the yokes of bondage and fear. Paul responds to this cry of anguish by a strong, positive assertion: "I thank God through Jesus Christ our Lord" (Rom. 7:25a). Victory is obtained through the grace of our Lord Jesus Christ.[27]

When Christ comes into one's heart, fear of death and hell are gone. The light of heaven breaks in upon the soul so that one sees his sins being laid upon Christ who takes them all away. Bondage is utterly broken and the soul is set free. There is now a genuine peace through Christ. No longer is there any consciousness of "the spirit of bondage ...to fear, but rather there is a blessed awareness of the presence of "the Spirit of adoption," through whom we cry, "Abba, Father."[28] What a marvelous transition from bondage to adoption.

Spirit of Adoption. The term "adoption" does not appear in the Old Testament. It is found only five times in the New Testament, and in each instance it is used by the Apostle Paul.[29] In four of these usages he is referring to a spiritual adoption through which one enters the kingdom of God. However, there is a different setting in mind when the Apostle speaks about adoption in Romans 8:23. Here Paul is projecting into the future, to a time when the physical bodies of Christians will be redeemed.

Doubtless the greatest verification of adoption into God's family is found when one obtains the Spirit of adoption: "You received the Spirit of adoption by whom we cry out, 'Abba, Father'" (Rom. 8:15b NKJ). Paul includes himself among the adopted ones as he changes pronouns from the second person plural "you" to the first person plural "we."[30] Paul had been addressing his readers when he wrote: "You received the Spirit of adoption," but he suddenly switched persons so that he might also testify as he added these words: "by whom we cry out, 'Abba, Father.'" Perhaps the Apostle became overwhelmed with emotion as he remembered the time when he first received "the Spirit of adoption" and thus felt constrained to join his fellow Christians at Rome in crying out, "Abba, Father."

The verb "κράζομεν" is a strong word. According to Arndt and Gingrich it carries a variety of meanings, such as to cry out, scream, shriek, call, call out, and cry; but in Romans 8:15 it points to fervent prayer.[31] According to Wesley, the word expresses "vehement speaking, with desire, confidence, constancy."[32]

The fervent cry or prayer of the one who receives the Spirit of adoption is manifested in the address, "'Αββά ὁ πατήρ." Paul's use of both the Aramaic and Greek words for "Father" may "point out the joint cry both of the Jewish and Gentile believer," as Wesley suggests.[33] Or, it may be that Paul is borrowing the words Jesus used in His agonizing prayer in the Garden of Gethsemane when He addressed God as "'Αββά ὁ πατήρ." Since the first word that a young baby utters is usually "Da-da," it is most fitting that when one becomes a child of God the first cry of the heart and lips is, "Father, Father."

Romans 8:16

Like its preceding verse, Romans 8:16 has two occurrences of the Greek word πνεῦμα. Unlike the preceding verse, there is no question in verse sixteen as to whose spirit Paul is trying to describe in each usage of πνεῦμα. When he begins the verse with these words, "αὐτὸ τὸ πνεῦμα," Paul is definitely referring to the Spirit of God or the Holy Spirit. But when the Apostle writes about "τῷ πνεύματι ἡμῶν," he is identifying human spirits, including his own.

The Greek form πνεῦμα is very common in the New Testament.[34] It is found more than 150 times in the Gospels and about 130 times in the Pauline epistles.[35] It has been translated by such English words as wind, breath, spirit, blowing, breathing, spiritual state, disposition, and state of mind.[36]

Two Johannine passages will help us understand Romans 8:16. The first is John, chapter four. That God is essentially spiritual in nature is affirmed in Jesus' words to the Samaritan woman: "God is Spirit" (Jn. 4:24a NKJ). In each of the Greek New Testaments cited earlier in this chapter, the wording is the same, namely this: "πνεῦμα ὁ θεός." In two of these texts πνεῦμα begins with a capital letter. "Π."[37] The KJV also uses an indefinite article before "Spirit" thus: "God is a Spirit." Perhaps the translators are trying to identify the Holy Spirit as "a Spirit" in this verse.

On the other hand, the New International Version and the New American Standard Bible use a small "s" for spirit and thus render the clause: "God is spirit." Apparently these translators understand these words to express, not His personality, but rather His nature.[38] Since God is spiritual in nature and human beings are both physical and spiritual, it does seem that Turner and Mantey are correct when they assert that God and humans "come closest together in the realm of the spirit."[39]

The point is this: when John states that "God is spirit (or Spirit)," it is not synonymous with saying "God is the Holy Spirit." While the latter statement is indeed factual, it does not seem to be John's purpose to make such an assertion in this verse. Rather, he is affirming that God's essence is spirit, not matter. Therefore, "Those who worship Him must worship in spirit and in truth" (Jn. 4:24b NKJ). God is spiritual in nature. Human beings are partly spiritual in nature. Hence relationships are effected between Creator and creature when God's Spirit contacts and communicates with human spirit.

The third chapter of John's Gospel also helps explain Romans 8:15, 16. Jesus shocked Nicodemus by stressing the necessity of one's being born again in order to see the kingdom of God (Jn. 3:3). The idea of a new or second birth seemed utterly strange to Nicodemus. In unfolding further light on this matter of the new birth, Jesus said: "Unless one is born of water and the Spirit, he cannot enter into the kingdom of God" (Jn. 3:5 NASB). Nicodemus was having a difficult time understanding the words of Jesus, so He contrasted one type of birth with another: "Flesh gives birth to flesh, but the Spirit gives birth to spirit" (Jn. 3:6 NIV). The Holy Spirit is thus seen to be the initiator of the new birth or a spiritual birth, even as human parents are the progenitors of human children comprised of flesh like that of their parents.

In his discourse to Nicodemus Jesus used the word πνεῦμα twice in John 3:8 when He said (NKJ): "The wind (πνεῦμα) blows where it wishes, and you hear the sound of it, but cannot tell where it comes from and where it goes. So is everyone who is born of the Spirit (τοῦ πνεύματος)." Although one can hear and feel the wind, there is something mysterious about it. On the other hand, that which results from the blowing of the wind can be seen and felt. The same is true concerning the movings of the Spirit. Bruce has expressed it thus: "The hidden work of the Spirit in the human heart cannot be controlled or seen, but its effects are unmistakably evident."[40]

There is one other New Testament passage which demands brief attention preparatory to an analysis of Romans 8:16. Paul's teaching on the work of the Holy Spirit in 1 Corinthians chapter two provides new insights which will sharpen the focus of one's understanding of the witness of the Spirit.

The Apostle may have been alluding to and/or paraphrasing parts of two or three verses in the Old Testament when he penned these words in 1 Corinthians 2:9 NKJ:

> *Eye has not seen, nor ear heard,*
> *Nor have entered into the heart of man*
> *The things which God has prepared for*
> *those who love Him.*[41]

This verse refers not to future blessings in heaven, but to the spiritual blessings a child of God experiences in this life, as indicated in the words which immediately follow: "But God has revealed them to us through His Spirit" (1 Cor. 2:10a NKJ). The revelations of God had been given "to us," i.e., to Paul, the writer and to the Corinthian Christians, the readers, all of whom were recipients of God's grace while living upon earth. According to the context the blessings which one cannot receive by means of physical senses are those inward, spiritual blessings of salvation.[42]

The thrust of Paul's argument is this: the blessings which relate to salvation in this life go far deeper than sights, sounds, or mental pursuits; they are revealed to us "through the Spirit" (διὰ τοῦ πνεύματος).[43] It is through the ministry of the Holy Spirit that spiritual realities are made known to those who have found Christ. "Now we have received, not the spirit of the world, but the Spirit who is from God, that we might know the things which have been freely given to us by God" (1 Cor. 2:12 NKJ). The verbs "received" and "given" point to the free gifts of God's grace, to that which cannot be earned or merited. The reason the Spirit is given or received is succinctly expressed "that we might *know* the things which have been freely given to us by God" (emphasis mine).

Paul stresses two or three facts about the Holy Spirit. First, He "searches all things, yea, the deep things of God" (1 Cor. 2:10b). Second, He "knows the things of God" (1 Cor. 2:11b). Consequently, one would expect the Holy Spirit to be the Person of the Godhead to reveal the things of God to the recipients of salvation, as disclosed in 1 Corinthians 2:9, 12.

To what faculty in human beings are the things of God revealed by the Spirit? That they are not revealed to one's physical eyes, ears, or mind is most evident (v. 9). Is it not one's spirit that becomes the receiver of spiritual blessings made known by the Holy Spirit? Since a person's spirit knows that which is within that person (1 Cor. 2:11a) it is most fitting that one's human spirit would serve as the natural faculty to both receive and "know the things which have been freely given to us by God" (v. 12).

Paul describes the person who has received "the things of God" as ὁ πνευματικός, which literally means "the spiritual one" (v. 15). This kind of individual is contrasted with what Paul calls a ψυχικός, which literally means "a soulish—or earthly—person" (v. 14). A few Bible versions translate ψυχικός, as a "natural man" (KJV, NKJ, NASB, and CON). The New International Version identifies this person as "the man without the Spirit." This person "does not accept the things that come from the Spirit of God, for they are foolish to him, and he cannot understand them because they are spiritually discerned" (1 Cor. 2:14 NIV). Like the earthly—or soulish—person, the spiritual individual is able to discern physical matters by means of bodily senses. However, since the former is not spiritual, he is unable to discern spiritual things even as a deaf person cannot judge the sounds of an orchestra. Carter states the contrast thus:

> The great difference in the two classes is simply that in one the natural man has been touched, awakened, reborn, and energized by the dynamic of God's Spirit. His awakened spiritual nature has responded to and harmonized with the Spirit of God. Thus he is a spiritual man by reason of the operation of God's Spirit. On the other hand, the other class consists of those who remain on the purely natural level by reason of the fact that their lives remain untouched by God's Spirit.[44]

With the Johannine and Pauline passages as a backdrop, it is now possible to approach the meaning of Romans 8:16 from a much better vantage point. Paul's statement is at once both simple and sublime. "The Spirit Himself bears witness with our spirit that we are the children of God" (NKJ). No attempt is made to explain how God's Spirit bears witness with one's human spirit. On the other hand, the purpose of the witness is unmistakable: to notify the seeker after God that he is now a member of God's family. It should be noted that Paul uses the present tense " ...that we *are* the children of God" (v. 16b, emphasis mine).

Direct and Indirect Witness of the Spirit. Of particular significance is the Greek verb συμμαρτυρέω, which means "testify or bear witness with."[45] This compound verb appears only three times in the New Testament and each of these is in Romans.[46] According to A. A. Trites, in these three passages συμμαρτυρέω expresses "a confirmatory, reinforcing, or accusatory co-testimony of the spirit or of human conscience."[47]

Hermann Strathmann claims that συμμαρτυρέω always carried the idea of confirmation in non-biblical Greek.[48] For the classical Greek writers "it means to confirm in the sense of the correspondence of a second or further piece of evidence which is added to the one already given."[49] Confirmation is thus strengthened by the presentation of dual evidence.

How can one know for certain he is a child of God? According to Romans 8:16 there are two distinct witnesses: (1) the witness of God's Spirit and (2) the witness of one's own spirit. For Wesley, the former witness was sometimes called the direct witness and the latter, the indirect witness.[50] The witness of one's own spirit is seen to be the testimony of one's conscience, "and is the result of reason or reflection on what we feel in our souls," as well as "a conclusion drawn partly from the Word of God, and partly from our own experience."[51]

Unlike Wesley, Wilber Dayton refers to both witnesses as "direct witnesses."[52] He sees each witness as complementing and supplementing the other:

> Being self-conscious and self-determining beings we have some valid knowledge of ourselves and of our condition. This is not to be despised. But in a matter of so great importance it is well to have it confirmed. This the Holy Spirit does. My spirit says, "It is well with my soul." The Holy Spirit responds, "Yes, you are a son." He does not witness contrary to but, rather, **with** our spirits.[53]

It should be carefully noted that Romans 8:16 does not say God's Spirit bears witness *to* one's human spirit, but rather *with* it. W. H. Griffith Thomas discusses this matter as follows:

> This means that the Spirit of God bears witness *to God* alongside of our own spirit's witness. We look up to God and call Him Father while at the same time the Holy Spirit Himself bears witness to God to the same effect that we are God's children... Thus, there is a double testimony; that of the Holy Spirit and of our own spirit, that we are the children of God, ...It is one of those absolute facts of the Christian position which are independent of our particular emotions or sentiments at any given moment, and, as such, it constitutes one of the most precious realities and assurances of our relation to God.[54]

In order to be saved one must cooperate with God by meeting certain conditions enumerated in Scripture. These conditions are summarized in Acts 20:21 as "repentance toward God and faith toward our Lord Jesus Christ" (NKJ). Since it is the human spirit which knows what transpires within one's inner being, one's spirit knows when a thorough repentance has taken place and when a simple, trusting confidence has been placed in the person and provisions of Jesus Christ. When this transpires, one's spirit affirms it or testifies that it is so. The Holy Spirit also testifies *with* the human spirit that the transaction has indeed taken place and the sinner who has just been saved is now a child of God. No two experiences are exactly alike, but when one is born again, condemnation is gone (Rom. 8:1), and there is "peace with God" (Rom. 5:1).

Since the Bible does not give us a step-by-step exposition of all the workings of the Spirit in conjunction with all of man's pursuits in seeking divine favor, it is not likely that any student of Scripture has every aspect in unmistakable order. J. A. Beet sees the interactions between God's Spirit and man's spirit to take place thus:

> Our spirit cried (v. 15) *Abba, Father:* and just as a similar cry from a child is a testimony—though possibly a mistaken one—that he is a son of the man whom he calls Father, so the cry to God of *our spirit,* the highest part of our being, *bears witness* **that we are children of God.** That this cry was prompted by the Spirit of God, adds His infallible testimony to the testimony of our own spirit, and assures us that our confidence is no delusion. Thus *the Spirit Himself* confirms the testimony of *our spirit.* In the order of cause and effect, the witness of God's Spirit precedes that of our own spirit; for He reveals to us the fatherly love of God, and thus moves us to call Him *Father.* But, in the order of our thought, our own cry comes first. We are first conscious of our own filial confidence, and then observe that it is wrought in us by the Holy Spirit.[55]

Beet continues by noting that "the word *witness* is a favourite in Greek for whatever affords proof.... It is especially used in reference to the Holy Spirit; and is very appropriate here because it is by a voice put into our lips that the Holy Spirit gives proof that we are sons of God."[56]

Regardless of the position one may prefer as to the precise working of God's Spirit upon or with man's spirit, it is obvious that the Holy Spirit is the key Agent. Man's spirit can only bear witness as a result of the prevenient action and witness of God's Spirit.

The Bible does not necessarily connect the Spirit's witness with "feelings." The witness of one's own spirit is normally associated with the fruit of the Spirit, which indeed has a clear connection with feelings, particularly love, joy, and peace (Gal. 5:22a).

The inward or direct witness of the Spirit would better be described by such terms as "consciousness," "awareness," or "knowledge." Nevertheless, would anyone seriously question whether an awareness or consciousness of sins forgiven would precipitate good and pleasant feelings?

Operations of the Spirit Restated

The Holy Spirit is actively engaged in the processes through which a sinner passes as he is translated from the kingdom of Satan to the kingdom of God.

At each stage the ministry of the Spirit may be observed.

It is the Spirit of God who takes the initiative to awaken and arrest the "natural person" who has previously lived on an earthly plane, being motivated by his bodily senses (Rom. 8:15a). Through the law of God the Spirit reveals the reality of sin (Rom. 7:7) and its universality (Rom. 3:23). As the awakened sinner struggles to follow God's law, he soon discovers that there is not sufficient strength in oneself to do so (Rom. 7:8-24). The Holy Spirit not only convinces of sin and of coming judgment upon it, but also of the righteousness of Christ and His grace which provides justification and redemption to those who believe in Him (Jn. 16:7-11; Rom. 3:24-28; 5:1-11; 7:25). When the sinner believes on Jesus, His blood becomes efficacious for one's pardon (Rom. 3:25-26; 5:8-9). Saving faith entails believing with one's heart, and this is followed by confession with one's mouth (Rom. 10:9-10). It is the Holy Spirit who takes the things of God and reveals them to the one who seeks God (Jn. 16:13-15; 1 Cor. 2:7-14). At the point of conversion one receives the Spirit of adoption into the family of God and is thereby enabled to cry: "Abba, Father" (Rom. 8:15b). One's own spirit is conscious of the changes which have been effected in one's inner being; and alongside of this testimony is the Spirit's personal and direct witness that all is now well, that one has been born again (Rom. 8:16). These two witnesses join together to confirm the miracle of the new birth and to provide the needful assurance that one is now a child of God.[57]

Perhaps Fanny Crosby had Romans 8:15, 16 in mind when she penned these words:

> *Blessed Assurance, Jesus is mine!*
> *Oh, what a foretaste of glory divine!*
> *Heir of salvation, purchase of God,*
> *Born of His Spirit, washed in His blood![58]*

Endnotes

1. *Works*, 1:104-5.

2. Ibid., 105, "A man of one book."

3. See *The Greek Text of Stephens*, 1550 (Samuel Bagster and Sons, Limited, 1896), 418. Hereafter cited as *Gr. N.T.-Stephens*, 1550. *The New Testament in the Original Greek*, eds. B. F. Westcott and F. J. A. Hort (New York: The Macmillan Company,. 1928), 363. Hereafter cited as *Gr. N.T.-Westcott and Hort*, 1928. *Novum Testamentum Graece*, eds. D. Eberhard Nestle, D. Erwin Nestle, and D. Kurt Aland (Stuttgart: Privileg. Wurtt, Bibelanstalt, 1956), 407. Hereafter cited as *Gr. N.T.-Nestle and Aland*, 1956. *The Greek New Testament According to the Majority Texts*, eds. Zane C. Hodges and Arthur L. Farstad (Nashville: Thomas Nelson Publishers, 1985), 491. Hereafter cited as *Gr. N.T.-Majority Texts*. *The Greek New Testament*, eds. Barbara Aland, Kurt Aland, Johannes Karavidopoulos, Carlo M. Martini, and Bruce M. Metzger (Stuttgart: Deutsche

Bibelgesellschaft, 1994), 539. Hereafter cited as *Gr. N.T.-UBS*, 1994.

4. Henry George Liddell and Robert Scott, "σύν," *A Greek-English Lexicon* (New York: Oxford University Press, 1983), 1691.

5. Or it may be that Wesley made an alteration in the Greek text, as he sometimes did. See John Wesley, *Explanatory Notes Upon the New Testament* (San Francisco: Carlton & Lanahan, n.d., repr., Salem, OH: Schmul Publishers, 1976), 382 (hereafter cited as *Explanatory Notes*).

6. J. Gresham Machen, *New Testament Greek for Beginners* (New York: The Macmillan Company, 1965), 53.

7. Joseph Agar Beet, *A Commentary on St. Paul's Epistle to the Romans* (London: Hodder and Stoughton, 1902; repr. Salem, OH: Allegheny Publications, 1982), 24.

8. George Allen Turner, *A Vision Which Transforms* (Kansas City: Beacon Hill Press of Kansas City, 1964), 85.

9. For an excellent discussion see William M. Greathouse, *The Epistle to the Romans*, vol. 8, *Beacon Bible Commentary* (Kansas City: Beacon Hill Press of Kansas City, 1968), 41-45.

10. W. F. Moulton, A. S. Geden, and H. K. Moulton, *A Concordance to the Greek Testament* (Edinburgh: T. & T. Clark, 1984), 821.

11. Ibid., 821-22. For an interesting discussion of the Holy Spirit in Romans 8, see Roger L. Hahn, "Pneumatology in Romans 8: Its Historical and Theological Context," *Wesleyan Theological Journal* 21, nos. 1 and 2 (spring-fall 1986): 74-90.

12. W. F. Arndt and F. W. Gingrich, *A Greek-English Lexicon of the New Testament and Other Early Christian Literature* (Chicago: The University of Chicago Press, 1957), 750-52. For other possible Pauline meanings of "flesh," see an interesting study by Richard E. Howard, *Newness of Life: A Study in the Thought of Paul* (Kansas City, MO: Beacon Hill Press, 1975), 28-33.

13. Moulton, Geden, and Moulton, 821, 887.

14. For a helpful discussion on various biblical terms which describe the sinful nature, see Adam Clarke, *Clarke's Commentaries*, vol. 6 (Nashville: Abingdon Press, n.d.), 77.

15. In three of the Greek New Testaments cited above, Rom. 7:25 begins thus: "Χάρις τῷ θεῷ" However, in both the *Gr. N.T.-Stephens*, 1550, and the *Gr. N.T.-Majority Texts* the verse begins, "εὐχαριστῶ τῷ θεῷ, which supports the translation found in both the KJV and the NKJ: "I thank God." While χάρις is often translated "grace," it can also be rendered as "thanks" or "gratitude," which many translators have used in either a noun or verb form. On the other hand, χάρις has also been translated "grace" in this verse. In response to the question in 7:24, "Who shall deliver me from the body of this death?" Ronald Knox answers thus in his translation of the first part of verse twenty-five: "Nothing else than the grace of God." See also *Works*, 1:260.

16. *Works*, 1:248-66; 267-84; 285-98.

17. William Sanday and Arthur C. Headlam, *The Epistle to the Romans, International Critical Commentary* (Edinburgh: T. & T. Clark, 1930), 196.

18. Beet, 218.

19. W. H. Griffith Thomas, *St. Paul's Epistle to the Romans* (Grand Rapids: Wm. B. Eerdmans Publishing Company, 1947), 215.

20. *Explanatory Notes*, 382.

21. Matthew Henry, *Acts to Revelation*, vol. 6, *A Commentary on the Whole Bible* (original data not listed; repr. Old Tappan: Fleming H. Revell Company, n.d.), 418.

22. See Sanday and Headlam, 202. Concerning "the Spirit of bondage" they have written: "From meaning the human spirit under the influence of the Divine Spirit πνεῦμα comes to mean a particular state, habit, or temper of the human spirit, sometimes in itself ...but more often as due to supernatural influence, good or evil..."

23. *Works*, 1:249. Outler is the editor of Volumes I-IV (Wesley's sermons) of the Bicentennial Edition of *The Works of John Wesley*.

24. *Works*, 1:250.

25. Ibid., 1:251-54.

26. Ibid., 1:255.

27. Ibid., 1:255-60.

28. Ibid., 260-62.

29. Moulton, Geden, and Moulton, 966. υἱοθεσίας is only found in Rom. 8:15, 23; 9:4; Gal. 4:5; and Eph. 1:5. See APPENDIX A for a discussion of the procedure used in the adoption of a son in the Roman world into which the New Testament came.

30. See Beet, 225.

31. Arndt and Gingrich, 448-49.

32. *Explanatory Notes*, 382.

33. Ibid.

34. According to Moulton, Geden, and Moulton, 819-23, πνεῦμα appears approximately 350 times.

35. Ibid.

36. Arndt and Gingrich, 680-81.

37. See *Gr. N.T.-Stephens*, 1550, 250, and *Gr. N. T.-Majority Texts*, 301.

38. George Allen Turner and Julius R. Mantey, *The Gospel According to John*, vol. 4, *The Evangelical Commentary on the Bible* (Grand Rapids: Wm. B. Eerdmans Publishing Company, n.d.), 112, 117.

39. Ibid., 112.

40. F. F. Bruce, *The Gospel of John* (Grand Rapids: William B. Eerdmans Publishing Company, 1983), 85.

41. It does appear that Paul may have constructed 1 Cor. 2:9 from parts of Isa. 52:15, 64:4, and 65:17.

42. See 1 Cor. 1:18, 30; 2:2, 4-5.

43. Two of the Greek texts cited above add the word "αὐτοῦ," but this addition does not change the force of meaning.

44. Charles W. Carter, *The First Epistle of Paul to the Corinthians*, vol. 5. *The Wesleyan Bible Commentary* (Grand Rapids: Baker Book House, 1966), 141.

45. Arndt and Gingrich, 786.

46. Moulton, Geden, and Moulton, 922. συμμαρτυρέω is only found in Romans

2:15; 8:16; and 9:1.

47. A. A. Trites, *Witness, Testimony,* Vol. 3, *The New International Dictionary of New Testament Theology*, ed. Colin Brown (Grand Rapids: Zondervan Publishing House, 1978), 1042.

48. Hermann Strathmann, συμμαρτυρέω, vol. 4, *Theological Dictionary of the New Testament*, ed. Gerhard Kittel (Grand Rapids: Wm. B. Eerdmans Publishing Company, 1983), 509.

49. Trites, 1039.

50. *Works*, 1:288; 270-74.

51. Ibid., 273; 287-88.

52. Wilber T. Dayton, *The Epistle of Paul to the Romans*, vol. 5. *The Wesleyan Bible Commentary* (Grand Rapids: Baker Book House, 1966), 55.

53. Ibid.

54. Thomas, 216.

55. Beet, 226.

56. Ibid.

57. For additional insights on "Spirit of adoption" and "beareth witness with," see D. D. Whedon, *Acts—Romans,* vol. 3, *Commentary on the New Testament* (New York: Nelson & Phillips, 1871; repr., Salem, OH: Schmul Publishers, 1977), 340. See also W. B. Godbey, *Acts—Romans: Paul the Champion Theologian*, vol. 5, *Commentary on the New Testament* (Cincinnati: Revivalist Office, n.d.), 133, for claiming that the witness of the Spirit to regeneration is not "the clear, constant, abiding and overwhelming witness" found in entire sanctification. Although he refers to Wesley, the two men are not in full accord on this matter.

58. Fanny Crosby, *Worship in Song* (Kansas City, MO: Lillenas Publishing Company, 1972), 437.

Chapter Two

A Biblical Basis for the Witness of the Spirit: Part II

The purpose of this chapter is to continue an analysis of key biblical passages which either assert or suggest that there is a witness of the Holy Spirit with the spirit of one who has come to God to receive justification/regeneration. Since Romans 8:15-16 is considered to be the most significant passage on the doctrine, and since it was given extensive treatment which will have some application to the passages under discussion in this chapter, less attention will be given to each of them. For the most part, the same format used in Chapter 1 will be utilized here.

Galatians 4:4-7

This passage bears some similarity to Romans 8:15-16, particularly in verses 5 and 6. Emphasis will be given to those aspects which add new dimensions to the doctrine of the witness of the Spirit.

Greek Texts

A comparison of the five Greek texts cited in Chapter 1 reveals uniform agreement in nearly every verse of Galatians 4:4-7. The differences are extremely minor.

In verse 6 these words appear in three of the texts: "τὰς καρδίας ἡμῶν," while the following words appear in the other two: "τὰς καρδίας ὑμῶν."

The participle κρᾶζον (v. 6) is accented with a circumflex in three of the texts but with an acute in the other two (κράζον).

In verse 7 ἀλλὰ appears in this form in three texts, but in the others the final vowel is elided (ἀλλ᾽).

Also in verse 7 these words are found in three of the texts: "κληρονόμος διὰ θεοῦ." But in the other two texts the words are expanded thus: "κληρονόμος θεοῦ διὰ Χριστοῦ."

It is of interest to note that in each of the above-mentioned passages, Westcott and Hort, Nestle and Aland, and the United Bible Societies' text are in agreement with the first position.[1] On the other hand, Stephens' text and the Majority Text are united in the second position.[2]

However, the consistent pattern revealed above is not followed in the accenting of ἀββά in verse 6. Nestle and Aland, as well as the Majority Text, use the grave accent and are the only two that agree with each other. Westcott and Hort use an acute, Stephens a circumflex, but the United Bible Societies' text uses no accent.

Since variations in accents and vowel elisions do not alter the meanings of a given passage, it is obvious that the most significant differences are in verses 6 and 7. In the first passage three of the texts opt for "into our hearts," while the other two render it "into your hearts." In either case Paul is talking about the hearts of Christians. Nothing is essentially gained or lost if one uses either the first person or the second person.

In verse 7 the distinction is more pronounced. Three of the texts speak about "an heir through God," while the other two record it as "an heir of God through Christ." Since Christ is God and came to do the work and will of His Father, there seems to be no essential gain or loss in whichever text one may use.

Thus, as in the examination of the Greek texts on Romans 8:15, 16, none of the variations in Galatians 4:4-7 affects the basic meaning of the passage. In God's scheme of redemption believers are adopted into His family and receive a divine witness as an assurance of a new relationship with God.

Context

Galatians 4:4-7 may be the second most important New Testament passage which treats the witness of the Spirit to one's conversion. In order to better understand this passage, an examination of the context in which it appears will be pursued.

Broad Context

As noted in Chapter 1 Paul had not yet visited the saints at Rome when he wrote his epistle to them. This was not true regarding the Galatians, for Paul and his missionary colleagues were the human agents God used for the conversion of the Galatians. It was sometime later, after he had departed from Galatia, that Paul heard about the Judaizing Christians who had entered the Galatian churches, preaching a different Gospel than he had proclaimed to them (1:6-9).

Unfortunately, most, if not all, of Paul's converts were already yielding to at least part of the message being proclaimed in this perverted gospel. Consequently, all the work which Paul and his fellow-laborers had wrought was being undermined; hence the need to send a strong, terse epistle to his converts in hopes of salvaging them from utter apostasy.

Scholars are not in agreement regarding the precise recipients of the epistle and the time frame in which it was written. There does seem to be stronger support for the so-called "South Galatian" theory than for the "North Galatian" theory.[3] The southern cities of Lystra, Derbe, Iconium, and Antioch in Pisidia were important places in Paul's ministry during each of his missionary journeys, whereas only brief mention is made of Paul's visits into northern Galatia (Acts 16:6; 18:23).

It would also appear that Paul wrote to the Galatians prior to the time of the Jerusalem conference (Acts, chapter 15). In this meeting it was decided that Gentiles need not be circumcised in order to be saved. If Paul had written to the Galatians after the Jerusalem conference, he would have surely pressed the results of that gathering into his epistle, since it would have provided a powerful conclusion to his other arguments. But this is not the case.

The epistle to the Galatians shares many similarities with the epistle to the Romans. But there are also several dissimilarities. Since he had not yet visited the church at Rome when he wrote to them, Paul provided them with the "most general and complete" of all his epistles.[4] For the most part, Paul limits his message to the Galatians to the immediate problems at hand. Since the Judaizers had attacked his apostleship, Paul weaves a great deal of autobiographical data into the first two chapters in which he recounts his former life as a persecutor of the Christians, his conversion, call to preach, and brief interactions with a few of the apostles. The Gospel which Paul proclaimed was not imparted to him by any human being; it was revealed to him by Christ Himself (1:12). In dealing with the problems in Galatia there are five matters to which Paul gives special attention.

Circumcision. Judaizing teachers insisted that Gentiles be circumcised as one of the conditions requisite for conversion. But this message could only precipitate confusion and chaos, since it did not correlate with the Gospel of Christ as proclaimed by Paul.

The noun "circumcision" (περιτομή) appears seven times in Galatians and the verb form (περιτέμνω) is found six times.[5] Twice Paul asserts that neither circumcision nor uncircumcision has any value or meaning in regard to a right relationship with God (5:6a; 6:15a). What really counts is "faith working through love" (5:6b NKJ) and being made "a new creation" (6:15b NKJ). What the Galatians need for salvation is not Christ *and* circumcision, but rather Christ *without* circumcision. The Apostle faithfully warned them thus: "If you let yourselves be circumcised, Christ will be of no value to you at all" (5:2 NASB). This would place the Galatians under an unbearable yoke.[6] Paul wisely noted that his Greek friend Titus had not been "compelled to be circumcised" (2:3 NIV).

Law. Circumcision was one aspect of Old Testament ceremonial law. But even under the old covenant adherence to the exact prescription of the law was not, in and of itself, the fulfillment of God's purpose for His people. The meaning of circumcision was expanded to include moral and spiritual connotations. For example, Jeremiah was concerned about circumcised ears (Jer. 6:10) and circumcised hearts (Jer. 9:26).

God gave the children of Israel three kinds of law: civil, ceremonial, and moral. Ceremonial laws passed away with the coming of Christ. Civil laws change in accordance with policies established by government. But moral laws are applicable for all people in all places at all times. One must be careful to identify the particular kind of law being addressed when dealing with biblical passages on law.

Paul used the word "law" (νόμος) approximately thirty-one times in Galatians.[7] No person can ever be justified by "observing the law" (2:16a NIV) because there is a curse upon everyone "who does not continue to do everything written in the Book of the Law" (3:10 NIV). Paul doubtless had both moral and ceremonial law in mind when he penned these passages. In commenting upon the latter verse Wesley noted that the law "requires what no man can perform; namely, perfect, uninterrupted, and perpetual obedience."[8]

While "the law is not based on faith" (3:12a NIV), neither is it "opposed to the promises of God" (3:21a NIV). The fact is, "If a law had been given that could impart life, then righteousness would certainly have come by the law" (3:21c NIV).

Salvation is not obtained by both observing the law and trusting in Christ. It is rather "by faith in Jesus Christ" (2:16b NKJ). The matter at hand was so serious that those who had sought to be justified by keeping the law had actually lost Christ and His grace: "You have been severed from Christ, you who are seeking to be justified by law; you have fallen from grace" (5:4 NASB).

Why, then, was the law given? "It was added because of transgressions, till the Seed should come to whom the promise was made" (3:19b NKJ). In Romans 5:20a Paul wrote this: "The Law came in that the transgression might increase" (NASB). In commenting upon the purpose of the law Professor G. G. Findlay wrote:

> Transgression presupposes law. It is the specific form which sin takes under law—the reaction of sin against law. What was before a latent tendency, a bias of disposition, now starts to light as a flagrant, guilty fact. By bringing about repeated transgressions the Law reveals the true nature of sin, so that it "becomes exceeding sinful." It does not make matters worse, but it shows how bad they really are. It aggravates the disease, in order to bring it to a crisis. And this is a necessary step towards the cure.[9]

Another purpose of the law is stated in Galatians 3:24, as follows: "The law was put in charge to lead us to Christ, that we might be justified by faith" (NIV). In this setting the law is personified and, as such, harks back to the household servant known as the paidagogos in the Greek world. One of his regular daily tasks was to accompany his master's children to and from the school. The paidagogos was not involved in the actual work of teaching. The law is like the paidagogos in that it leads to the Lord Jesus Christ.[10] While the law cannot save, it points to Christ the Giver of grace so that "we might be justified by faith" (3:24b).

After one is converted there is an important law to observe called "the law of Christ," which can be fulfilled by bearing "one another's burdens" (6:2a). The principle underlying this law actually encompasses the purpose of all law, "For all the law is fulfilled in one word, even in this: 'You shall love your neighbor as yourself'" (5:14 NKJ).

Faith. The doctrine of faith has a preeminent place in the theology of Paul. It is crucial for both obtaining and retaining salvation. In Galatians the Apostle uses the noun "faith" (πίστις) approximately twenty-two times and the verb "believe" (πιστεύω) four times.[11]

Paul's message is crystal clear: salvation is obtained not by observing the law, but by exercising faith in Jesus Christ (2:16; 3:24, 26). As in Romans, Abraham is cited as the father of believers, for he "believed God, and it was accounted to him for righteousness. Therefore know that *only* those who are of faith are sons of Abraham" (3:6-7 NKJ). Genuine faith will reveal itself by "working through love" (5:6b NKJ).

Spirit. The work of the Holy Spirit in bringing assurance to the seeker of justification/regeneration is at the heart of this study. Paul uses the word "spirit" (πνεῦμα) approximately eighteen times in Galatians.[12] In most instances Paul is referring to the Spirit of God. In only two passages does he mention the human spirit (6:1, 18).

Paul asked three pertinent questions in chapter three. The first one is this: "Did you receive the Spirit by observing the law, or, by believing what you heard?" (3:2b NIV). A second question follows: "After beginning with the Spirit, are you now trying to attain your goal by human effort?" (3:3b NIV). A third question Paul raised was this: "Does God give you his Spirit and work miracles among you because you observe the law, or because you believe what you heard?" (3:5 NIV).

The answers to each of these questions were obvious. It was by faith, not by works of the law, that they had entered into the kingdom of God and continued therein, providing God a channel to work mightily among them. When

Paul asked them if they had received the Spirit "by observing the law, or by believing," (3:2b) he must have meant receiving the Spirit when they first believed and were thereby ushered into the new birth.[13] The language of this verse is reminiscent of Romans 8:15b, where Paul wrote, "Ye have received the Spirit of adoption."

Freedom. In working with the problems at Galatia there was one more crucial issue with which Paul had to deal. This was the matter of freedom or liberty. When the Galatians had found Christ they were liberated from the bondage of sin. Jesus had clearly taught that "everyone who sins is a slave to sin" (John 8:34 NIV), but He also said: "If you hold to my teaching, you are really my disciples. Then you will know the truth, and the truth will set you free" (John 8:31b, 32 NIV).

The term "freedom" (ἐλευθερία) appears four times in Galatians.[14] Paul warned his converts that false brothers had slipped into their midst "to spy on our liberty which we have in Christ Jesus, that they might bring us into bondage" (2:4). In light of the subtle work of the Judaizers Paul reminded the Galatians that "it is for freedom that Christ has set us free" (5:1a NIV). He then exhorted: "Stand firm, then, and do not let yourselves be burdened again by a yoke of slavery" (5:1b NIV). If the Galatians succumbed to the message of the legalists, they would forfeit the freedom they had found in Christ. Nevertheless, there was also the ever-present danger of abusing freedom; hence, the admonition: "You, my brothers, were called to be free. But do not use your freedom to indulge the sinful nature; rather, serve one another in love" (5:13 NIV).

Immediate Context

For the purpose of this study the immediate context will encompass the passage found in chapter three, verse twenty-five through chapter four, verse three. In the opening part of chapter four, Paul is further expounding and illustrating the message he has given in chapter three.

Galatians 3:25-29. A new era has dawned. Christ has come and with His coming faith has a new meaning. Prior to Christ's coming the law acted somewhat like a prison guard, confining and yet protecting the sinner (3:23). The law was also like the child's escort or nanny who accompanied and protected him during childhood years.[15] But "now that faith is come, we are no longer under the supervision of the law" (3:25 NIV).

Faith is the means whereby one becomes a child of God. "For you are all sons of God through faith in Christ Jesus" (3:26 NIV). The contrast between works and faith is most obvious. Findlay comments thus: "The efficacy of faith lies in *its object.* 'Works' assume an intrinsic merit in the doer; faith has its virtues in Him it trusts."[16]

Baptism is also an important matter in Christianity. "For as many of you as were baptized into Christ have put on Christ" (3:27 NKJ). In and of itself baptism has no more merit than circumcision. On the other hand, baptism "presupposes faith" and is often used by Paul as being synonymous with faith.[17]

A Jewish man often thanked God that He had not made him a Gentile, a woman, or a slave; but in the family of God ethnic, cultural, class, and gender distinctions are not significant, "For you are all one in Christ Jesus" (3:28d NKJ). Consequently, the message of the Judaizers was utterly misleading and dangerous. Findlay has clearly expressed the issues at hand for the Galatians.

> "Faith in Christ Jesus" is a condition that opens the door to every human being,— "Jew or Greek, bond or free, male or female." If then baptized, believing Gentiles are sons of God, they stand already on a level higher than any to which Mosaism raised its professors. "Putting on Christ," they are robed in a righteousness brighter and purer than that of the most blameless legalist. What can Judaism do for them more? How could they wish to cover their glorious dress with its faded, worn-out garments? To add circumcision to their faith would be not to rise, but to sink from the state of sons to that of serfs.[18]

Coming into God's family by faith in Jesus Christ brought with it the privilege of being part of "Abraham's seed, and heirs according to promise" (3:29). Abraham was a man of faith and the promises made to him were particularly fulfilled in Christ. The Galatians, like other Gentile Christians, are in "the true Abrahamic succession of faith."[19]

Galatians 4:1-3. Cole may be correct when he suggests that the connecting link of the previous chapter with the early part of chapter four may be the reference to the paidagogos who leads the child "to and from school ...while still in his minority."[20] In Galatians 4:1-8 Whedon sees "the development from Judaism or Gentilism to Christianity," as being "parallel to the development from childhood into manhood."[21] Unfortunately, the Galatians had moved in the wrong direction and had, therefore, "advanced backwards."[22]

Paul painted two pictures to show the Galatians the folly of adding circumcision to Christ. The first is that of a child who is heir to his father's estate, but until he reaches the age of maturity set by his father, he is much like a servant or slave since he (the child) is under the supervision of guardians. It is understood that a child cannot make decisions and function like a mature adult. Time is an important factor in progressing from childhood to adulthood.

In the second portrait Paul, the Galatians, and other Christians appear. He identifies himself and other Christians as having been "children" prior to coming to Christ, thus in a parallel relation to "child" in verse one. In this pre-Christian state Paul says they had been "in bondage under the elements of the world" (v. 3b). There is not a uniform agreement among scholars as to the meaning of "elements (στοιχεῖα) of the world." The term στοιχεῖον is found only seven times in the New Testament, and two of these are in Galatians.[23] According to Arndt and Gingrich the term can bear several possible meanings, such as: elements (of learning), fundamental principles, letters of the alphabet, elemental substances, basic elements (in the natural world), elemental spirits, and heavenly bodies.[24]

Since most of the Galatians had doubtless been Gentile pagans prior to their conversions, one can see how the various meaning of "elements" might apply to their previous worship. However, since Paul includes himself in the statement, "even so, we, when we were children, were in bondage under the elements of the world," and since Paul had been a devout Jew prior to his conversion, it seems best that a meaning for στοιχεῖον be found that could apply to the worship of both paganism and Judaism. In this setting it would appear that the term "elements" denotes the beginning lessons Jews or Gentiles learned in their respective religious experiences, but which have now been outmoded by Christ.[25] No doubt the "bondage" connected with these "elements of the world" involved various rituals and ceremonies which placed heavy burdens upon both Jewish and pagan worshipers. For the Jews the "elements" point back to the law in Galatians 3:23. For the Galatian Gentiles it involved the observation of special occasions throughout the year (4:10). To return to "the weak and worthless elemental things" of their previous worship would be to return to bondage (4:9c, d NASB).

Text

A significant transition is noted in verse four: "But when the fullness of the time was come, God sent forth His Son, made of a woman, made under the law." Just as the heir child had to pass through various stages and experiences in order to mature into adulthood, so Judaism had to pass through elemental stages in the unfolding of progressive revelation until the fullness of time should strike when Christ would be sent into the world. The father of the heir determined the exact time when he should pass into maturity and be invested with all his filial rights. Even so, the heavenly Father determined the exact time when Christ should come. "The revelation made to Paul could not have been received by Moses, or David, or Isaiah. His doctrine was only possible after and in consequence of theirs."[26]

Christ was "born of a woman" in order that He might be fully human. He was "born under law" so that He might be in subjection to it. Findlay penned these words: "The Son of God who was to end the legal bondage, was sent into it Himself. He wore the legal yoke that He might break it."[27]

The purpose in Christ's coming was to provide redemption, to bring one from the servitude of bondage under law to adoption into God's family as a full-fledged son (4:5). One is reminded of Paul's language in Romans 8:15b, when he stated: "You received the Spirit of adoption" (NKJ). In each of these passages there are both receivers and givers. Sinners are the recipients and God, or Christ, is the Giver. Thus salvation is a gift, freely bestowed by God's grace on all who believe. "For it is by grace you have been saved, through faith—and this not from yourselves, it is the gift of God—not by works, so that no one can boast" (Eph. 2:8-9 NIV).

Paul had already told the Galatians that justification is by faith (3:24) and that we become "children of God by faith in Christ Jesus" (3:26). Even as revelation was progressive in the Old Testament era, there is a sense in which the work of salvation is progressive. The work of the Holy Spirit in awakening and convicting the sinner is prerequisite to salvation. Without His work of conviction no one would seek the Lord. God's plan of salvation involves at least three important and successive stages, namely, regeneration, entire sanctification, and glorification.

Sometimes regeneration is called the first work of grace. William M. Smith offers an interesting discussion on three changes which are effected in this first work of grace.[28] He points out that each of these follows a logical sequence, even though all three of them seems to take place simultaneously in the experience of the seeker. Smith calls justification a "changed record," regeneration a "changed nature," and adoption a "changed relation." He claims that in point of time regeneration must take place prior to adoption, since only a living person would be adopted. Justification must take place prior to regeneration, since only a person whose record has been made right is a candidate for the new birth.[29]

Thus when Paul talks about those who "receive the adoption of sons" (4:5), it is understood that justification and regeneration are also included in this so-called "first work of grace," since one cannot become a child of God without being justified and regenerated.

If Smith is correct in affirming the work of God in bringing about one's conversion to unfold in this order—justification, regeneration, and adoption—the next step is revealed in Galatians 4:6. It entails confirmation of one's conversion, which is attested when God sends forth "the Spirit of His Son into our hearts, the Spirit who calls out, 'Αββα, Father'" (4:6b, c NIV).

Paul does not say that receiving the Spirit of Christ makes one a son; rather, he asserts that "because you are sons, God sent the Spirit of his Son into your hearts" (4:6a, b). Opting for a different sequence of divine operation in bringing one into the Kingdom of God than that which is given by Smith, J. A. Beet sees regeneration as taking place after one has received the Spirit since the Spirit is the agent in bringing about the new birth (Jn. 3:5; Titus 3:5).[30] Whatever the exact sequence may be is not worth splitting hairs over. The following facts are clearly stated in Scripture: sonship is obtained by faith in Christ; in consequence of that faith, and subsequent to it, the Spirit of Christ is sent into one's heart "crying Abba, Father."

Another parallel is most obvious. God had sent His Son into the world after it had become fully prepared through the progressive experiences of both Judaism and Gentilism (Gal. 4:4). Even so, there comes a "fullness of time" in the experiences of a seeker after God when confession of need has been made and faith has been exercised. When one's preparatory experiences have ripened into a true heart faith (Rom. 10:8-10), God again becomes a Sender. This time God the Father sends "the Spirit of His Son into our hearts."

"The Spirit of His Son" is none other than the Holy Spirit. At any rate, the Holy Spirit and the Spirit of Christ are one and the same in essence. The Father, Son, and Spirit have a distinction in personality but a sameness in essence, as noted in various Biblical passages.

Jesus is God (Matt. 26:64; Phil. 2:6) and the Holy Spirit is God (Acts 5:3-4). Jesus referred to the Holy Spirit as "the Spirit of your Father" (Matt. 10:20b), and, since Jesus and God the Father are one with each other (Jn. 17:22), the Father, Son, and Spirit must be one. Jesus told His disciples that He must depart in order for the Comforter to come. "But if I depart, I will send Him to you" (Jn. 16:7e NKJ). Jesus had promised His disciples that He would send them "another Comforter" who would abide with them forever (Jn. 14:16). Jesus called this Comforter the "Spirit of truth" (Jn. 14:17; 15:26); 16:13), yet Jesus declared this of Himself: "I am ...the truth" (Jn. 14b). In conjunction with His promise to send the Comforter, Jesus said: "I will not leave you comfortless: I will come to you" (Jn. 14:18). If Jesus were leaving this world to return to the Father, how then could He come to His disciples? Simply by means of His "other Self," the Holy Spirit Who would teach them (Jn. 14:26), guide them (Jn. 16:13), and show them the things of both the Father and the Son (Jn. 16:15).

"The Spirit of His Son" is the "the Spirit of adoption" in Romans 8:15. However, upon receiving the Spirit of adoption in this passage Paul says, "We cry, Abba, Father." But in Galatians 4:6 it is "the Spirit of His Son" Who cries, "Abba, Father." Why would both the Holy Spirit and the newborn child of God cry, "Abba, Father?" This is doubtless due to the dual witness in Romans 8:16: "...the Spirit Himself bears witness with our spirit that we are the children of God." Perhaps the Holy Spirit is called "the Spirit of His Son" in order to emphasize His work in bringing one into sonship. As God's only begotten Son,

Jesus often addressed Him as "Father." The first words of a young child are often "Da, da." It would appear that the logical sequence would unfold thus: when the sinner confesses his sins and exercises faith in the Lord Jesus, he is forgiven, made a new creature, and adopted into God's family. Then the Holy Spirit cries, "Abba, Father," in the heart of the believer. Upon hearing the Spirit's cry, the one finding Christ immediately cries out, "Abba, Father." The two witnesses are in agreement with each other, thus assuring the seeker that his sins are forgiven. Huxtable thinks that believers provide the Spirit with "organs of utterance" in Romans 8:15.[31] But since there are two distinct witnesses in Romans 8:16, it would seem best to interpret them as two distinct cries, with the first prompting the second.

The great transformation wrought in the heart of the believer brings about a transition from the bondage of servanthood or slavery to the freedom and blessing of sonship. Wesley once thought he would have gone to hell should he have died prior to his Aldersgate experience in 1738, but in later reflection he recognized that he had been a servant of God for many years before he became a son.[32]

One other point where the Galatians passage is similar to that of Romans should be noted. Both passages discuss elementary things—sonship, adoption, and the cry of "Abba, Father"—but each of them also notes that these experiences lead onward toward an inheritance. One becomes an heir as a consequence of being a child (Rom. 8:17; Gal. 4:7).

In an earthly setting an heir is a child who receives the property and possessions of the father at the time of his death. In the setting of a child/heir of God the parallelism does not carry through, since God will never die. Rather, it will be at the death of God's child or at the time of Christ's advent that God's children will receive their inheritance. Peter identifies a Christian's inheritance as one which is" imperishable and undefiled and will not fade away, reserved in heaven for you" (1 Pet. 1:6 NASB). In its fullest meaning the inheritance is the Lord Himself as He affirmed in Ezekiel 44:28, "I am their inheritance: ...I am their possession."

When Paul wrote to the Church at Ephesus, he noted the role of the Holy Spirit in regard to their inheritance. As one would expect, hearing the Word and believing in Christ were important elements in obtaining salvation (Eph. 1:13a, b).

As a result of their faith, Paul wrote: "You were sealed with the Holy Spirit of promise, who is the guarantee of our inheritance until the redemption of the purchased possession, to the praise of His glory" (1:13c, d—14 NKJ). The Ephesians had been sealed (ἐσφραγίσθητε) by the Spirit. The verb σφραγίδω can be translated as mark, seal up, acknowledge, attest, or certify.[33] The "earnest or guarantee" (ἀρραβών) of our inheritance is an interesting word. It means a pledge, first installment, down payment, or deposit.[34]

It is the Holy Spirit who seals, marks, or certifies the one who hears the Word of truth and believes in Christ (Eph. 1:13). The Spirit becomes the "first installment of our inheritance" (1:14). Since the Holy Spirit is the Spirit of adoption (Rom. 8:15b) who cries, "Abba, Father," and since a child of God becomes an heir of God (Rom. 8:17a; Gal. 4:7b), it would seem to follow that when Paul talks about the Spirit sealing a believer and being a first installment of our inheritance, it is simply another way of saying this: "The Spirit Himself bears witness with our spirit that we are children of God" (Rom. 8:16 NKJ).[35]

The witness of the Spirit provides a foretaste of final blessing when the inheritance comes to its full fruition. Paul assured the Corinthians that God "set his seal of ownership on us, and put his Spirit in our hearts as a deposit, guaranteeing what is to come" (2 Cor. 1:22 NIV).

1 John 3:24; 4:13; 5:10

In 1 John the Apostle repeatedly uses the words "we know." He describes the Christian life as one of certitude. A Christian knows God (2:3, 13-14), truth (2:21), and the fact that he dwells in God and God in him (3:24; 4:13).

Greek Texts

The five Greek texts cited earlier are in virtual agreement in these three verses with the exception of the last word in 5:10a. In three of the texts the one who believes on the Son of God is said to have "the witness in him" (αὐτῷ, but in Westcott and Hort, αὑτῷ),[36] while in the other two texts the witness is said to be "in himself" (ἑαυτῷ).[37] Whichever text one may choose, the meaning is basically the same.

As in the Pauline passages in Romans and Galatians the essential agreement of the Greek texts in these Johannine verses provides a solid biblical foundation for the doctrine of the witness of the Holy Spirit to one's conversion.

Context

Only brief attention will be given to the context of 1 John. Since John's style is different from Paul's, no attempt will be made to divide the context into the categories of "broad" and "immediate" as had been done for the passages in Romans and Galatians. Perhaps an overview of John's teaching in his first epistle can best be seen by observing several contrasts which he sets forth in vivid language.

Light and Darkness. "God is light and in Him is no darkness at all" (1:5c

NKJ). In commenting upon these words Clarke states that God is the "source of wisdom, knowledge, holiness and happiness; and *in him is no darkness at all—* no ignorance, no imperfection, no sinfulness, no misery."[38] Since light dispels darkness, walking in the light of God brings a right relationship and fellowship with Him (1:7).

If one claims to have fellowship with God but walks in darkness, i.e., sin, he is not telling the truth (1:6). One who hates his brother is in darkness and walks in darkness because his eyes are blinded (2:11).

Love and Hate

John is fond of using the term "love" in both its noun and verb forms. Whether he is talking about God's love for human beings or their love for Him and one another, it is always the loftiest Greek word (ἀγαπάω, ἀγάπη).

Another predicate of God is asserted by John when he declares that "God is love" (4:8b, 16b). He is the source and originator of love. "In this is love, not that we loved God, but that He loved us and sent His son to be the propitiation for our sins" (4:10 NKJ). "We love Him because He first loved us" (4:19 NKJ).

Love for others is an evidence that God's love is in one's heart (4:12). On the other hand, "If someone says, 'I love God,' and hates his brother, he is a liar; for he who does not love his brother whom he has seen, how can he love God whom he has not seen?" (4:20 NKJ). If one hates his brother, that hatred places him in the classification of "a murderer" (3:15).

Truth and Lies

The truth is contrasted with a lie (2:21). John refers to "the spirit of truth, and the spirit of error" (4:6d). God the Father and Christ the Son are identified as being "true" (5:20).

Truth is commonly defined as "reality." Hence a lie is marked by unreality—it pretends to be what it is not.

In his Gospel John noted that Jesus claimed to be "the truth" (Jn. 14:6b). Jesus also said: "You shall know the truth, and the truth shall make you free" (Jn. 8:32 NKJ). Since Christ is truth in its highest meaning, could not one rewrite John 8:32 thus: "You shall know Christ and He shall make you free."

Jesus Christ and Antichrists

Jesus Christ is at the heart of 1 John. The Incarnation is highlighted at the outset (1:1). Gnosticism had made insidious inroads into the early church.[39] The Gnostics taught that matter is basically evil and spirit alone is good. Since the human body is composed of matter, Gnostics regarded it as evil. Therefore, the Incarnation could not have been real, as they saw it. There were two major schools of thought which developed. The Docetists taught that Jesus did not have a physical body like human beings have; rather, he had a spiritual essence, but only appeared or seemed to have a physical body.

Another theory was apparently developed by Cerinthus, a contemporary of John. Cerinthus claimed that Jesus and Christ were two separate beings. Jesus was born as an ordinary human being. At the time of Jesus' baptism the divine Christ came upon him and then toward the end of Jesus' life the Christ departed from him. According to this theory, the divine Christ never suffered.

John clearly attacked both the Docetists and the followers of Cerinthus. In no uncertain terms John asserted that Jesus Christ had a real physical body (1:1) and He was divine (5:1). "Who is a liar, but he who denies that Jesus is the Christ?" (2:22a NKJ).

The Holy Spirit and Evil Spirits

The Holy Spirit is seen to be the One who imparts knowledge to God's child that God dwells in him (3:24; 4:13). One work of the Spirit is to "bear witness, because the Spirit is truth" (5:6c).

An evil spirit is identified as one who "does not confess that Jesus Christ has come in the flesh" (4:3a), whereas "the Spirit of God… confesses that Jesus Christ has come in the flesh" (4:2).

Obedience and Disobedience

Gnostics claimed to have a secret knowledge whereby they could release their spirits from the incarceration of evil, physical bodies.[40] However, for John it was not enough to say, "I know God," if they did not keep His commandments/Word (2:4, 5) and walk as Christ walked (2:6).

Some of the Gnostics became ascetics, but others became antinomians and thus believed they could use their bodies any way they desired.[41] John may well have had these kinds of Gnostics in mind as he cried out against those who say but do not do. "Everyone who sins breaks the law; in fact, sin is lawlessness" (3:4 NIV). "He who sins is of the devil" (3:8a NKJ). "We know that whoever is born of God does not sin" (5:18a NKJ).

Belief and Unbelief

In order to obtain the new birth one must believe that Jesus is the Christ, the Messiah (5:1a). To overcome the world one must believe that "Jesus is the Son of God" (5:5 NKJ).

On the other hand, one who does not believe the testimony God has given concerning Jesus has made God a liar "because he has not believed the testimony that God has given of His Son" (5:10b, c NKJ).

Texts

Since 1 John 3:24b and 1 John 4:13 are nearly identical, both passages will be treated together. A discussion of 1 John 5:10a will follow.

1 John 3:24b and 1 John 4:13

Prior to each of these verses John exhorts his readers to love one another (3:23c; 4:11). Before the exhortation to love in 3:23 is an admonition to believe in Christ: "We should believe on the name of His Son Jesus Christ" (NKJ).

Emphasis is placed upon keeping God's commandments in 3:24: "Now he who keeps His commandment abides in Him, and He in him. And by this we know that He abides in us, by the Spirit whom He has given us" (NKJ). To know that one dwells in God and God in him is dependent upon the keeping of His commandments. The inward assurance of this mutual indwelling is provided by the Holy Spirit Who "witnesses with our spirits, that we are his children, and brings forth his fruits of peace, love, holiness."[42] Whedon sees a dual testimony at work in this passage with the Holy Spirit involved as "the direct testimony given by him in our hearts uniting with the testimony of our open practical life."[43]

In 4:12b John states that "if we love one another, God abides in us" (NKJ). We have an inward knowledge of this indwelling "because He has given us of His Spirit" (4:13 NASB). Adam Clarke sees 1 John 3:24b and 4:13 as involving the direct witness of the Spirit, but he admits that one cannot explain "how this testimony is given and confirmed."[44]

1 John 5:10a

John uses the term "witness" in both its noun and verb forms (μαρτυρία μαρτυρέω) in 1 John 5:6-11. The Holy Spirit "bears witness, because the Spirit is the truth" (v. 6 NASB). The Spirit, the water, and the blood are in agreement with each other and they also bear witness (v. 8). Both humans and God bear witness, but God's testimony is greater because it is the testimony of God, which he has given about his Son" (v. 9b NIV).

This promise then follows: "The one who believes in the Son of God has the witness in himself" (v. 10a NASB). What is the witness John is describing in this verse? According to verse eleven, "The witness is this, that God has given us eternal life, and this life is in His Son" (NASB). Does the witness pertain to God's written record which He has given us concerning His Son? Doubtless it does, but it must not be limited to God's written Word. God's Word is truth (Jn. 17:17), but so is Christ (Jn. 14:6a), and the Holy Spirit (1 Jn. 5:6c).

At the outset of this chapter John explains how one may enter the new birth: "Whoever believes that Jesus is the Christ is born of God; and whoever loves the Father loves the child born of Him" (v. 1 NASB). Faith and love are important elements in the Christian life, as noted in 1 Jn. 3:23; 4:11; 5:1). If the keeping of God's commandments to believe and to love leads to a knowledge of God's indwelling one's heart, which is then certified by the witness of the Spirit (1 Jn. 3:23, 24); if believing that Jesus is the Christ or the Son of God is a condition for obtaining the new birth; would it not be reasonable to expect an inward verification of this new birth by a witness of the Spirit? And since one of the Spirit's tasks is to bear witness (1 Jn. 5:6), would it not follow that "the one who believes in the Son of God has the witness [of the Spirit to his conversion] in himself" (v. 10a)?

In commenting upon this matter of having "the witness in himself" Adam Clarke states that it is "the Spirit bearing witness with his spirit that he is a child of God," thus aligning 1 John 5:10a with Romans 8:16.[45]

Summary Statements

Throughout this and the previous chapter an attempt has been made to analyze key biblical passages which either assert or suggest that there is such a phenomenon as the witness of the Holy Spirit with the spirit of one who has come to God through Jesus Christ in order to be justified/regenerated. It is now in order to form, by way of summary, conclusions which have been drawn from an analysis of the whole.

1. There are clear biblical affirmations that attest to the reality of the witness of the Holy Spirit with the spirit of one who comes to God through Christ in order to obtain the new birth, as noted in Romans 8:15, 16; Galatians 4:4-7; 1 John 3:24; 4:13; 5:10. This conclusion is based upon both contextual and syntactical relations.

2. The witness of the Spirit does not testify in isolation of, but rather in conjunction with, the testimony of one's own spirit (Rom. 8:16a), which provides a check-and-balance system.

3. The dual witness is further seen by the joint cry that goes forth in the convert's heart: (1) the Spirit cries, "Abba, Father," when He comes into one's heart (Gal. 4:6b); and (b) the newborn babe in Christ also cries, "Abba, Father," as a consequence of being made a child of God (Rom. 8:15b; Gal. 4:6a).

4. The purpose of the witness is to confirm a right relationship as a son or daughter in the family of God (Rom. 8:16b).

5. This witness provides comfort and certainty in being rightly related to God.

6. Faith exercised in one's heart is the means whereby one enters into the new birth and subsequently receives the witness of the Spirit (Rom. 10:10a; 1 Jn. 5:1, 10a).

Endnotes

1. See *Gr. N.T.-Westcott and Hort*, 424; *Gr. N.T.-Nestle and Aland*, 484-85; *Gr. N.T.-UBS*, 646-47.

2. *Gr. N.T.-Stephens*, 496; *Gr. N.T.-Majority Texts*, 576.

3. For an excellent discussion on these two theories see Merrill C. Tenney, *Galatians, The Charter of Christian Liberty* (Grand Rapids: Wm. B. Eerdmans Publishing Co., 1950), 46-55.

4. Beet, 24.

5. Moulton, Geden, and Moulton, 799. Paul does not use the verb form in Romans, but he does employ the noun form fourteen times.

6. At the Jerusalem conference (Acts 15) Peter protested against the Judaizers' requirement of circumcision for salvation by saying: "Why do you try to test God by putting on the necks of the disciples a yoke that neither we nor our fathers have been able to bear! No! We believe it is through the grace of our Lord Jesus that we are saved" (Acts 15:10-11 NIV).

7. Moulton, Geden, and Moulton, 668-69. By contrast Paul uses "law" (νόμος) nearly seventy times in Romans.

8. *Explanatory Notes*, 478.

9. G. G. Findlay, *The Epistle to the Galatians, The Expositor's Bible* (New York: George H. Doran Company, n.d.), 214-15.

10. William Barclay, *The Letters to the Galatians and Ephesians*, 2nd ed., The Daily Study Bible Series (Philadelphia: The Westminster Press, 1954), 33-34.

11. Moulton, Geden, and Moulton, 809, 808. In Romans Paul uses πίστις about forty-one times and πιστεύω approximately twenty-one times: Moulton, Geden, and Moulton, 809, 807-8.

12. Ibid., 822. By contrast πνεῦμα is used by Paul about thirty-four times in Romans: Ibid., 821.

13. See *Explanatory Notes*, 477, where Wesley interprets the matter of receiving the Spirit to mean receiving both the witness and the fruit of the Spirit.

14. Moulton, Geden, and Moulton, 325.

15. For a helpful discussion on the paidagogos, see Alan Cole, *The Epistle of Paul to the Galatians*, vol. 9 of *Tyndale New Testament Commentaries*, ed. R. V. G. Tasker (Grand Rapids: Wm. B. Eerdmans Publishing Company, 1965), 108.

16. Findlay, 228.

17. Ibid., 231.

18. Ibid., 234.

19. Ibid., 242.

20. Cole, 112.

21. Whedon, D. D., *1 Corinthians—2 Timothy*, vol. 4, *Commentary on the New Testament* (New York: Nelson & Phillips, 1875; repr. Salem, OH: Schmul Publishers, 1977), 230.

22. Ibid.

23. Moulton, Geden, and Moulton, 905.

24. Arndt and Gingrich, 776.

25. For an excellent treatment of the elements of the world see Joseph Agar Beet, *Commentary on St. Paul's Epistle to the Galatians* (no city or publisher listed, 1897; repr. Salem, OH: Schmul Publishers, 1981), 103-4.

26. Findlay, 245-46.

27. Ibid., 251.

28. William M. Smith, *Bible Doctrines* (Westfield, IN: Union Bible Seminary, repr. 1970), 109-10.

29. Ibid.

30. Beet, *Galatians*, 107.

31. E. Huxtable, *Galatians*, vol. 2, *The Pulpit Commentary*, eds. H. D. M. Spence and Joseph S. Excell (Grand Rapids: Wm. B. Eerdmans Publishing Company, 1953 repr.), 186.

32. See *Works*, 3:497.

33. Arndt and Gingrich, 803-4.

34. Ibid., 109.

35. See Clarke, 434, as an advocate for this position.

36. *Gr. N.T.-Westcott and Hort,* 342; *Gr. N.T.-Nestle and Aland,* 606; and *Gr. N.T.-Majority Texts,* 713.

37. *Gr. N.T.-Stephens,* 616; and *Gr. N.T.-UBS,* 820.

38. Clarke, 903.

39. The following overview of Gnosticism is drawn from William Barclay, *The Letters of John and Jude* (Edinburgh: The Saint Andrews Press, 1958; 1 repr., Philadelphia: The Westminster Press, 1960), 5-12.

40. Ibid., 6.

41. Ibid., 11.

42. *Explanatory Notes,* 637.

43. Whedon, D. D., *Titus—Revelation,* vol. 5, *Commentary on the New Testament* (New York: Phillips & Hunt, 1880; repr. Salem, OH: Schmul Publishers, 1978), 272.

44. Clark, 918.

45. Ibid., 924.

Chapter Three

Puritan Teaching on the Witness and Its Influence on Wesley

Both of John Wesley's parents were born into Puritan families and each of these was headed by a distinguished minister. We also know that both of John's great-grandfathers were Puritans. It is possible that the lineage extended back even farther. According to Edmund Calamy, John Wesley's grandfathers, Dr. Samuel Annesley and John Westley,[1] and his great-grandfather, Bartholomew Westley, were ejected in 1662 from the Church of England along with approximately two thousand other ministers who were not willing to fully accept the revised *Book of Common Prayer*.[2] Calamy includes a brief history of each of Wesley's grandfathers.[3]

Given their long and devoted ecclesiastical heritage, it would have seemed inevitable for Samuel Wesley and Susanna Annesley to have continued in the Puritan tradition. But, the fact is, as teenagers and prior to their marriage, Samuel and Susanna chose to break away from the Nonconformists (or the Dissenters as the Puritans were sometimes called) and join the Church of England.

Since Samuel and Susanna were converted to Anglicanism, it was to be expected that they would train up their children to be fully committed to the Church of England. While Samuel and Susanna had made a decisive choice to separate from Dissent, it was not possible for them to be utterly emptied of the principles and practices of Puritanism with which they had been ingrained during their childhood and youthful years. Consequently, the influence of Puritanism was bound to impact Samuel Wesley's family in good, yet subtle, ways. Their biblical and theological emphases coupled with disciplined, daily living reflected Puritan heritage.

John Wesley grew up in an Anglican parsonage and obtained a formal education which would naturally be biased toward theological positions held by the Church of England. In 1740 Wesley wrote an article entitled "The Principles of a Methodist," in which he admitted that he had been trained to interpret the Scriptures relating to assurance in a manner different from that of the Puritans:

When Peter Böhler, as soon as I came to London, affirmed of true faith in Christ, (which is but one,) that it had these two fruits inseparably attending it, "dominion over sin, and constant peace from a *sense* of forgiveness," I was quite amazed, and looked upon it as a new gospel. If this was so, it was clear I had no faith. But I was not willing to be convinced of this. Therefore I disputed with all my might, and laboured to prove that faith might be where these were not; especially, where that *sense* of forgiveness was not; for, all the scriptures relating to this I had been long since taught to construe away, and *to call all Presbyterians who spoke otherwise.*[4]

For the purposes of this study the term "Puritan" is used in a broad sense to include the sixteenth- and seventeenth-century Englishmen who were united with a common objective to "purify" Christian doctrine and life. In this context some of the Puritans were members of the Church of England, others included Baptists and Independents who opted to separate from the Church, and yet others were Presbyterians and Independents who had been ejected through the Act of Uniformity in 1662. Although the Puritans were identified by various religious name tags, they were united in a belief that the Bible is the authoritative source for faith and practice. They also believed in experiential religion which involves a vital, living faith and assurance of sins forgiven.

Since Wesley was reared and educated in Anglicanism it is indeed amazing that he became a serious student of Puritan literature and published so many of their writings, albeit in modified form. Exactly how or when Wesley became interested in Puritan writers is not clear. In his excellent study on Wesley and Puritanism, Robert Monk concludes that Wesley's "openness to truth wherever he found it is the clue to his accepting so much from the Puritan divines, who were certainly outside the scope of his formal education."[5]

Religious crises affect one's interests and directions. Although Wesley had read the writings of several Puritans prior to 1738, it was not until after his Aldersgate experience that he "came to a genuine appreciation of the Puritans and their teachings...."[6] No doubt the greatest single area of interest for both Wesley and the Puritans was their genuine concern for practical Christian living.

Among the doctrines embraced by the Puritans and Wesley perhaps none was more significant than that of assurance of salvation. Wesley must have been surprised as he read Puritan after Puritan and found that they had placed much emphasis upon the privilege of being a recipient of the witness of the Spirit to one's salvation.

Wesley is well known for his teaching on the doctrine of assurance. He is often credited with recovering this doctrine which was nearly lost during the

Middle Ages; but the fact is, the sixteenth- and seventeenth-century Puritans had been stressing this biblical teaching long before Wesley's birth.

The purpose of this chapter is to examine the doctrine of the witness of the Spirit as taught by the Puritans, particularly the writings of those whom Wesley included in *A Christian Library*, in order to see what influence, if any, they appear to have had upon Wesley's understanding and teaching of this doctrine. In order to better appreciate the influence of the Puritans, a brief background will be given concerning *A Christian Library* before noting the specific teaching of the Puritans on the witness of the Spirit.

A Christian Library

Wesley knew the value of placing good Christian literature in the hands of his converts. If they were to grow in grace and the knowledge of the Lord, it was imperative for them to fill their minds with truths from God's Word and good books. Wesley was convinced that "reading Christians will be knowing Christians."[7]

Both poverty and illiteracy abounded in Wesley's day, so he provided wholesome literature in simple language for his people. Not only did he himself write many books, pamphlets, and tracts; he also published in abridged form the works of numerous writers.

The largest publishing task undertaken by Wesley took place during the years of 1749-55 when he edited *A Christian Library* which was originally printed in fifty volumes.[8] According to Wesley Tracy a second issue was published in 1772 or 1773 which was followed by a third edition appearing in thirty volumes during the years of 1819-26.[9] This latter edition will be used for this study.

Purpose

In the preface of *A Christian Library* Wesley expressed his purpose in editing the numerous writings which he included in this collection:

> I have particulary endeavored to preserve a consistency throughout, that no part might contradict any others; but all conspire together, "to make the man of God perfect, throughly furnished unto every good word and work."
>
> But in order to do this, I have been obliged, not only to omit the far greatest part of several eminent authors, but also to add what was needful, either to clear their sense, or to correct their mistakes. And in a design of this nature, I apprehend myself to be at full liberty so to do. I therefore take no author for better, for worse; ...but endeavor to follow each so far as he follows Christ. And not (knowingly) one step farther.[10]

As already noted in the full title of *A Christian Library*, Wesley's goal was to publish "the Choicest Pieces of Practical Divinity Which Have Been

Published in the English Language." Wesley appreciated the need for careful biblical and theological studies, but he also knew that a proper understanding of Scripture should lead to daily, practical Christian living. For Wesley, Practical Divinity simply meant "Christianity reduced to practice."[11]

Composition

In a letter to a friend, dated August 14, 1748, Wesley expressed a desire which he had had for some years to print "a little library" of eighty to one hundred volumes.[12] At that time he had several books prepared for publishing and a printer who was ready to begin as soon as Wesley was able to purchase a printing press.[13] Thus he must have been doing extensive reading and editing for *A Christian Library* in the early 1740's or at the latest by the middle 1740's, since the initial printing began in 1749.

Wesley never reached his projected goal of eighty to one hundred volumes but settled for fifty volumes, doubtless due to the lack of sales and his own loss of money in the project as revealed in a solemn entry in his *Journal*, dated November 6, 1752: "In the remaining part of this and in the following month, I prepared the rest of the books for the *Christian Library*, a work by which I have lost above two hundred pounds. Perhaps the next generation may know the value of it."[14]

Writers

In his first edition Wesley incorporated the writings of more than seventy authors which included (1) four of the Ancient Fathers; (2) at least five foreign writers; (3) an unknown number of authors of anonymous writings; (4) twenty-eight authors from the Church of England; and (5) thirty-two Puritans.[15]

Since Wesley was a minister in the Church of England, it is amazing that he chose more writers from the ranks of Puritanism than from his own church. It is even more amazing that the total number of pages given to Puritan writers is approximately double that which is given to Anglicans.[16]

Most of the Puritans used in *A Christian Library* had active ministries from about 1640-1700 (exceptions were Robert Bolton, John Preston, Richard Sibbes, and William Whately), but none were contemporary with Wesley.[17]

Content

A cursory examination of the Table of Contents reveals a wide variety of literary genre which includes sermons on many topics, prayers, letters, accounts of persecution and martyrdom among God's people, devotional tracts, practical admonitions for Christian living, and numerous biographies of godly people.

Wesley wanted to help his converts live up to all their privileges in Christ Jesus and to be more than conquerors through Him. There seemed to be no better way to do this than to give them stories about saints who lived victoriously. Hence the inclusion of the accounts of so many people of deep piety.

Once again the pattern that emerges is not what one would expect, yet it is consistent with what has been discovered earlier. Puritan biographies far outnumber those of the Church of England.[18] Since daily, victorious Christian living is closely connected to an assurance of personal salvation, it is not surprising that Wesley chose so many Puritan biographies in light of the fact that the writers emphasized the witness of the Spirit far more than did the Anglican ministers.

Abridgement

In his preface to the writings of the Puritans Wesley speaks highly of "those holy men, who sealed the ancient religion with their blood" and others who "took joyfully the spoiling of their goods, ...being branded with the nickname of Puritans, and thereby made a bye-word and a proverb of reproach."[19]

The Puritan writers are commended by Wesley for their strengths. Their writings are characterized by an earnestness and seriousness, with eternity's values in view; they treat the subjects upon which they write in a thorough manner; they magnify Christ; they honor the Scriptures and study it carefully; they expose the fallacies of antinomianism; and they teach their converts how to live and walk by faith, especially when good feelings subside.[20]

On the other hand Wesley does not overlook the weaknesses in the Puritan writers. They tend to be repetitious and verbose; sentences are often long and lack a smooth flow; some words and expressions are obsolete and unintelligible; controversies are regularly incorporated; and their teaching of holiness is not adequate.[21]

Methods

In both the preface to the Puritan writers and the preface to the entire *Christian Library*, Wesley discusses his methods of abridgement.[22] The most common method was simply omission, sometimes of words or phrases, and in other cases paragraphs and large sections.[23] He tended to update obsolete words and delete foreign terms and statements which were added for the purpose of illustration or embellishment.[24] Sometimes Wesley would add words to clarify meaning, but generally speaking, the additions are few.[25] Rearranging words and paraphrasing are more common.[26] As one would expect, Wesley changed the language when the subject at hand was that of predestination or election.

Comparative Study

To determine the Puritans' understanding of the witness of the Spirit, one cannot assume that a careful reading of Puritan writers in *A Christian Library* will suffice, since Wesley took liberty to make many changes in the original writings. However, one may assume that Wesley is in general agreement with the teachings as they appear in *A Christian Library,* since he did the work of abridgment.

It is imperative that one compare the Puritans' original treatises with Wesley's abridged edition in order to discern areas in which he agreed or disagreed with positions embraced by the Puritans. For the purpose of this study selected portions from three Puritans will be compared with the corresponding abridgements in *A Christian Library.* In each case the selections relate to the doctrine of assurance or the witness of the Spirit.

Robert Bolton, General Directions for a Comfortable Walking with God. [27] A passage of approximately forty-eight pages in Bolton's original writing has been selected for the comparative study. [28] In his abridgment of these pages Wesley reduced the total number to about twenty-three pages. [29] Sometimes Wesley omitted entire pages from Bolton's original writing. [30] In other instances large portions of pages were struck out. [31] Personal pronouns originally given in the plural number are sometimes changed to the singular. [32] It is not always easy to understand why Wesley changed some words. For example, he changed Bolton's statement, "...his present *degree* of grace ...," to read like this: "...his present *pitch* of grace..." [33] One can only ask if "pitch" is clearer than "degree." Certainly not in this century.

In most cases it does appear that Wesley's omissions and word changes make for easier and more relevant reading. He often strikes out descriptive, modifying words as in this example of Bolton's statement: "I threw myself into the merciful and meritorious arms of my crucified Lord," which is reduced to these words: "I threw myself into the arms of my crucified Lord." [34]

Wesley is definitely interested in shorter and less embellished sentences. Bolton goes to great length in using picturesque language to describe the witness of the Spirit:

> A sound and undeceiving persuasion that thou art everlastingly locked in the arms of God's mercy and love, grounded upon the word, seconded and set on by the Spirit, is a most rare and rich jewel, which doth infinitely outshine and overweigh in sweetness and worth any rock of diamond, crystal mountain, or this great creation were it all converted into one invaluable pearl; and therefore is infinitely envied, and assaulted mightily on all sides. [35]

Wesley abridged this lengthy description to read thus: "The real testimony of the Spirit, is a most rare jewel, which doth infinitely outweigh in worth any rock of diamond; and therefore is infinitely envied, and assaulted mightily on all sides." [36]

In some instances Wesley will include the Scripture passages used by Bolton but omit the references.[37] Perhaps these kinds of omissions were oversights since biblical references are always helpful to a serious reader.

John Preston, The Breast-Plate of Faith and Love.[38] Four passages have been selected from Preston's treatise, *The Breast-Plate of Faith and Love*, for a comparative study. The total pages comprising these passages number approximately forty.[39] In abridging these passages for *A Christian Library* Wesley reduces them to about nineteen pages.[40]

Since Wesley does not usually enlarge upon another's writing, it is to be expected that the reduction in pages is largely due to striking out words, paragraphs, and entire pages. Omissions may involve theological positions with which Wesley disagreed, such as eternal security.[41] In other cases he may simply omit numerous comments and replace them with a Scripture.[42]

John Owen, On Communion with God the Father, Son, and Holy Ghost.[43] A similar pattern emerges in a comparative study of John Owen's treatise, *On Communion with God the Father, Son, and Holy Ghost*. In a selected passage consisting of about eleven pages[44] which deal with the work of the Holy Spirit, particularly in relation to the doctrine of assurance, Wesley reduces the material in *A Christian Library* to approximately six pages.[45]

Since the pages in Owen's original writing contain about fifty percent more words than the pages in *A Christian Library*, the number of omissions are even more significant. It is understandable that Wesley would strike out several Greek words,[46] but difficult to justify the retention of Latin terms.[47] Not only does Wesley often strike out numerous words in each paragraph from the original writing; he sometimes unites two paragraphs into one.[48]

Puritan Emphases on the Witness
and Agreement/Disagreement with Wesley

The fact that Wesley included so many Puritan writers in *A Christian Library* and also reprinted many other Puritan treatises in abridged forms reveals his high esteem for their literary contributions for the enhancement of practical Christian living. A study of Wesley's abridgments in the above-mentioned treatises by Robert Bolton, John Preston, and John Owen with their original writings makes it clear that, except for a few matters such as election, predestination, and eternal security, he was in essential agreement with them regarding the doctrine of assurance. He affirmed a basic agreement in a letter written in 1760.[49] For the most part Wesley's abridgments did not change the basic teaching of the Puritans; they mainly resulted in the omission of words and paragraphs which he perceived to be unnecessary embellishments to their core messages.

The Puritan writers took a special interest in the person and work of the Holy Spirit, writing upon the doctrine of assurance in a thorough manner.[50] It is doubtful if any religious group throughout church history has written as often and as extensively on the subject of assurance/the witness of the Spirit as did the seventeenth century Puritans.

Attention will now be given to the teaching of several Puritans, most of whom impacted Wesley enough that he reprinted their comments, albeit an abridged form.

Robert Bolton

Robert Bolton was born in 1572 and died in 1631. According to Monk's list of Puritan writers and their particular writings chosen by Wesley for inclusion in the first edition of *A Christian Library*, more treatises were included from Bolton than from any Puritan, namely six.[51]

For this study Bolton's work, *General Directions for a Comfortable Walking with God*, will be explored. The very title would suggest that assurance of one's salvation would be an integral part of "a comfortable walking with God."

Bolton rehearses the manner in which the Holy Spirit and the Word of God worked upon his soul when he was a sinner, bringing him to a place of deep conviction and sorrow for his sins; then leading him to a strong desire for salvation through Christ, whereupon he cast himself upon the Savior and found a glorious experience of conversion.[52] Bolton describes the changes wrought in him as being more than moral, formal, mental, temporary, and partial; rather, as expressed in II Cor. 5:17, "Old things are passed away, behold, all things are become new": this newness involved his "heart, affections, thoughts, words, actions, delights, desires, sorrows, society, and all things."[53]

A consciousness of these changes along with other inward and outward fruits would constitute a testimony or witness of his own spirit or conscience.[54] Bolton also refers to "a secret application of the promises of the Gospel in form of an experimental syllogism" which he sets forth in the following propositions: "Whosoever believes and repents is a child of God: I believe and repent; therefore, I am a child of God."[55] Wesley likewise utilizes syllogism in describing the witness of one's own spirit.[56]

Bolton notes that the first proposition is easy to understand because it is based on Scripture, but a difficulty arises when one asks how the second proposition, based on personal knowledge, can be known for certain? Bolton gives two answers as to how one may know he is a child of God: (1) "by the certainty of internal vision" which he seems to identify with the witness of the Spirit;[57] and (2) "by the testimony of a renewed conscience."[58] If indeed by these two responses Bolton is identifying the witness of the Holy Spirit and the witness of one's spirit, he and Wesley are in strong agreement.

As to the order in which the witnesses are given, however, Bolton and Wesley are not in agreement. For Bolton, the witness of one's spirit comes first and is thereafter confirmed by God's Spirit:

> When we, by these means, have assured our souls that we are the children of God, which is the testimony of our own renewed spirits; the Spirit of God, as another witness, secondeth and confirmeth this assurance by divine inspiration, and by sweet motions and feelings of God's special goodness, and glorious, savingpresence; and so, according to the apostle's phrase, "beareth witness with our spirit," Rom. VIII:16.[59]

On the other hand, Wesley opts for the opposite order by insisting that logic requires the witness of the Spirit to precede the witness of one's spirit:

> That this "testimony of the Spirit of God" must needs, in the very nature of things, be antecedent to the "testimony of our own spirit" may appear from this single consideration: we must be holy of heart and holy in life before we can be conscious that we are so, before we can have "the testimony of our spirit" that we are inwardly and outwardly holy. But we must love God before we can be holy at all; this being the root of all holiness. Now we cannot love God till we know he loves us: "We love him because he first loved us." And we cannot know his pardoning love to us till his Spirit witnesses it to our spirit. Since therefore this "testimony of his Spirit" must precede the love of God and all holiness, of consequence it must precede our inward consciousness thereof, or the "testimony of our spirit" concerning them.[60]

Arthur Yates claims that Wesley's argument is invalidated inasmuch as he used the word "know" in two different senses without realizing it. The phrase "know He loves me" denotes "intellectual knowledge" while "know His love" points to "experiential knowledge."[61] One must also question Wesley's statement, "We must love God before we can be holy at all." If he means that one must first love God in order that he might become holy, the statement is confusing, because the very opposite is obvious: one must be made holy so that he can then love God.

Perhaps Bolton and Wesley were both wrong in their endeavors to establish which witness comes first. Since Romans 8:15 describes a conjoining of God's Spirit with man's spirit, should not these two witnesses bear testimony at the same time rather than in sequence? Monk makes this observation: "Although the two witnesses may therefore be logically distinguished, with God's witness preceding that of the believer, in actual fact that event is simultaneous."[62] In personal experience it may be that for some there is a consciousness of a fruit of the Spirit before there is an awareness of the direct witness of the Spirit. Wesley would seem to be open to this kind of possibility, at least in the last twenty years of his ministry.[63] In reality it is difficult to separate the fruits of the Spirit from His witness. "The consciousness of joy, peace, and love comes with, and is a part of, the consciousness of acceptance."[64]

Bolton sees the two witnesses as a check-and-balance system, so that one is tested by the other. If one claims to have the witness of the Spirit and is at the same time living in even one known sin, that person is greatly deceived.[65] Wesley heartily concurs.[66]

For Bolton, the true witness of the Spirit is always answerable to God's Word, is marked by a pursuit of holiness and a hatred of sin, is attended by a spirit of prayer, and inspires one to use all the means of grace.[67] Wesley is in esential agreement on these issues.

John Preston

John Preston was born in 1587 and died in 1628. Two of his works were included, in an abridged form, in *A Christian Library* by Wesley.

Preston's treatise, *The Breast-Plate of Faith and Love*, will be examined regarding content which is relevant to the doctrine of the witness of the Spirit. As one might expect, the title points to the significant themes of faith and love. The former has a close relationship with assurance.

Preston sees Christ as the object of faith and man's entire heart (which includes his mind and his will) as the subject of faith.[68] Faith involves two acts: (1) the direct act is founded upon God's Word and entails taking Christ and His righteousness for forgiveness as revealed in Scripture; and (2) the reflex act, by which one knows he has taken Christ; this latter act is based upon personal experience and is dependent on the Holy Spirit Who "witnesses with our spirit that we are the children of God."[69] In order to lay hold upon Christ and lean wholly upon Him, one must first be emptied of all else, for faith "cannot fill the heart with Christ, unless the heart be emptied first."[70]

Both faith and assurance admit degrees so that a Christian can and should grow from one degree to another.[71] The Bible speaks about little faith and great faith. Preston urges his readers to "labour to be filled full of faith, by studying the Word," and also to "labour to get full assurance; for the more assurance you have the more love you shall have."[72]

Wesley likewise places much emphasis upon faith. A cursory reading of his first seven sermons in Volume I of his *Works* reveals the fact that Wesley strongly emphasized salvation by faith.[73] He also taught that there are degrees in both faith and assurance.[74]

Faith is made effectual in one's heart by the Holy Spirit Who applies the law to one's conscience, reveals the gracious provisions of Christ, and then bears witness with one's spirit that these provisions of grace are his.[75]

Like other Puritan writers Preston refers to the work and witness of the Spirit by quoting I Corinthians 2:12 as well as Romans 8:16. The work of the Spirit is absolutely essential if the Word of God and the minister's sermon are to be effectual to those to whom they are given.[76]

The Holy Spirit bears witness with a person's spirit in two specific ways: (1) "by clearing of the promises, and shining into our hearts, with such a light as makes us able to discern and believe them;" and (2) "by an immediate voice, by which he speaketh immediately to our spirits..."[77]

By "clearing of the promises" Preston means that God's Spirit joins with us in a "soft voice" as we open the Scripture and thus gives a "secret witness to them" so that we can build upon the promises.[78]

When he speaks of "an immediate voice" Preston is referring to the direct witness of the Spirit. And when this takes place the believer can say, as the disciples said to Jesus in John 16:29, "Now thou speakest plainly, and speakest no parable; we understand thee fully."[79]

As Preston sees it, a "work of humiliation" always precedes the witness of the Spirit and the witness of the Word always accompanies the Spirit's witness.[80] True, saving faith will bring with it purity of heart, the spirit of prayer, peace, love, joy, and humility.[81] One can only wonder if Preston's comments influenced Wesley to include, in his first sermon on the witness, similar characteristics which precede and accompany the Spirit's witness.[82]

John Owen

John Owen was born in 1616 and died in 1683. While serving as Vice-Chancellor of Oxford he had a significant influence upon Wesley's grandfather, John Westley, during his university years.

In the first edition of *A Christian Library* Wesley incorporated five of Owen's writings. The treatise used in this study is entitled, *Of Communion with God the Father, Son, and Holy Ghost.*

Owen presents an excellent discussion on the witness of the Spirit by giving direct attention to Romans 8:16, noting that the issue to which the Spirit bears witness is "that we are the children of God." This transaction from being a child of Satan to a child of God takes place when one receives "the Spirit of adoption."[83]

When one is put to a severe test as to whether he is a child of God, it is the testimony of God's Spirit which settles the issue. To illuminate this point, Owen uses an illustration from a judicial setting, which appears in Wesley's abridged form as follows:

The judge being set, the person concerned lays his claim, produceth his evidences, and pleads them; his adversaries endeavoring all that in them lies to disannul his plea. In the midst of the trial, a person of known and approved integrity comes into the court, and gives testimony fully and directly on behalf of the claimer, which stops the mouths of all his adversaries, and fills the man with joy and satisfaction.[84]

Owen continues the illustration by making a spiritual application:

So is it in this case. The soul, by the power of its own conscience, is brought before the law of God; there a man puts in his plea, that he is a child of God, that he belongs to God's family; and for this end produceth all his evidences, every thing, whereby faith gives him an interest in God. Satan, in the mean time, opposeth with all his might; many flaws are found in his evidences; the truth of them all is questioned, and the soul hangs in suspense as to the issue. In the midst of the contest the Comforter comes; and overpowers the heart with a comfortable persuasion, and bears down all objections, that his plea is good, and that he is a child of God.[85]

In yet another illustration Owen describes the work of the Spirit in bearing witness with one's spirit.[86] He refers to the time when Jesus was asleep in a ship and a great storm arose until the waves covered the vessel. The disciples earnestly implored Jesus to save them before they would perish. Jesus asked them, "Why are ye fearful, O ye of little faith?" Then He "rebuked the winds and the sea, and there was a great calm" (Mt. 8:26).[87] Indeed, the Spirit's witness brings great calm to the storm-tossed soul seeking assurance from God.

Owen and Wesley had much in common in their teaching about the witness. It may be that Wesley borrowed the illustration of the stormy sea brought to a calm.[88]

Other Puritan Writers

Only brief attention can be given to a few other Puritan writers with whom Wesley was acquainted. He included various treatises from some of them in *A Christian Library*.

Isaac Ambrose

Isaac Ambrose was born in 1604 and died in 1663. Wesley incorporated three of Ambrose's writings in *A Christian Library*. One of them, "Looking Unto Jesus," deals with the doctrine of assurance.

Ambrose asserts that the Spirit bears witness both "immediately" and also "mediately."[89] The immediate testimony refers to the direct witness of the Spirit concerning which two extreme positions emerged: (1) that of the Antinomians, who claimed this was the only valid testimony; and (2) that of other professors of religion, who denied that there is such a testimony as the direct witness of the Spirit because of the fanatical extremes to which Antinomians had gone.[90]

Rejecting these extreme positions, Ambrose opted for a middle course which recognizes both the direct witness of the Spirit and also the graces of the Spirit implanted in one's heart.[91] He described the immediate witness as follows:

> Certainly there is a work wherein the Spirit acts as in illumination, and infusion of good motions into us, wherein by a secret influence upon the heart, he quiets and calms the troubled soul concerning its condition by his own immediate power, without any grounds from Scripture outwardly, or graces within.[92]

Ambrose declares that the Spirit witnesses while one is engaged in duty or has just completed a duty, while one is praying, or partaking of the ordinances.[93] Wesley would strongly support Ambrose's emphasis upon availing oneself of the means of grace.

Richard Sibbes

Richard Sibbes was born in 1577 and died in 1635. Three of his writings were chosen by Wesley for inclusion in *A Christian Library*. In two of these, namely, "The Fountain Opened" and "The Nativity of Christ," he gives brief attention to the work of the Spirit in assurance.

In the former treatise he particularly stresses the personal aspect: "Now the Spirit doth not only teach the truths of the Gospel, but the application of those truths, that they are *ours*: this truth of the gospel is *mine*..."[94] This kind of emphasis reminds one of Wesley's definition of the witness when he states: "...the Spirit of God directly witnesses to *my* spirit, that *I* am a child of God; that Jesus Christ hath loved *me*, and given himself for *me*; and that all *my* sins are blotted out, and *I*, even *I*, am reconciled to God."[95]

It is rather surprising that Wesley did not include some of Sibbes' writings, in which he has much to discuss concerning assurance, in *A Christian Library*, since the two men have much in common regarding this doctrine. For example, in his treatise, "Salvation Applied," Sibbes notes that faith involves a two-fold act: "1. An act of faith, trusting and relying; and 2. An act of assurance upon that act of relying."[96] Sibbes carefully distinguishes belief from assurance but strongly urges his readers to strive for both:

> For it is one thing to believe and cast myself upon Christ for pardon of sins, and another thing upon that act to feel assurance and pardon. The one looks to the word more principally; the other is founded upon experience, together with the word. We ought to labor for both, ...to cast ourselves upon Christ for salvation; and then upon believing we ought to find and feel this assurance. But these many times are severed, and sometimes the first is without the second. The first brings us into the state of grace. A man may be in the state of grace, by giving consent to Christ and relying on him for mercy, and yet want assurance of pardon and reconciliation in the second place.[97]

At one time Wesley believed that justifying faith and assurance were coupled together. During the Conference in June of 1747 the question was asked, "Is justifying faith a divine assurance that Christ loved *me* and gave himself for *me*?" To which this answer was given, "We believe it is."[98] However, Wesley's thinking was to undergo a change in the weeks following the 1747 Conference. In a letter to his brother Charles dated July 31, 1747, Wesley stated that he could not necessarily connect justifying faith to assurance.[99] In the letter he defined "justifying faith" as "that faith which whosoever hath not is under the wrath and curse of God," and "a sense of pardon" as "explicit assurance that my sins are forgiven."[100] Wesley went on to correctly base his position on this argument: "if justifying faith *necessarily* implies such an explicit sense of pardon, then every one who has it not, and every one so long as he has it not, is under the wrath and under the curse of God. But this is a supposition contrary to Scripture as well as to experience."[101] Wesley's change of position relative to faith and assurance will be treated more fully in a subsequent chapter.

In his treatise on "Salvation Applied" Sibbes offers several reasons why one could trust Christ and rely upon Him and yet not have a consciousness of assurance.[102] Among the reasons are these: having a physical/mental problem; not understanding the nature of faith; not giving a priority to assurance; and fellowshiping with people who are not deeply spiritual.

It is even more surprising that Wesley did not place in *A Christian Library*, Sibbes' sermon on Romans 8:15, 16, entitled "The Witness of Salvation."[103] This detailed exposition deals with the spirit of bondage, the witness of God's Spirit, and the witness of one's spirit. Sibbes' treatment of "the spirit of bondage," as the Holy Spirit awakening and convicting the sinner, is much like Wesley's position.[104] Much more space is given to a discussion of the witness of one's spirit than that of the witness of God's Spirit.[105]

As Sibbes sees it, a recipient of the witness of the Spirit will manifest three characteristics: (1) humility; (2) watchfulness unto prayer; and (3) love.[106] Once again Wesley is seen to be in agreement with Sibbes' assessment.[107]

Richard Baxter
Richard Baxter was born in 1615 and died in 1691. Only one of his writings, "The Saints' Everlasting Rest," was placed by Wesley into *A Christian Library*.

Baxter affirms that God has provided "sound assurance" or "certainty of salvation" for those who will strive to obtain it.[108] He does not seem to be addressing conscientious readers as much as careless people who do not seek God with all their hearts.

Baxter declares that the reason many live in spiritual uncertainty is "wilfulness and negligence."[109] The means for overcoming this uncertainty is to engage in rigorous examination of oneself.[110]

While hindrances to self-examination and spiritual certainty do come from Satan and ungodly men, the biggest problem arises from one's own heart and life, often manifested in a love of self, sin, and worldly matters.[111] There is always a gulf between sin and assurance.[112]

Another interesting assessment made by Baxter: some lack assurance simply because they are spiritually lazy, but on the other hand, "the way of painful duty is the way of fullest comfort."[113]

Baxter urged his readers who lack assurance to become proactive in their desire to find certainty: "As a man therefore that is cold should not stand still and say, I am so cold that I have no mind to labour, but labour until his coldness be gone, and heat excited; so he that wants the comfort of assurance must not stand still, and say, I am so doubtful and uncomfortable that I have no mind for duty; but ply his duty, and exercise his graces, until he finds his doubts and discomforts vanish."[114]

Wesley had great respect for Baxter and could heartily agree that one must earnestly pursue spiritual certainty and not "rest in any supposed fruit of the Spirit without the witness."[115]

Walter Marshall

The last Puritan writer to be explored in this chapter is Walter Marshall who was born in 1628 and died in 1680. Wesley does not include any of Marshall's treatises in *A Christian Library*. In a letter to Thomas Davenport dated January 19, 1782, Wesley wrote: "It is, I believe, near forty years ago that a friend recommended to me Mr.Marshall's *Gospel Mystery of Sanctification*. A few passages I found scattered up and down which I thought leaned toward Antinomianism. But in general I approved of it well and judged it to be an excellent book."[116]

Marshall divides his book into fourteen chapters which he describes as "Directions." Chapter ten is titled *Direction X*, which opens with these introductory comments: "That we may be prepared by the Comforts of the Gospel to perform sincerely the Duties of the Law, we must get some Assurance of our Salvation, in that very Faith whereby Christ himself is received into our Hearts: therefore we must endeavor to believe on Christ confidently, persuading and assuring ourselves, in the Act of believing, that God freely giveth to us an Interest in Christ and his Salvation, according to his gracious promise."[117]

Marshall is not easy to follow, since his word order and sentence structure are often cumbersome. However, repeated readings open a wealth of spiritual guidelines to a sincere seeker after God.

Throughout the entire chapter Marshall continually highlights the themes of "assurance" and "faith." Like Wesley he had sought in vain for God's salvation because "he sought it not by faith, but by the works of the law."[118] Hence it is understandable that once he found salvation by faith he would be a strong advocate for its proclamation.

For Marshall, assurance and saving faith must necessarily be connected, because "the nature of saving faith...always hath in it some assurance of salvation by Christ, . . ."[119] Marshall taught that there are degrees of assurance just as there are degrees of faith.[120] He often speaks of "some assurance"[121] in contrast with "much assurance."[122] Thus a weak or little faith would have some assurance, although it would necessarily be of a less degree than that which is coupled with strong faith.[123]

If Marshall is correct in asserting that saving faith is inseparably connected with assurance or the witness of the Spirit, then it naturally follows that assurance is necessary for salvation since one can only be saved "by grace" and "through faith" (Eph. 2:8a).

During one period of his ministry Wesley, like Marshall, believed that justifying faith and divine assurance were one and the same and, therefore, if one did not have the witness of the Spirit, he was necessarily unsaved and under the wrath of God. As noted earlier in this chapter Wesley came to see the absurdity of embracing these positions.[124]

Like other Puritan writers, Marshall refers to both "the direct act of faith" and "the reflex acts of faith." Unlike some, such as John Preston, Marshall connects the witness of the Spirit with the "direct act" rather than the "reflex act" of faith.[125] For Marshall, the "reflex act" would fit both Wesley's understanding of the indirect witness and the sequence of following the direct witness, as stated in these words: "...we must necessarily have some assurance of our salvation in the *direct* act of faith, whereby we are justified, sanctified, and saved, before we can, upon any good ground, assure ourselves, that we are already in a state of grace, by that which we call the *reflex* act."[126]

Marshall does not place much emphasis upon the reflex act of faith or the witness of one's own spirit. He does admit that Christians may get "some assurance by the *reflex* act of faith," but he then states that "they often soon lose it again by sins and temptations."[127]

Marshall's closing comments give clear directions to those who have sought assurance only by means of the reflex act and have fallen into sins and spiritual problems by so doing:

The way to avoid these evils, is to get your *assurance*, and to maintain it, and renew it upon all occasions by the *direct* act of faith, by *trusting* assuredly *on the name of the Lord, and staying yourself upon your God, when you walk in darkness, and see no light* in any of your qualifications (Isa. 50:10). I doubt not but the experience of choice Christians will bear witness to this truth.[128]

Although Wesley was deeply indebted to the Moravians for their personal interactions and guidance in his life leading him to an assurance of sins forgiven, he was especially indebted to the Puritans for their prolific writings on the witness of the Spirit which doubtless helped him develop his own theological statements on the doctrine. There was not unanimous agreement among the Puritans as to the detailed meaning of the witness of the Spirit, yet they did have much in common in their understanding of the doctrine and in the emphasis they placed upon assurance.[129]

A study of the Puritan literature of the witness alongside that of Wesley's writings leads one to the conclusion that he had much in common with them and was doubtless influenced much by their contributions on the doctrine. This assessment is supported by the fact that Wesley read and abridged numerous Puritan treatises dealing with the witness of the Spirit in order to incorporate them into *A Christian Library*. Perhaps he would have included other Puritan writings in *A Christian Library* if he would have published eighty to one hundred volumes as he had originally planned, instead of just fifty volumes.[130]

Summary Statements

It does seem fitting to close this chapter by enumerating the areas in which the Puritans and Wesley are in essential agreement regarding assurance/the witness of the Spirit:

(1) Assurance or the witness of the Spirit is a biblical doctrine which needs to be understood and experienced.

(2) The witness of the Spirit to one's salvation is preceded by the Spirit serving as "The spirit of bondage again to fear" (Rom. 8:15) in which He awakens and convicts a sinner of his lost condition.

(3) There is such a phenomenon as the direct and immediate witness of the Holy Spirit with a person's spirit (Rom. 8:16) which may or may not be accompanied by the Word of God.

(4) There is also the witness of one's spirit which is basically the testimony of one's conscience, reason, or understanding.

(5) Salvation is obtained by faith, but justifying faith and assurance are not synonymous; they are not necessarily connected.

(6) It is possible that one might possess justifying faith and yet lack assurance for a time, perhaps due to some mental or physical difficulty.

(7) However, the normal Christian experience for believers is to enjoy both the witness of the Holy Spirit and the witness of one's own spirit.

(8) The witness of the Spirit brings peace and calm to the storm-tossed soul, much like Jesus brought calm to the storm-tossed sea.

(9) Both the witness of the Spirit and the witness of one's own spirit are essential in providing a check-and-balance system wherein each is tested by the other.

(10) Sin and assurance are incompatible; true assurance is never given to anyone who is involved in a known sin.

Endnotes

1. An early spelling of the name included a "t" which was apparently dropped by Samuel when he attended Oxford; see Robert C. Monk, *John Wesley: His Puritan Heritage* (Nashville: Abingdon Press, 1966), 20. A second edition has recently been published at Lanham, MD.: Scarecrow Press, c. 1999. However, by the time the new edition was published the research and writing of this chapter was completed. The second edition is an expansion on the first but contains the same essential content.

2. Edmund Calamy, *The Nonconformist's Memorial*, 2nd ed., 3 vols. (London: Printed for Button and Son, and T. Hurst, Paternoster-Row, 1802-3), 1:124-28; 2:115, 164-75.

3. Ibid. Since Dr. Annesley was a well-known leader among the Puritans, one would have expected Calamy to have devoted more space to him than to the other grandfather; however, less than five pages is given to Annesley, while more than ten pages is granted to John Westley.

4. John Wesley, *The Works of John Wesley*, 14 vols., ed. Thomas Jackson (Grand Rapids: Baker Book House, 1978), 8:366 (italics mine). Since the Bicentennial Edition of *The Works of John Wesley* is not available in all its volumes at the time of this writing, it will be necessary to use the edition edited by Thomas Jackson for some references (hereafter cited as *Works*, ed. Jackson).

5. Monk, 36.

6. Ibid., 23.

7. John Wesley, *The Letters of the Rev. John Wesley*, A.M., ed. John Telford (London: Epworth Press, 1960), 6:201 (hereafter cited as *Letters*).

8. The complete title is *A Christian Library: Consisting of Extracts From and Abridgements of the Choicest Pieces of Practical Divinity Which Have Been Published in the English Tongue.*

9. Wesley D. Tracy, *The Wesleyan Way to Spiritual Formation: Christian Spirituality in the Letters of John Wesley* (doctoral dissertation, 1987), 10.

10. John Wesley, *A Christian Library*, 30 vols., 3rd ed. (London: Printed by T. Cordeux, for T. Blanshard, 1819-26), I, IX (hereafter cited as *CL*).

11. As quoted by Monk, 33.

12. *Letters*, 2:152.

13. Ibid.

14. *Works*, 20:443.

15. See Monk, 256-62 for a complete list of the writers as they are placed in the first edition of *A Christian Library*.

16. See Monk, 38, and Tracy, 24.

17. Monk, 39-40.

18. According to Monk, 263-64, there were only eight biographies of men from the Church of England, while there were twenty-five from the Puritans. But this latter number does not include eleven other Puritans for whom brief biographies were given (see Monk, 259).

19. *CL*, 4:105.

20. Ibid., 4:106-8.

21. Ibid., 4:106.

22. Ibid., 4:106; 1:ix.

23. Wesley reduced Isaac Watt's *Treatise on Passions* of one hundred and seventy-seven pages to a tract of twenty-four pages; see *Works*, ed. Jackson, 3:353.

24. See Monk, 50-51.

25. Ibid., 51.

26. Ibid.

27. Robert Bolton, *General Directions for a Comfortable Walking with God* (Ligonier, PA: Soli Deo Gloria Publications, 1991 reprint). This treatise was first published in 1626.

28. Bolton, 344-91.

29. *CL*, 4:396-419.

30. Bolton, 360-61, 367, 385, 388-89. *CL*, 4:404-6, 417-19.

31. Bolton, 366, 371, 381-82. *CL*, 4:408-11, 415-19.

32. Bolton, 362, 379. *CL*, 4:406, 414.

33. Bolton, 382. *CL*, 416.

34. Bolton, 346. *CL*, 4:398.

35. Bolton, 375.

36. *CL*, 4:412.

37. Bolton, 363, 386. *CL*, 4:407,417.

38. John Preston, *The Breast-Plate of Faith and Love*, 5th ed., (London: Imprinted by R.Y. for Nicholas Bourne, 1634; reprint, Carlisle, PA: The Banner of Truth Trust, 1979).

39. Preston, 44-59, 99-117, 159-66, 190-98.

40. *CL*, 5:346-51, 362-67, 378-81, 386-88.

41. Preston, 54. *CL*, 5:349-50.

42. Preston, 54-55. *CL*, 5:349-50.

43. John Owen, *The Works of John Owen*, ed. William H. Goold, Vol. 2, *On Communion with God the Father, Son, and Holy Ghost* (London: The Banner of Truth Trust, reprint 1966).

44. Owen, 239-49.

45. *CL*, 11:94-99.

46. Owen, 239, 241. *CL*, 11:94-95.

47. Owen, 242. *CL*, 11:96.

48. Owen, 240-41, 242-43. *CL*, 11:94-95, 96-97.

49. See *Letters*, 4:126, where Wesley writes to the editor of *Lloyd's Evening Post* in response to criticisms given by a "Mr. T. H. alias E. L." Part of Wesley's comments are as follows: "…you say: 'No Protestant divine ever taught your doctrine of Assurance.' I hope you know no better; but it is strange you should not. Did you never see Bishop Hall's works? Was not he a Protestant divine? Was not Mr. Perkins, Bolton, Dr. Sibbs, Dr. Preston, Archbishop Leighton? …By assurance …I mean 'a confidence which a man hath in God that by the merits of Christ his sins are forgiven and he reconciled to the favor of God.'"

50. See J. I. Packer, *A Quest for Godliness: The Puritan Vision of the Christian Life* (Wheaton, IL, Crossway Books, 1990), 179, where he states, "The work of the Holy Spirit is the field in which the Puritans' most valuable contributions to the church's theological heritage were made, and the subject of assurance in particular is treated with great fullness and profundity by some of the finest Puritan minds…"

51. Monk, 259.

52. Bolton, 344-47. *CL*, 4:396-99.

53. Bolton, 347-48. *Cl*, 4:399.

54. Bolton, 365-66. *CL*, 4:408.

55. Bolton, 362. *CL*, 4:406.

56. See *Works*, 1:288, where Wesley gives this syllogism: "Experience or inward consciousness, tells me that I have the fruit of the Spirit. And hence I rationally conclude: therefore I am a child of God." See also *Works*, 1:272, for another syllogism.

57. See Bolton, 355, where he connects "the evidence of internal vision" with I Cor. 2:12, "We have received, not the spirit of the world, but the spirit which is God; that we might know the things that are freely given to us of God."

58. Bolton, 362. *CL*, 4:406.

59. Bolton, 368. *CL*, 4:408.

60. *Works*, 1:274-75.

61. Arthur Yates, *The Doctrine of Assurance* (London: The Epworth Press, 1952), 135.

62. Monk, 84.

63. See *Letters*, 5:235, 6:272 ff.

64. Monk, 84.

65. Bolton, 368. *CL*, 4:408-9.

66. *Works*, 1:286.

67. Bolton, 370-79. *CL*, 4:410-14.

68. Preston, 44-48. *CL*, 5:346-48.

69. Preston, 53-55. *CL*, 5:349-51.

70. Preston, 57-58. *CL*, 5:351.

71. Preston, 99-105. *CL*, 5:362-64.

72. Preston, 109-10. *CL*, 5:365-66.

73. *Works*, 1:117-232. It is interesting to note that the first sermon is entitled, "Sal-

vation by Faith."

74. *Letters*, 3:305.
75. Preston, 159-62. *CL*, 5:378-79.
76. Preston, 164-65. *CL*, 5:380-81.
77. Preston, 164. *CL*, 5:380.
78. Preston, 164-66, 190-96. *CL*, 5:380-81, 386.
79. Preston, 164. *CL*, 5:380.
80. Preston, 192, 197. *CL*, 5:387-88.
81. Preston, 191 f. *CL*, 5:388-94.
82. *Works*, 1:277-81.
83. Owen, 241.
84. *CL*, 11:95.
85. Ibid.
86. Owen, 242. *CL*, 11:96.
87. Ibid.
88. *Works*, 1:287.
89. *CL*, 9:30.
90. Ibid.
91. Ibid.
92. Ibid.
93. Ibid., 31,33.
94. *CL,* 6:65 (italics mine).
95. *Works,* 1:274 (italics mine).
96. Richard Sibbes, *Works of Richard Sibbes*, ed. Alexander B. Grossart (Carlisle,
PA: The Banner of Truth Trust, 1977 reprint), 5:393.
97. Ibid.
98. *Letters*, 2:108.
99. Ibid.
100. Ibid.
101. Ibid.
102. Sibbes, 5:393-400.
103. Ibid., 7:367-85.
104 Ibid., 7:370-76. *Explanatory Notes*, 382.
105. Ibid., 7:376-81.
106. Ibid., 7:383-85.
107. *Works*, 1:279-81.
108. *CL*, 22:150-51.
109. Ibid., 22:150.
110. Ibid.
111. Ibid., 22:152-55.
112. Ibid., 22:159.
113. Ibid.
114. Ibid., 22:161.

115. *Works*, 1:298.

116. *Letters*, 7:101-2. See also *Works*, 22:110 and *Letters*, 3:239.

117. Ibid., 110.

118. Ibid., 250-51.

119. Ibid., 126.

120. Ibid., 114-15.

121. Ibid., 110,115,126-27,129,132.

122. Ibid., 115.

123. Ibid.

124. See *Letters*, 2:108-9.

125. Ibid., 125-26. Cf. with Preston, 53-55, and *CL*, 5:349-51.

126. Ibid., 130. Cf. *Works*, 1:272-75.

127. Ibid., 132-33.

128. Ibid., 133.

129. For further insights and helpful assessments regarding Puritan literature on the witness of the Spirit, see Forest T. Benner, *The Immediate Antecedents of the Wesleyan Doctrine of the Witness of the Spirit* (Ph.D. Dissertation, Temple University, 1966), 23-149; Howard Watkin-Jones, *The Holy Spirit from Arminius to Wesley* (London: The Epworth Press, 1929), 305-321; and Geoffrey F. Nuttall, *The Holy Spirit in Puritan Faith and Experience* (Oxford: Basil Blackwell, 1947), 48-61.

130. See *Letters*, 2:152, and *Works*, 20:443.

Chapter Four

Wesley's Journal Entries Regarding
the Witness

John Wesley began writing his diaries in 1725 and continued to do so until nearly the end of his long life in 1791.[1] Unfortunately, parts of the diaries 1727-29, 1734, 1737, and 1738 are missing as well as all the diary notes from 1742 to 1783.[2]

On the other hand, it is fortunate that Wesley's complete *Journal* has been published in several editions over a period of approximately two hundred years. The *Journal* covers the most important period of Wesley's life from October 1735 to October 1790.

Although some scholars have dated the publication of the first volume of the *Journal* to 1738 or 1739, it seems more likely the date was 1740.[3] Unlike much of the autobiographical writing of Wesley's time, his *Journal* was written to be published.[4] However, as Reginald Ward notes, "Wesley's *Journal* has much more in common with its literary predecessors than with its successors."[5]

It appears that Wesley was careful to compile, on a daily basis, brief diary notes which would later be enlarged for compilation in his *Journal*.[6] In the midst of an extremely busy schedule he would snatch time here and there to write up portions of the *Journal* which would then be sent off to the printer, but there might be delays of two or three years between the installments.[7] These delays would have afforded Wesley the opportunity to make corrections or additions.[8]

Like some autobiographies prior to and during his lifetime, Wesley incorporated such matters as conversion testimony, travel and landscape data, defense against allegations, religious news, the work of revival, and "thumb-nail sketches of the new birth."[9] Ward asserts that "Wesley reduced the conversion narrative to an insignificant proportion of a huge work running to a million words..."[10] Apparently Ward is referring to Wesley's account of his own conversion. While the total pages dealing directly with his conversion may seem small in contrast to the total pages of the *Journal*, Wesley draws from his own experience lessons and principles which he applies throughout his ministry as he seeks to bring lost humanity to the Savior. In Ward's opinion "the principal theme was his service to the Kingdom of God and the gathering of the Methodist people."[11] But one might well ask, "Does not this theme denote conversion narrative in a broad sense?"

The purpose of this chapter is to explore the major part of Wesley's adult life regarding the significance of the witness of the Spirit in these areas: (1) his own search for assurance of sins forgiven; (2) the development of the doctrine in Wesley's own mind and experience; and (3) the emphasis of the witness in his ministry.

The main divisions for this chapter will be the dates attached to the volumes identified as *Journals and Diaries* in the Bicentennial Edition of *The Works of John Wesley*.

1735-1738

In many respects this is the most important period in Wesley's life concerning his search for and obtainment of assurance of salvation. It was in the spring of 1725 that Wesley started to keep a diary. He had been inspired to do this after reading Bishop Taylor's *Rules for Holy Living and Dying*, but it also seems that Wesley's interest in a diary was the direct outflow of his determination to make religion the chief business of his life.[12]

By the time Wesley began to compile the data for his first *Journal*, he had already been a serious seeker after God for over ten years and would yet have a journey of more than two and one-half years to his Aldersgate experience. Tuttle observes that Wesley's search for assurance from 1725-1735 was centered upon asceticism which was manifested in various phases as follows: (1) as a tutor at Oxford Wesley practiced self-denial (1725-1727); (2) as a parish minister at Wroot he gave himself to solitude (1727-1729); (3) as a leader in the Holy Club he tried works of love (1730-1732); and (4) as a reader after the mystics he stressed the interior life (1732-1735).[13] Ten years of earnest struggles had not brought him to the full assurance of faith.

It is at this point in time that his *Journal* begins as he prepares to sail to Georgia as a missionary.

Voyage to Georgia

The *Journal* opens with this date: Tuesday, October 14, 1735. At the outset Wesley identifies the three men who were traveling with him to America as Mr. Benjamin Ingham, Mr. Charles Delamotte, and his own brother, Charles Wesley. These men had one basic purpose in going to Georgia, namely this, "to save our souls, to live wholly to the glory of God."[14]

In the afternoon of October 14, Wesley and his three companions boarded the *Simmonds* which would not set sail for another week. When he discovered there were twenty-six Moravians on board, Wesley decided to learn German and at least three of the Moravians began to study English so that they might converse with each other.[15]

Less than a week after boarding, Wesley and his friends chose to practice self-denial by giving up meat and eating vegetables only, mainly rice and biscuits. They also gave themselves to a rigorous daily schedule which began at 4:00 a.m. and concluded between 9:00 and 10:00 p.m., involving time for private and public prayers, Bible reading and study, language study, sermon preparations, meals, sharing of activities accomplished, lessons for children, and public worship.[16]

During the voyage to America Wesley revealed a deep-seated fear, especially during a storm. On November 23, 1735, he penned these words: "At night I was waked by the tossing of the ship and roaring of the wind, and plainly showed I was unfit, for I was unwilling to die."[17]

On January 17, 1736, Mr. Wesley wrote: "About eleven I lay down in the great cabin, and in a short time fell asleep, though very uncertain whether I should wake alive, and much ashamed of my unwillingness to die.[18]

Then on January 23 he noted that another storm began in the evening and increased in force the next morning until he recorded these words: "I could not but say to myself, 'How is it that thou hast no faith?' being still unwilling to die."[19]

Tuttle refers to Wesley's fear of death as "the enemy" and further states that "for nearly twenty-five years (1714-1738) Wesley would pursue the kind of assurance that would deliver him from his fear of death and dying." Sin was also an enemy, but for Wesley a fear of death became his greatest observable enemy.[20]

On January 25 the most violent storm of all came upon them. The ship was shaken and jarred with such severity that it appeared the planks would be dashed into pieces. While the Moravians were engaged in a worship service, the sea poured in upon them, splitting the mainsail and causing some of the English-speaking people to scream out of fear; but the Germans remained calm and continued to sing.[21] Later Wesley asked one of them if they were not afraid during the storm. The man answered, "I thank God, no." Wesley then asked if their women and children were not afraid, to which he calmly responded, "No; our women and children are not afraid to die."[22]

After encountering a couple more storms the passengers aboard the *Simmonds* finally came within sight of American trees on February 1. Then, on Friday, February 6, 1736, they set foot upon an American island about 8:00 a.m., where they knelt to give thanks unto God.[23]

Experiences in Georgia

Mr. James Edward Oglethorpe (1696-1785), friend of Samuel Wesley and philanthropist, was the founder of the Colony of Georgia.[24] It was Oglethorpe who urged Wesley to participate in the second trip to Georgia by serving as a missionary to the Indians.[25]

Oglethorpe traveled on to Savannah sometime after the passengers assembled on the small island, but he returned the next day with a Moravian pastor, August Gottlieb Spangenberg.[26] Wesley was concerned about his own conduct and asked Spangenberg to give him counsel; to which the latter responded thus: "My brother, I must first ask you one or two questions. Have you the witness within yourself? Does the Spirit of God bear witness with your spirit that you are a child of God?" Wesley was surprised at the questions and did not respond, so Spangenberg continued by asking, "Do you know Jesus Christ?" Wesley hesitated and then said, "I know he is the Savior of the world;" to which Spangenberg replied, "True, but do you know he has saved you?" Wesley answered, "I hope he has died to save me." Spangenberg then asked Wesley one more question, "Do you know yourself?" Wesley answered, "I do," but in retrospect he expressed his own doubts by saying, "I fear they were vain words."

It appears that Wesley was greatly impressed with Spangenberg as a person and a spiritual leader from the time of their first meeting on February 7. Two days later Wesley asked him many questions about himself and the Moravian Church.[27]

No doubt he began to observe the lives of the Moravians with even greater interest after his dialogues with Spangenberg. For a period of time Wesley spent entire days with the Moravians in one room, except for a little time when he took a walk. In commenting upon their demeanor he wrote these words: "They were always employed, always cheerful themselves, and in good humor with one another. They had put away all anger and strife and wrath and bitterness and clamour and evil-speaking. They walked worthy of the vocation wherewith they were called, and adorned the Gospel of our Lord in all things."[28]

Wesley does not share in the *Journal* much about his spiritual status after his initial meeting with Spangenberg until nearly the end of his sojourn in America, nearly two years after his first discussions with him.[29] What he does record in the *Journal* is a brief overview of his activities which included preaching, giving communion, praying, catechizing children, and dividing the saints into little societies.[30]

When Wesley met Miss Sophy Hopkey in March of 1736, little did he realize that problems would arise between them which would lead to his departure from America about one year and nine months later. On August 23, 1737, Wesley refused to serve her communion and this refusal precipitated anger in Mrs. Sophy Hopkey Williamson which finally brought pressure on Wesley to return to England.[31]

Voyage Back to England

As Wesley began his long voyage back to Britain in December of 1737, he again opened his heart to his spiritual condition regarding his lack of faith and his fear of death:

> Let me observe hereon, (1) that not one of these hours ought to pass out of my remembrance, till I attain another manner of spirit, a spirit equally willing to glorify God by life or by death; (2) that whoever is uneasy on any account (bodily pain alone excepted) carries in himself his own conviction that he is so far an unbeliever. Is he uneasy at the apprehension of death? Then he believeth not that "to die is gain."[32]

On January 8, 1738, he penned these words of confession: "By the most infallible of proofs, inward feeling, I am convinced: 1. Of unbelief, …2. Of pride, …3. Of gross irrecollection, …4. Of levity and luxuriancy of spirit, . . ."[33]

Wesley wrote his oft-quoted admission on January 24: "I went to America to convert the Indians; but Oh! who shall convert me? …I have a fair summer religion. I can talk well; nay and believe myself, while no danger is near: but let death look me in the face, and my spirit is troubled.… O who will deliver me from this fear of death!"[34]

On January 25 Wesley prepared a detailed summary concerning his struggles over many years as he sought for assurance of sins forgiven. Although this incident is rather lengthy, it provides an excellent overview of the various teachings which he had encountered and interacted with over a period of time which probably encompassed about thirteen years.

> 1. For many years have I been tossed about by various winds of doctrine. I asked long ago, What must I do to be saved? The Scripture answered, "Keep the commandments. Believe, hope, love; follow after these tempers till thou has fully attained, that is, till death, by all those outward works and means which God hath appointed, by walking as Christ walked."
>
> 2. I was early warned against laying, as Papists do, too much stress either on outward works or on a faith without works, which, as it does not include, so it will never lead to, true hope or charity. Nor am I sensible that to this hour I have laid too much stress on either, having from the very beginning valued both faith, the means of grace, and good works, not on their own account, but as believing God, who had appointed them, would by them bring me in due time to the mind that was in Christ.

3. But before God's time was come I fell among some Lutheran and Calvinist authors, whose confused and indigested accounts magnified faith to such an amazing size that it quite hid all the rest of the commandments. I did not then see that this was the natural effect of their overgrown fear of popery, being so terrified with the cry of "merit and good works" that they plunged into the other extreme. In this labyrinth I was utterly lost, not being able to find out what the error was, nor yet to reconcile this uncouth hypothesis either with Scripture or common sense.

4. The English writers, such as Bishop Beveridge, Bishop Taylor, and Mr. Nelson, a little relieved me from these well-meaning, wrong-headed Germans. Their accounts of Christianity I could easily see to be, in the main, consistent both with reason and Scripture. Only when they interpreted Scripture in different ways I was often much at a loss. And again there was one thing much insisted on in Scripture—the unity of the Church—which none of them I thought clearly explained, or strongly inculcated.

5. But it was not long before providence brought me to those who showed me a sure rule for interpreting Scripture, viz., *consensus veterum*—"quod ab omnibus, quod ubique, quod semper creditum." At the same time they sufficiently insisted upon a due regard to the One Church at all times and in all places. Nor was it long before I bent the bow too far the other way: (1) by making antiquity a co-ordinate (rather than subordinate) rule with Scripture; (2) by admitting several doubtful writings as undoubted evidences of antiquity; (3) by extending antiquity too far, even to the middle or end of the fourth century; (4) by believing more practices to have been universal in the ancient Church than ever were so; (5) by not considering that the decrees of one provincial synod could bind only that province, and the decrees of a general synod only those provinces whose representatives met therein; (6) by not considering that most of those decrees were adapted to particular times and occasions, and consequently when those occasions ceased, must cease to bind even those provinces.

6. These considerations insensibly stole upon me as I grew acquainted with the mystic writers whose noble descriptions of union with God and internal religion made everything else appear mean, flat, and insipid. But in truth they made good works appear so too; yea, and faith itself, and what not? These gave me an entire new view of religion, nothing like any I had had before. But alas! It was nothing like that religion which Christ and his apostles lived and taught. I had a plenary dispensation from all the commands of God. The form ran thus: "Love is all; all the commands beside are only means of love; you must choose those which you feel are means to you, and use them as long as they are so." Thus were all the bands burst at once. And though I could never fully come into this, nor contentedly omit what God enjoined, yet, I know not how, I fluctuated between obedience and disobedience: I had not heart, no vigor, no zeal in obeying; continually doubting whether I was right or wrong, and never out of perplexities and entanglements. Nor can I at this hour give a distinct account how or when I came a little back toward the right way,. Only my present sense is this: all the other

enemies of Christianity are triflers; the mystics are the most dangerous of all its enemies. They stab it in the vitals, and its most serious professors are most likely to fall by them. May I praise him who hath snatched me out of this fire likewise, by warning all others that it is set on fire of hell.[35]

Four days later, on January 29, Wesley recorded these words: "...I who went to America to convert others, was never myself converted to God."[36] However, in 1774, Wesley responded to this statement by adding this comment: "I am not sure of this,"[37] thus raising a serious question mark about the accuracy of his earlier statement.

In his *Journal* notes for January 29 Wesley raised several questions and made many affirmations regarding his study of philosophy, languages, and theology; he also enumerated his numerous labors and sufferings for the Lord. He then asked, "Does all this give me a claim to the holy, heavenly, divine character of a Christian?" To which he responds: "By no means. If the oracles of God are true, if we are still to abide by 'the law and the testimony,' all these things, though when ennobled by faith in Christ they are holy, and just and good, yet without it are dung and dross..."[38]

Wesley continued by asserting that he was "a child of wrath and hell."[39] In adding a corrective comment to these words in 1774 he wrote these words: "I believe not."[40] He went on to express the kind of faith he wanted as "a sure trust and confidence in God, that through the merits of Christ my sins are forgiven, and I reconciled to the favor of God'..."[41] I want that faith which none can have without knowing that he hath it (though many imagine they have it who have it not)...And he is freed from doubt, 'having the love of God shed abroad in his heart through the Holy Ghost which is given unto him'; which 'Spirit itself beareth witness with his spirit, that he is a child of God.'"[42]

England to Aldersgate

On February 1, 1738, Wesley again set foot on British soil, having been gone for nearly two and one-third years. Six days later, on February 7, he met for the first time Mr. Peter Böhler, a Moravian minister who, along with others, had just come from Germany en route to Georgia for missionary labors.[43] In the next three months Böhler would be used of God to direct Wesley to faith in Christ through which he would obtain assurance of sins forgiven on May 24, 1738, at Aldersgate Street.

Böhler traveled with both John and Charles Wesley from London to Oxford on February 17.[44] In a letter written to Count Zinzendorf concerning this journey with the Wesley brothers, Böhler declared that John "is a good-natured man: he knew he did not properly believe on the Saviour, and was willing to be taught."[45]

Wesley visited with his friend John Gambold on February 18 and noted that Gambold had broken away from his mystic connections. In so doing Wesley revealed his own displeasure with the teachings of mysticism.[46]

The next day he spent much time conversing with Böhler but admits he did not understand Böhler, especially when he said, "My brother, my brother, that philosophy of yours must be purged away."[47]

On March 4 and 5 Wesley again engaged in conversations with Böhler, by whom on the latter day Wesley was "clearly convinced of unbelief, of the want of 'that faith whereby alone we are saved.'"[48] Being convinced of his lack of faith Wesley asked Böhler if it would be better for him to stop preaching until he obtained faith; to which Böhler responded, "By no means…Preach faith *till* you have it, and then *because* you have it, you *will* preach faith."[49]

The following day Wesley offered a condemned prisoner named Clifford the message *of salvation by faith alone.*[50] Although he is not mentioned by name, it appears that Clifford is "the condemned man" with whom Wesley and Mr. Kinchin prayed on March 27, after which he testified that Christ had taken away his sins and condemnation.[51]

On Thursday, March 23, Wesley met with Böhler who asserted that holiness and happiness accompany a living faith. This motivated Wesley to search the Greek Testament to see if this were indeed the doctrine of God.[52]

About one month later, on April 22, Wesley and Böhler met and discussed the nature of faith. The two men agreed on a definition of faith, but Wesley struggled with the concept of faith being "an instantaneous work" as something "given in a moment" so that one "could at once be thus turned from darkness to light, from sin and misery to righteousness and joy in the Holy Ghost."[53] Once again Wesley searched the Scriptures, especially the Acts of the Apostles, and was quite amazed to discover that nearly all the conversions were instantaneous, but he was still not sure God was working in the eighteenth century as He did in the first, until he made this confession the next day:

> I was beat out of this retreat too, by the concurring evidence of several living witnesses, who testified God *had thus wrought in themselves*; giving them in a moment such a faith in the blood of his Son as translated them out of darkness into light, out of sin and fear into holiness and happiness. Here ended my disputing. I could now only cry out, 'Lord, help Thou my unbelief!'"[54]

On April 26 Wesley may have met with Böhler for the last time prior to his departure for America, at least as far as quality time for the two men to be alone. As they walked together across several miles, Böhler exhorted Wesley "not to stop short of the grace of God."[55]

Under the date of May 4, Wesley noted that Böhler left London to embark for America. From the second edition (1743) onwards Wesley affixed these words to the reference of his departure: "O what a work hath God begun since his coming into England!"[56]

From May the 10th till the 13th Wesley lamented that he was "sorrowful and very heavy, being neither able to read nor meditate, nor pray, nor do anything." A letter from Mr. Böhler encouraged him to believe in Christ and to conquer unbelief.[57]

On Friday, May 19, Charles Wesley was stricken a second time with pleurisy. John, along with others, spent Saturday night in prayer. On Sunday John received the unexpected news that Charles had found spiritual victory and subsequently had his physical strength restored as well.[58]

For John, however, Monday through Wednesday, May 22-24, were days of "continual sorrow and heaviness," which is somewhat reflected in questions and answers that he presents in a letter to a friend: "Do we already feel 'peace with God,' and joy in the Holy Ghost?" Does his "Spirit bear witness with our spirit, that we are the children of God'? Alas, with *mine* he does not. Nor, I fear with yours. O thou Saviour of men, save us from trusting in anything but *thee*!"[59]

Before giving a description of his Aldersgate experience on May 24, 1738, Wesley inserted into his *Journal* a review of his life and spiritual conditions, which is divided into twelve periods.[60]

1. Until he was about ten years of age he was very careful to obey the commandments of God, concerning which he had been instructed as the only way to be saved. Wesley admits that his obedience related particularly to outward responsibilities, since he was ignorant of "inward obedience or holiness."

2. The next time frame covered six or seven years (1714-1720) when Wesley was a student in Charterhouse, a boarding school for boys located in London. Being away from home he became careless and often engaged in outward, but not scandalous, sins.

He kept reading his Bible, saying prayers, going to church, and because of these deeds he hoped to be saved.

3. During the next five years Wesley was enrolled as a university student at Christ Church, Oxford. He continued to say prayers and read his Bible along with other religious books, but he also continued to engage in known sins from time to time. Perhaps he now hoped to be saved by having a shallow kind of repentance before and after communion, which he received three times a year.

4. In 1725, when he was twenty-two years of age, Wesley was ordained a deacon in the Church of England. He began reading after Thomas à Kempis and also began to alter his lifestyle, setting apart an hour or two each day

for spiritual matters and praying for inward holiness. As a consequence of now living a good and earnest life, he believed he was a good Christian.

5. In 1726 Wesley was elected a fellow of Lincoln College. He became acquainted at this time with William Law's books, *A Practical Treatise on Christian Perfection* and *A Serious Call to a Devout and Holy Life*. He saw the importance of redeeming time and being more disciplined in his daily life. Because he earnestly strove to keep God's law, both inwardly and outwardly, he was convinced that he was in a saved state.

6. A few years later, in 1730, Wesley got involved in ministering to both the spiritual and the physical needs of prisoners and poor people. He gave himself to fasting and other kinds of self-denial. Yet for all of his good works in behalf of others and his life of self-denial, he could not find "any comfort, nor any assurance of acceptance with God."

7. In this time period Wesley said he met "a contemplative man" (apparently William Law, whom Wesley first visited on July 3, 1732) who discouraged him from engaging in outward works, but rather encouraged him to give himself to mental prayer and similar exercises in order to unite his soul with God. However, the teaching of the mystics did not bring Wesley an assurance of such union with God.

8. This next time frame took place in late 1735 and early 1736 when Wesley was traveling on board the *Simmonds* en route to Georgia. He met twenty-six Moravians who greatly influenced him by their lives and testimonies. They showed him "a more excellent way." He admits he did not understand them at first, but the real problem involved his own preconceived ideas, that he "was too learned and too wise."

9. When engaged in his Georgia ministry, Wesley confessed that he sought to establish his own righteousness, not the righteousness of Christ, which is obtained by a living faith in Him. He was therefore fitting into Romans chapter 7 as the man "under the law."

10. During this time period Wesley is still in Georgia (1736-1737), striving against sin but not conquering; serving sin but doing so unwillingly, living, not under grace, but under the law. This struggle had been going on by now for more than ten years. "Neither had I 'the witness of the Spirit with my spirit.' And indeed could not; for I 'sought it not by faith, but (as it were) by the works of the law.'"

11. While traveling back to England in early 1738 Wesley was convinced that the reason for his uneasiness in the face of possible death was due to his unbelief. Thus the one thing he most needed was a true and living faith, yet he still failed to see that this faith must be in and through Christ, not simply a faith in God. In God's good providence Wesley met Peter Böhler who taught him

that faith has two inseparable fruits attached to it, namely "dominion over sin" and "constant peace from a sense of forgiveness." Wesley was shocked at Böhler's comments, for if he were correct, Wesley had no faith. But Wesley was not ready to believe this without a struggle. Indeed he labored to prove that one might have faith "especially where that sense of forgiveness was not." Wesley went on to say, "For all the Scriptures relating to this I had been long since taught to construe away, and to call all 'Presbyterians' who spoke otherwise. Besides, I well saw no one could (in the nature of things) have such a sense of forgiveness and not *feel* it. But I felt it not. If then there was no faith without this, all my pretensions to faith dropped at once."

12. In this final time frame just before his heart-warming experience Wesley is being led, step by step, through the human instrumentality of Böhler to clearly see from both Scripture and living witnesses that "a true, living faith in Christ is inseparable from a pardon for all past, and freedom from all present sins." Consequently, Wesley resolved to seek God's saving grace by both "renouncing all dependence ...upon *my own* works of righteousness" and by using every means of grace "for this very thing, justifying, saving faith, a full reliance on the blood of Christ shed for *me*; a trust in him as *my* sole justification, sanctification, and redemption."

An Unforgettable Day: May 24, 1738

As noted earlier, Wesley experienced much heaviness Monday through Wednesday, May 22-24. But all this was to change before the 24th would end. In fact, encouraging signs would appear during the day.

About 5:00 a.m. Wesley opened his Bible to 2 Peter 1:4, "There are given unto us exceeding great and precious promises, even that ye should be partakers of the divine nature." It may have been only a few minutes later that he opened the Scripture to Mark 12:34, "Thou art not far from the kingdom of God."[61] Each of those Scriptures must have been a means of encouragement to Wesley in the midst of his heaviness.

At any rate, that afternoon he went to St. Paul's where he heard this anthem:

> Out of the deep have I called unto thee, O Lord. Lord, hear my voice. O Let thine
> ears consider well the voice of my complaint. If thou, Lord, wilt be extreme to
> mark what is done amiss, O Lord, who may abide it? But there is mercy with
> thee; therefore thou shalt be feared. [...] O Israel, trust in the Lord: For with the
> Lord there is mercy, and with him is plenteous redemption. And he shall redeem
> Israel from all his sins.[62]

How fitting were these words from Psalm 130. Wesley must have wondered how soon he would be conscious of "a sense of forgiveness."

In the evening Wesley attended a society meeting on Aldersgate Street, but he did so "very unwillingly," probably out of a sense of obligation. Whatever the case might have been, acting on volition rather than on emotion was soon to bring a long-sought-after blessing. While a man was reading Luther's Preface to his commentary on Romans, something happened. No one can tell it as well as Wesley himself:

> About a quarter to nine, while he was describing the change which God works in the heart through faith in Christ, I felt my heart strangely warmed. I felt I did trust in Christ, Christ alone for salvation, and an assurance was given me that he had taken away *my* sins, even *mine*, and saved *me* from the law of sin and death.[63]

Wesley's testimony deserves careful analysis. Just a few months earlier he had confessed that the "one thing needful" for him was "the gaining a true, living faith" which he identified as "faith in or through Christ."[64] While Wesley was listening to a description of what God does in the heart of one whose faith is in Christ, his own faith blossomed into a true, living confidence in Christ for his own salvation so that he could then affirm, "I felt I did trust in Christ, Christ alone for salvation." His faith brought with it the two concomitants mentioned by Böhler, namely "dominion over sin and constant peace from a sense of forgiveness."[65] The latter blessing was immediately made manifest to Wesley: "—an assurance was given me that he had taken away my sins;" the earlier blessing, "dominion over sin," would be verified that night and over and over again in the days and weeks following May 24.

That God had wrought a marvelous work of grace in Wesley's heart was most evident in what he did immediately after obtaining assurance of sins forgiven: he prayed fervently for those who had persecuted him and despitefully used him.[66]

Wesley then testified to those present what he had first felt in his heart, but soon the enemy suggested to him, "This cannot be faith; for where is thy joy?" The Lord helped Wesley to see that "*peace and victory over sin are essential to faith in the Captain of our salvation, but that as to the transports of joy* that usually attend the beginning of it, especially in those who have mourned deeply, God sometimes giveth, sometimes withholdeth them, according to the counsels of his own will."[67]

After he returned home that evening Wesley was strongly bombarded with temptations; but, as he cried unto the Lord, he was delivered from them. He summed up the basic difference between his new state and his former state like this: "I was striving, yea fighting with all my might under the law, as well as under grace. But then I was sometimes, if not often, conquered; now, I was always conqueror."[68] What clear evidence that Wesley was now a genuine Christian!

Aldersgate to Germany

As one would expect, the tenor of Wesley's *Journal* is noticeably different after May 24, 1738, especially in regard to his own spiritual standing.

On the day following his heart-warming experience Wesley was again buffeted by Satan who said, "If thou didst believe, why is there not a more sensible change?" In his response Wesley was conscious that the Lord gave him words to say as he replied thus: "That I know not. But this I know, I have *now peace with God,* and *I sin not today*, and Jesus my Master has forbid me to take thought for the morrow."[69]

During the next few days Wesley testified to having peace, victory over sin, and many temptations.[70] He also acknowledged a lack of joy at the same time he possessed peace, which is the same lesson the Lord taught him after his Aldersgate experience on May 24.[71] He does admit that one reason for his lack of joy was due to his lack of prayer.[72]

On June 6 Wesley recorded this testimony: "I had still more comfort, and peace, and joy." He needed this blessing because that evening he received a letter from Oxford which stated that if one had any doubt or fear it was evident that he did not have weak faith, but rather "no faith at all." This comment troubled Wesley, for he did not see it to be in alignment with Scripture.[73]

Visit with Moravians

In the closing part of the first volume of his *Journal*, Wesley records the testimonies of several Moravians whom he met in Germany during the months of July and August, 1738. He was pleased to find "living proofs of the power of faith: persons 'saved from *inward as well as outward* sin,' …and from all doubt and fear by the abiding 'witness of the Holy Ghost given unto them.'"[74]

On July 12 Wesley heard Count Zinzendorf respond to this question, "Can a man be justified and not know it?" Part of Zinzendorf's reply is as follows:

1. Justification is the forgiveness of sins.
2. The moment a man flies to Christ he is justified.
3. And has peace with God, but not always joy.
4. Nor perhaps may he know he is justified till long after.
5. For the assurance of it is distinct from justification itself.
6. But others may know he is justified by his power over sin, …and his "hunger and thirst after righteousness,…"[75]

Upon hearing Zinzendorf, Wesley remembered what Peter Böhler had often taught on this subject, namely these points:

1. When a man has living faith in Christ, then he is justified.
2. This is always given in a moment.
3. And in that moment he has peace with God.
4. Which he cannot have without knowing that he has it.

5. And being born of God, he sinneth not.

6. Which deliverance from sin he cannot have without knowing that he has it.[76]

It is obvious that Zinzendorf and Böhler are in agreement that a justified person has peace with God and victory over sin. On the other hand, Böhler seems to necessarily connect justification with assurance, whereas Zinzendorf clearly distinguishes the one from the other. It will be seen in Chapter 6 that Wesley came to the conclusion that justifying faith is not necessarily connected with assurance.

The fact is, some of the men whom Wesley interviewed testified that they did not receive assurance until some time after their burden of sin was removed and their hearts had at least a measure of peace.[77] On the other hand, for some of those whom Wesley interviewed, justification and assurance seemed to take place at the same time.[78]

For the Moravians, faith must be placed, not in one's own righteousness or good works, but in the righteousness and blood of Christ.[79] Arvid Gradin described the full assurance of faith in this manner:

> Repose in the blood of Christ. A firm confidence in God, and persuasion of his favour; serene peace and steadfast tranquility of mind, with a deliverance from every fleshly desire, and from every outward and inward sin. In a word, my heart, which before was tossed like a troubled sea, was still and quiet, and in a sweet calm.[80]

The remaining part of this chapter will involve a brief overview of Wesley's references to the doctrine of assurance/witness of the Spirit in his other *Journal* volumes. Volume 18 is the most important as well as most prolific of all the volumes treating this doctrine in that it deals with Wesley's own struggling and searching for personal assurance of sins forgiven.

1738-1743

The time period of 1738-1743 is covered in the *Journal* entries in volume 19. The discussions in this volume are particularly significant in that they mark Wesley's personal experiences subsequent to his heartwarming experience at Aldersgate and his interviews with several Moravians in Germany during the summer of 1738. It was also during this time that Wesley broke relations with the Moravians.[81]

Wesley's Personal Encounters

As noted earlier in this chapter, Wesley experienced strong Satanic attacks, temptations, and heaviness during the days immediately following the clear assurance of sins forgiven, which he received on May 24. No doubt he was processing several components in his mind as he analyzed his own experiences and those of the Moravians whom he had interviewed. Since there was not a consensus among all the Moravians concerning such matters as justifying faith, assurance, or the witness of the Spirit, Wesley was naturally engaged in a difficult task as he endeavored to bring reason, tradition, and experience into alignment with the teaching of Scripture as he understood it.

It is surprising—if not shocking—to read Wesley's *Journal* entry for October 14, 1738, less than five months after receiving a blessed assurance that his sins were forgiven, that he did not then possess a peace which "excludes the possibility either of fear or doubt."[82] He then made this confession:

> Yet, upon the whole, although I have not yet that joy in the Holy Ghost, nor that love of God shed abroad in my heart, nor the full assurance of faith, nor the (proper) witness of the Holy Spirit with my spirit that I am a child of God, much less am I, in the full and proper sense of the words, in Christ a new creature;...[83]

One must ask if Wesley might have been overly conscientious or introspective at this time. It may be that he gave too much weight to his feelings as he tended to do. Whatever the case may have been, Wesley was not ready to cast away his confidence in what God had already done for him, as he notes in a concluding statement affixed to the above question: "I nevertheless trust that I have a measure of faith and am 'accepted in the Beloved': I trust 'the handwriting that was against me is blotted out', and that I am 'reconciled to God through his Son.'"[84]

Even more shocking is Wesley's entry on January 4, 1739, when he wrote: "My friends affirm *I am mad*, because I said 'I was not a Christian a year ago.' I affirm, I am not a Christian now."[85] He seemed to base this affirmation on the fact that he was not conscious of possessing the love of God, the peace of God, or the joy of the Holy Ghost in his heart.[86] Between October 14, 1738, and January 4, 1739, Wesley found help through prayer, communion, and searching the Scriptures.[87] He continued to preach that his hearers should not be satisfied with anything less than "a clear assurance that God had forgiven their sins, bringing with it a calm peace, the love of God, and dominion over all sin."[88]

Witness of the Spirit

The term "witness of the Spirit" is found at least seven times in volume 19. Four of the occurrences are found in the testimonies of two Christians.[89] Two of the references appear in Wesley's discussions of the differences between him and some of the Moravians regarding justifying faith.[90]

Spirit of Adoption

The expression "Spirit of adoption" is found at least six times in Wesley's *Journal,* volume 19. In each of these instances he is preaching or teaching about the Spirit of adoption in Romans 8:15,[91] which is closely related to the witness of the Spirit in Romans 8:16.

Know/Knew

Throughout this volume the words "know" or "knew" appear approximately thirteen times in connection with assurance of salvation. In nearly every occurrence the word is used to describe personal testimonies of those who came to "know" the reality and joy of sins forgiven.[92] An example is a lady at Epworth who testified thus: I *know* I am saved through faith."[93]

Emphasis upon Feeling

It is interesting to note how often Wesley refers to "feeling" when he talks about "assurance." He used the word "felt" twice in describing his heart-warming experience on May 24, 1738: "...I *felt* my heart strangely warmed. I *felt* I did trust in Christ, Christ alone for salvation,..."[94]

On two occasions in volume 19 Wesley says he does not feel any love to God: therefore he knows he has no love to Him because he feels it not.[95] One wonders if Wesley placed too much stress on feelings. Yet it is difficult to find fault with his statement that the "*inward* 'fruits of the Spirit,' ...must be *felt,*' ..."[96] since love, joy, and peace are indeed emotions.

Degrees of Faith

Perhaps the single most important doctrine over which Wesley and the Moravians separated was their differences in understanding the matter of justifying faith. The Moravians in England, especially those who followed Philipp Heinrich Molther's teaching on faith, embraced a strong position on justifying faith which Wesley could not accept.

Molther and others taught that one either had a "full assurance of faith" or no faith at all and that there are "*no degrees of faith.*"[97] Wesley took issue with the Moravians on this concept and refuted it by pointing to Scripture which identifies those who were "weak in the faith" and "of little faith."[98] For Wesley "weak faith" is mixed with fear and doubt and is the faith nearly all believers possess for "a short time after they have first 'peace with God.'"[99] Many of the Moravians decried the use of the ordinary *means of grace,* insisting that one should simply *be still* until he obtains the full assurance of faith.[100]

Baptism, Lord's Supper, and Susanna Wesley's Experience

Wesley was a strong advocate for using every possible means of grace, including baptism and the Lord's Supper, in order to obtain full assurance of faith. In volume 19 he cites four examples of individuals who obtained assurance of salvation while partaking of communion.[101] The most touching story is that of Wesley's mother, Susanna, who received the witness of the Spirit with her spirit that all her sins were forgiven, about three years prior to her death.[102]

1743-1754, Volume 20

Volume 19 of the *Journal*, comprised of approximately three hundred and fifty pages of journal entries, has at least seven references to the *witness of the Spirit* and about six occurrences of the phrase *Spirit of adoption*. By contrast, volume 20 has nearly five hundred pages of journal entries but appears to have only two references to the *witness of the Spirit* and no references to the *Spirit of adoption*.

Witness of the Spirit
The only two direct references to the witness of the Spirit appear in a letter, dated November 27, 1750, that Wesley wrote to a friend. The letter involved detailed reasons why Wesley could not admire the teaching of the Moravians: "Those who before had the witness in themselves of redemption in the blood of Christ, who had the Spirit of God witnessing with their spirit that they were the children of God, after hearing these but a few times, began to doubt; then reasoned themselves into utter darkness;…"[103]

Know/Knew
There are several occurrences of the words *know, knew* or *knowledge* in conjunction with an assurance of salvation.[104] One example is found in a letter written to Wesley from John Haime who gave this testimony: "For now I *knew* there was no condemnation for me, believing in Christ Jesus."[105] In an entry dated December 27, 1749, Wesley speaks about more than six hundred people who "have given proof that they have a *saving knowledge* of God and of Jesus Christ whom he hath sent."[106]

Assured/ Full Assurance of Faith
In a letter written to Wesley on May 25, 1745, about a lady named Mary Cook who had been ill for more than six months and then found saving grace, this testimony was included: "I am *assured* of God's love to my soul. I am not afraid to die."[107] And in a letter dated July 29, 1747, a gentleman told Wesley that "for above two years I have known that God for Christ's sake had forgiven me all my sins. I lived in the full *assurance* of faith, which made me rejoice in all states."[108]

1755-1766, Volume 21

Volume 21 has approximately five hundred pages of journal entries. There are at least six references to the word *witness* as it relates to assurance of sins forgiven.[109]

Witness to Justification

In describing John Keeling's experience, dated July 29, 1759, Wesley wrote: "He *was* justified, it seems, on that memorable sabbath, but had not a clear witness of it till ten days after."[110]

Wesley includes the testimony of Elizabeth Longmore whom God had met in a special way at the Lord's Table and also following communion in her place of prayer when the Lord spoke to her in these words: "Go in peace; thy sins are forgiven thee."[111] Some time later she testified that "the witness that God had saved me from all my sins grew clearer every hour."[112] The other four references to the witness are references to Scripture.

In three instances Wesley does not use the term *witness* but states the same thing by speaking of those who had "a clear sense of God's pardoning love,"[113] a sense of God's pardoning mercy,"[114] and "a clear sense of being renewed."[115]

Witness to Entire Sanctification

Although it is not the purpose of this study to deal with the witness of the Spirit to a second definite work of grace, it is of interest to note that Volume 21 has more testimonies to the Spirit bearing witness to sanctification than to justification.[116] Only brief reference will be noted here.

On March 12, 1760, Wesley examined several believers who affirmed that "they have constantly as clear a *witness* from God of sanctification as they have of justification."[117] In an entry dated June 11, 1763, Wesley records an account given to him by Samuel Meggot about a man named George Story who was praying one morning when "God gave him a witness in himself that he had purified his heart."[118]

It was apparently in the early 1760's that God used John Manners to bring many into experiences of both justification and entire sanctification. Manners told Wesley of a lady who "was seized with so *keen* a conviction as gave her no rest till God had sanctified her and witnessed it to her heart."[119] Manners also gave an account of William Moore who had been seeking God for a pure heart for two hours "when he felt a glorious change and the Spirit of God witnessing that the work was done."[120]

Other Terminology

The term *knew* is used at least three times to describe assurance of salvation for three individuals.[121] The words *assured* and *assurance* are also employed to describe those who obtained either justification or sanctification.[122]

1765-1775, Volume 22

Volume 22 has approximately four hundred and eighty pages of journal accounts. As one might expect, this volume, like the preceding one, contains references to the witness of the Spirit to sanctification or perfect love, as well as to justification.

Witness to Justification

On July 10, 1766, Wesley met with a large society of believers who were spiritually alive, which prompted him to say: "I think not above two out of sixteen or seventeen whom I examined have lost the direct witness of that salvation ever since they experienced it."[123]

A few days later Wesley spoke to a congregation on this theme: "'We know that we are of God'; namely, 'by the Spirit which he hath given us' by the witness of the Spirit, and by the fruit confirming that witness."[124]

On July 21, 1767, Wesley told about a young lady who had "the uninterrupted witness of his Spirit" for seven years.[125]

Witness to Entire Sanctification

When Wesley tells about those who possessed the witness of the Spirit to entire sanctification, he was thereby affirming that they also had the witness to their conversion. He had preached in a marketplace to a large congregation on June 17, 1770, where he met a lady who told him about her obtaining a clean heart: "And on Sunday I was delivered and had as clear a witness of this as of my justification."[126]

Then, on August 16, 1775, Wesley was called to the bedside of a dying saint who for ten years "had the constant witness that God has taken up all her heart" and filled her with "perfect love."[127]

Other Terminology

As in other volumes of his *Journal*, Wesley employs the words *know* and *knew* to denote assurance of salvation.[128]

Spirit of adoption is found at least one time in volume 22.[129]

The words *assure* or *assurance* are used at least four times. One example is recorded on January 15, 1767, concerning Richard Morris who never saw his need of salvation until death stared him in the face; but then he called upon the Lord and "was soon assured of his love, and continued praising and rejoicing till his spirit returned to God."[130]

1776-1786, Volume 23

Volume 23 of the Bicentennial Edition of the *Works of John Wesley* has approximately four hundred and twenty-five pages of journal entries. There appears to be only two clear references to the witness of the Spirit, and both of these relate to entire sanctification.

On April 19, 1779, Wesley went to a place called Otley where the work of the Lord was advancing, especially in the matter of sanctification, concerning which he stated thus: "I think everyone who has experienced it retains a clear witness of what God has wrought."[131]

The second reference was recorded on June 19, 1784, when Wesley met a select society which he commended greatly:

> They were about forty, of whom I did not find one who had not a clear witness of being saved from inbred sin. Several of them had lost it for a season, but could never rest till they had recovered it. And every one of them seemed now to walk in the full light of God's countenance.[132]

One other reference is made to the "direct witness of the Spirit," not in the journal text but rather in a footnote supplied by the editors. The comments relate to a sermon preached by Wesley and recorded in the diary of a gentleman named Robert Roe (September 4, 1780).[133]

Wesley also uses other language to describe assurance of salvation, such as "full assurance of faith,"[134] "the experimental knowledge of God,"[135] "knew the pardoning of God,"[136] "a clear sense of the love of God,"[137] and "a sense of the pardoning love of God."[138]

1787-1790

Volume 24 of the Bicentennial Edition of Wesley's *Works* was not published at the time of this writing; thus it has been necessary to use the earlier edition edited by Thomas Jackson.

It appears that Wesley does not have any reference to the direct witness of the Spirit during these last four years. There is at least one account of assurance of sins forgiven recorded on March 29, 1787, where he writes: "Two declared, after bitter cries, that they knew their sins were just then blotted out by the blood of the Lamb;..."[139]

Summary Statements

The *Journal* accounts of Wesley give glimpses into the personal religious experiences of both Wesley and those with whom he was acquainted during his lengthy ministry. What vivid pictures are painted of those who sought and found a vital experience of grace:

1. They could not be satisfied until they had an inward assurance that their sins were forgiven.

2. This assurance was given when the Holy Spirit bore witness with their spirits, testifying to the fact that they were the children of God.

3. Added to this witness was a consciousness of possessing the fruit of the Spirit: love, joy, and peace filling their hearts.

4. This blessed assurance is seen to be the common privilege of God's children.

5. If the witness is lost, it may be recovered.

Endnotes

1. See Richard P. Heitzenrater's "Editorial Introduction" in *Works,* 18:302, 304.

2. Ibid., 18:304.

3. See W. Reginald Ward's "Introduction in *Works*, 18:81. Ward presents a detailed introduction of 119 pages in which he discusses autobiographical writings before, during, and after Wesley. He also deals with the nature and construction of Wesley's *Journal.*

4. Ibid., 18:2.

5. Ibid.

6. Ibid., 18:90.

7. Ibid., 18:40-41.

8. Ibid., 18:41.

9. Ibid., 18:14, 18, 27-31, 37, 40, 44-49, 42.

10. Ibid., 18:41.

11. Ibid.

12. For an interesting discussion of Wesley's resolve to make religion his major business, see Robert G. Tuttle, Jr., *John Wesley: His Life and Theology* (Grand Rapids: Zondervan Publishing House, 1978), 61-68.

13. Ibid., 145.

14. Ibid., 18:136-37.

15. Ibid., 18:137-38.

16. Ibid.

17. Ibid., 18:140. The Oxford/Bicentennial Edition of Wesley's Works retains his grammatical usages, even if they are now outdated. See *Works*, 25:120-22, 127-28.

18. Ibid., 18:141.

19. Ibid., 18:142.

20. Tuttle, 74-75.

21. *Works,* 18:142-43.

22. Ibid., 18:143.

23. Ibid., 18:145.

24. Ibid., 18:136, 145. See footnote 4.

25. Ibid., 18:136.

26. Ibid.,. See 146-47 for Wesley's dialogue with Spangenberg.

27. Ibid., 18:146.

28. Ibid., 18:151.

29. Wesley first met Spangenberg on February 7, 1736. He left Georgia on December 2, 1737.

30. *Works*, 18:153-54, 157, 187, 194.

31. Ibid., 18:187ff. See *Works*, 18:365-559 in the Manuscript Georgia Journal and Diary for details in Wesley's relationships with Miss Hopkey.

32. Ibid., 18:207.

33. Ibid., 18:288. It is of interest to note that, at this time, Wesley refers to "inward feeling" as the most infallible of proofs. What strange words, at least for a present-day Christian!

34. Ibid., 18:211.
35. Ibid., 18:212-13.
36. Ibid., 18:214.
37. Ibid. See footnote.
38. Ibid., 18:214-15. To this latter statement Wesley added these words in 1774: "I had even then the faith of a *servant*, though not that of a *son.*"
39. Ibid., 18:215.
40. Ibid. See footnote.
41. Ibid., 18:216, where Footnote 19 states that this is the definition of faith most oft-quoted by Wesley.
42. Ibid., 18:215-16.
43. Ibid., 18:223.
44. Ibid., 18:225.
45. Ibid. See footnote 25.
46. Ibid.
47. Ibid., 18:225-26.
48. Ibid., 18:228. In the 1774 correction sheet Wesley added these words: "with the full Christian salvation."
49. Ibid.
50. Ibid.
51. Ibid., 18:232-33.
52. Ibid., 18:232. After Aldersgate Wesley will often couple holiness and happiness.
53. Ibid., 18:233-34.
54. Ibid., 18:234.
55. Ibid.
56. Ibid., 18:237.
57. Ibid., 18:238-39.
58. Ibid., 18:241. See Appendix B for Charles' conversion story.
59. Ibid., 18:241-42.
60. The following discussion of Wesley's experiences prior to Aldersgate is largely drawn from *Works*, 18:242-49. See also Tuttle, 51-77, 85-155, 163-92.
61. *Works*, 18:249.
62. Ibid.
63. Ibid., 18:249-50.
64. Ibid., 18:247.
65. Ibid., 18:248.
66. Ibid., 18:250.
67. Ibid.
68. Ibid.
69. Ibid., 18:251. Since Wesley lived a careful, conscientious life for about thirteen years prior to Aldersgate, one would not expect to see any great preceptible change.
70. Ibid., 18:251-53.

71. Ibid., 18:242, 250.
72. Ibid., 18:251.
73. Ibid., 18:254.
74. Ibid., 18:260.
75. Ibid., 18:261.
76. Ibid.
77. Ibid., 18:280-85, 287-88.
78. Ibid., 18:285-87, 290-91.
79. Ibid., 18:271-72, 283-86, 289.
80. Ibid., 18:291. Nearly thirty years later Wesley will illustrate the witness of the Spirit by referring to "the stormy wind and troubled waves" subsiding into a "sweet calm." See *Works*, 1:287.
81. *Works*, 19:162.
82. Ibid., 19:18.
83. Ibid., 19:19.
84. Ibid.
85. Ibid., 19:29.
86. Ibid., 19:30.
87. Ibid., 19:20, 22, 28.
88. Ibid., 19:164.
89. Ibid., 19:23, 25, 26, 95.
90. Ibid., 19:131-32.
91. Ibid., 19:51, 102, 276, 278, 281, 314.
92. Ibid., 19:15, 93, 98, 105, 147, 177, 256, 267, 273, 280, 282, 284, 316.
93. Ibid., 19:273 (italics mine).
94. Ibid., 18:250 (italics mine).
95. Ibid., 19:18, 30.
96. Ibid., 19:85.
97. Ibid., 19:131-32, 217.
98. Ibid., 19:154-55.
99. Ibid., 19:154.
100. Ibid.
101. Ibid., 19:27, 93, 98, 151.
102. Ibid., 19:93, 283.
103. Ibid., 20:370.
104. Ibid., 20:8, 255, 317, 347, 383, 390, 429, 461.
105. Ibid., 20:8 (italics mine).
106. Ibid., 20:317 (italics mine).
107. Ibid., 20:82 (italics mine).
108. Ibid., 20:126 (italics mine).
109. Ibid., 21:211, 244, 286, 292.
110. Ibid., 21:211.
111. Ibid., 21:244.

112. Ibid.
113. Ibid., 21:179.
114. Ibid., 21:374-75.
115. Ibid., 21:380.
116. Ibid., 21:247, 331, 375-77, 417.
117. Ibid., 21:247.
118. Ibid., 21:416-17.
119. Ibid., 21:375.
120. Ibid., 21:377.
121. Ibid., 21:218, 331, 343.
122. Ibid., 21:133, 212, 381.
123. Ibid., 22:49.
124. Ibid., 22:51.
125. Ibid., 22:90-91.
126. Ibid., 22:235.
127. Ibid., 22:462.
128. Ibid., 22:9, 92, 169, 220.
129. Ibid., 22:357.
130. Ibid., 22:70.
131. Ibid., 23:125.
132. Ibid., 317.
133. Ibid., 23:185.
134. Ibid., 23:56.
135. Ibid., 23:109.
136. Ibid., 23:204.
137. Ibid., 23:162.
138. Ibid., 23:191.
139. *Works*, ed. Jackson, 4:365.

Chapter Five

Wesley's Sermons on the Witness

That John Wesley was a skillful organizer, astute leader, and competent writer few would deny, but as Albert Outler asserts, "It was preaching that defined his vocation preeminently."[1] In a brief note in his *Journal* dated July 28, 1757, Wesley highlighted the importance of preaching in his own ministry: "About noon I preached at Woodseats, in the evening at Sheffield. I do indeed *live* by preaching!"[2]

The purpose of this chapter is to compare and contrast Wesley's two sermons, The Witness of the Spirit, I, and The Witness of the Spirit, II, analyze and critique them, and draw conclusions in order to understand more fully his interpretation of this significant doctrine. However, prior to an examination of the sermons per se, it does seem fitting to give some attention to the Preface he affixed to his published sermons along with other salient matters regarding his preaching ministry.[3]

Wesley's Preface to His Sermons

The Preface to Wesley's sermons was reprinted, without revision, in each edition from 1746 to 1787.[4] In ten paragraphs he briefly summarizes the purposes, style, content, and spirit of his sermons. It may be that he was trying to attract a broad readership by affixing a rather general title to the sermons, namely this: *Sermons on Several Occasions.*[5]

Doctrinal Content

Wesley chose the medium of sermons to communicate his theology. In the first paragraph of the Preface he claims that his published sermons "contain the substance of what I have been preaching for between eight and nine years last past."[6] Since his first edition was published in 1746, the eight or nine years takes him back to the approximate time of his Aldersgate experience. Outler interprets the reference to "eight or nine years" as implying that Wesley's conversion was not to be connected to a specific crisis experience but rather to a series of events that unfolded in 1738.[7] One may seriously question whether Wesley is saying anything at all about his conversion in the above-mentioned statement. It may well be that Outler is reading more into Wesley's comment than was intended.

It is true that Wesley did undergo a radical shift in his thinking as a consequence of his Aldersgate experience. He had once held that holy living was a prerequisite for justifying faith, but later came to see that it was the exact opposite: justifying faith precedes holy living.[8] On the other hand, some of his teaching, even several years prior to 1738, remained essentially the same to the end of his life.[9]

In his Preface comments Wesley states that he had publicly spoken on every subject in his sermon volumes during the approximate time frame of 1738-1746. He then added: "Every serious man who peruses these will therefore see in the clearest manner what those doctrines are which I embrace and teach as the essentials of true religion."[10]

It was in 1739 that Wesley began his field preaching which brought him to "the discovery of his true vocation as an evangelist,"[11] and in that area of labor he saw his main work to be that of preaching, thus "his choice of the sermon as the chief genre for his theological expositions."[12]

Wesley's ministry bore little fruit until he engaged in field preaching in April of 1739 when the Lord thrust him out as the spiritual leader of a revival movement which would span more than half a century.[13] Since the Revival "outlasted all precedent and expectations,"[14] one might well have expected that Wesley's chief interest would be centered in a practical, not a systematic, theology. As converts were gathered into societies and classes for instruction and nurture, and as preachers were gathered into annual Conferences, it seemed most appropriate that Wesley's sermons should provide the basic format for communicating doctrine among the early Methodists. Outler expresses it in these words: "This decision that a cluster of sermons might serve as doctrinal standards for a popular religious movement is a significant revelation of Wesley's self-understanding of his role as spiritual director of the 'people called Methodists.'"[15]

Unadorned Style

In the second, third, and fourth paragraphs of the Preface to his sermons Wesley discusses his choice of sermon style. He emphatically affirms that his sermons have been purposefully constructed without "elaborate, elegant, or oratorical dress," since those to whom he writes are "the bulk of mankind ...who neither relish nor understand the art of speaking..."[16]

Wesley was well aware of the ornate styles some ministers had adopted. He deplored such and deliberately chose a plain style of preaching, based on principle, as stated in the Preface to his *SOSO (Sermons on Several Occasions)*, V—VIII (1788): "I could even now write ...as even the admired Dr. [Hugh] B[lair]. But I dare not.... I dare no more write in a 'fine style' than wear a fine coat.... I cannot relish French oratory—I despise it from my heart.... I am still for plain, sound English."[17]

For the most part Wesley labored among those who were poor and not well educated. Thus he was wise to follow the example of our Lord Jesus Christ who used simple language which even children could understand. "I design plain truth for plain people," Wesley wrote; "therefore ...I abstain ...as far as possible from even the show of learning, unless in sometimes citing the original Scriptures."[18] Nevertheless, while he sought to avoid words not easily understood, particularly technical terms, he admitted that he was probably not successful in doing so at all times.[19]

A rather strange statement appears at the outset of paragraph 4 in the Preface where Wesley writes: "...my design is in some sense to forget all that ever I have read in my life ...(always excepting the inspired)."[20] There is no indication that Wesley ever slackened the pace of his reading; to the contrary, he maintained a heavy reading schedule throughout his long life. As Outler sees it, "the only credible meaning for such a disavowal is that he was willing to forego any outward show of learning that might distract his readers."[21] Wesley goes on to explain why he wanted to forget much that he had previously read: "I am persuaded that, on the one hand, this may be a means of enabling me more clearly to express the sentiments of my heart, without entangling myself with those of other men; and that, on the other, I shall come with fewer weights upon my mind, ...either to search for myself or to deliver to others the naked truths of the gospel."[22]

Even a brief survey of the Bicentennial Edition of his sermons will convince one that Wesley drew from numerous writers and tended to leave uncited both biblical and non-biblical sources. Thanks to the diligent work of various scholars many sources have been located and cited in the footnotes. It seemed second nature for Wesley to borrow from others, but he also put his own stamp upon that which he borrowed.[23] He was extremely skillful in weaving the language of Scripture into the fabric of his own writing.[24]

The Way of Salvation

In the fifth and sixth paragraphs of the Preface Wesley unveils his deepest desires as being twofold: (1) he wants to know how to arrive safely on heaven's shore; and (2) he wants to help others land safely as well.[25]

Recognizing the brevity of life and the unending duration of eternity, Wesley discusses the need to read and study the Bible in order to know the way to heaven. "Let me be homo unius libri."[26] It is doubtful that many of his "plain people" would have had any familiarity with these Latin terms; however, such an insertion is an exception to his normal style of writing. By claiming to be "a man of one book," Wesley did not mean he would never read anything but the Bible. Rather, he meant that the Scripture would always have priority over all other writings and be the authoritative source for his beliefs and practices.[27] The amount of Scripture Wesley quotes, paraphrases, or alludes to in his sermons is astonishing. In his first ten sermons in Volume I (including the two sermons on the Witness of the Spirit) Wesley averages about 138 biblical quotations, paraphrases, or allusions per sermon!

Two purposes for his sermons are expressed in paragraph 6 regarding his desire to help others in their pursuit of heaven. First of all, Wesley wants to help new converts maintain a "heart-religion" and avoid having only a form of godliness. In the second place, he desires to warn those who have a heart-religion not to go to the other extreme and "make void the law through faith."[28] Wesley's life-long pursuit was to strike a proper balance by avoiding extremes on either side.

At the heart of Wesley's sermons is the theme of salvation. Outler aptly sums it up in these words: "The controlling theological inquiry throughout his life was into the meaning of becoming and being a Christian in all aspects of the Christian existence."[29] It was Wesley's goal to separate biblical teaching from manmade doctrines. "I have endeavored to describe the true, the scriptural, experimental religion, so as to omit nothing which is a real part thereof, and to add nothing thereto which is not."[30]

Wesley built his sermons/theology on the tried and proven pillars of Scripture, reason, and Christian antiquity, but he also added another important ingredient, namely that of experience or "experimental heart religion," which denotes "personal assurance of God's justifying, pardoning grace."[31]

Helping people both become and be Christian was not only the hallmark of Wesleyan sermons, but also of Wesleyan hymns, for the Methodists "sang the same doctrine in their hymns as they heard and read in their sermons."[32] It was in the Methodist hymnody that Charles Wesley's influence was immense, in his own lifetime and in subsequent church history to the present time. Outler observes that John's sermons and Charles' hymns coupled together provided the early Methodists with "practical tools for teaching and spiritual formation," and therefore as such "they constitute 'a small body of divinity' more accessible than any systematic treatise could have been."[33]

That Wesley gave a prominent place to the matter of salvation in his sermons is seen by glancing at the sermon titles in Volume I (*SOSO*). The first ten sermon titles (excluding Charles' sermon entitled "Awake, Thou That Sleepest") are as follows: "Salvation by Faith;" "The Almost Christian;" "Scriptural Christianity;" "Justification by Faith;" "The Righteousness of Faith;" "The Way to the Kingdom;" "The First-fruits of the Spirit;" "The Spirit of Bondage and of

Adoption;" "The Witness of the Spirit, I;" and "The Witness of the Spirit, II." One can readily see that Wesley's great emphasis is upon helping people enter into experiential, heart-religion.

Prefixed Sermons

In the seventh paragraph of the Preface Wesley acknowledges the fact that he had prefixed three of his own sermons plus one from his brother Charles to the first volume at the request of some of his friends.[34] One of the reasons for including these "prefixed sermons" was to refute those who claimed he did not at that time preach what he did at an earlier period.[35]

Priority of Love

The final four paragraphs of the Preface are a strong plea to place love above dogmatism in doctrine. Wesley admits he may not be entirely correct in teaching the way to heaven and confesses that he is open to be taught "a better way" if one can show him such by "plain proof of Scripture."[36] But he urges that there be much kindness and patience and a deliberate effort to set all anger and undue pressure aside, "For how far is love, even with many wrong opinions, to be preferred before truth itself without ove?"[37] What excellent admonition for professors of religion in any era of time who may differ with one another in regard to the interpretation of a particular passage of Scripture. Wesley's rationale for his plea is beyond debate: "We may die without the knowledge of many truths and yet be carried into Abraham's bosom. But if we die without love, what will knowledge avail? Just as much as it avails the devil and his angels."[38]

Wesley as a Preacher

In order to more fully appreciate and understand Wesley's sermons one needs to have some acquaintance with the man as a preacher. After Wesley came to the conclusion that God had called him to be an evangelist, and since the main work of an evangelist is preaching, it is not at all unusual that he chose the format of a sermon as the medium by which he would expound his theology.

As stated earlier, Wesley built his theology upon the commonly accepted triad of Scripture, reason, and Christian antiquity to which he added a fourth component, that of personal experience. Outler neatly summarizes Wesley's eclectic method by observing that for him "theology is the interpretation of spiritual and moral insights sparked by the prevenient action of the Holy Spirit, deposited in Holy Scripture, interpreted by the Christian tradition, reviewed by reason, and appropriated by personal experience."[39] What a brilliant summation of practical divinity!

Use of Scripture

Perhaps the most impressive thing about Wesley's sermons to first-time readers is the vast amount of Scripture incorporated into each sermon. His grasp of the written Word of God is such that he interconnects it with his own language in a smooth and natural flow. For Wesley the Bible is not to be viewed simply as "standing revelation" but also as a "speaking book."[40]

Use of Christian Tradition

John Wesley had a keen interest in the history of the church throughout his long life. For him tradition was discovered when he re-entered "the Christian past in order to appropriate its best treasures for his own time," since, no matter what changes had transpired, "he saw an essential continuity that had perdured."[41]

As a consequence of Wesley's desire to live in and learn from the writings of Church Fathers, "one cannot point to another popular theologian with as lively a sense of the normative role of Christian antiquity for contemporary theology."[42]

Use of Reason

Endowed by the Creator with a fertile mind and blessed with educational privileges both in homeschooling and formal classes, it is not unusual that Wesley would develop into an accurate thinker and a competent logician. He was careful to distinguish between theological knowledge which involves intuitive realities and empirical knowledge which entails tangible realities.[43]

Use of Experience

By adding experience to Scripture, Christian antiquity, and reason, Wesley formed his well-known quadrilateral. This new element points to a religion of the heart which Wesley found in his Aldersgate experience on May 24, 1738. Connected with it is a personal knowledge or assurance that one's sins have been forgiven by God's saving grace.

Use of Numerous Sources

Wesley's breadth of reading afforded him rich sources from which he could draw. He was acquainted with the Greek and Latin classics, Anglican and Puritan theology, the Hebrew and Greek Bible, English literature, scientific studies, biographies and explorations.[44] His reading was often done "in haste and on the run."[45] He tended to quote from memory, changing the originals if he saw fit;[46] consequently "his quotations are rarely exact and rarely identified,"[47] but, on the other hand, they are "rarely misleading."[48]

Busy and Lengthy Ministry

It is rather common knowledge that Wesley preached approximately forty thousand times (an average of fifteen sermons per week) and traveled some two hundred and fifty-two thousand miles (the same distance one would travel in circling the earth ten times) in his itinerant ministry that spanned about fifty years. When one considers the journal and diary records he kept, the vast number of letters and sermons he wrote, plus the many other volumes he either edited or penned, it is amazing that one man could ever have accomplished so much, even during such a lengthy ministry.

Not the Most Eloquent Orator

Based on statistical data alone, one may tend to think that John Wesley was the most gifted and eloquent preacher of his day. But such was not the case. He never seemed to be called in his day as Spurgeon was in his, "a prince of preachers." But, as noted earlier, Wesley frowned on putting "elaborate, elegant, or oratorical dress" on his sermons.[49] For him, preaching was serious business. (This is not to suggest that some ministers more gifted in communication than Wesley were not serious in their labors.) However, Wesley's goal was not to be an eloquent orator, but rather a spokesman for God whose chief business was to save souls.

On October 15, 1769, a Swedish professor, Johan Henrik Liden, met Wesley for the first time and heard him preach. In commenting on his preaching Liden said this: "He has no great oratorical gifts, no outward appearance, but he speaks clear and pleasant," and then the professor went on to complement Wesley as one who "has learning as a bishop and a zeal for the glory of God which is quite extraordinary."[50]

Thomas Haweis, an evangelical historian, contrasted Wesley with Whitefield from the eyewitness reports he had gathered: "His mode of address in public was chaste and solemn, though not illumined with those coruscations of eloquence which marked ...the discourses of his rival, George Whitefield;" however, Haweis also observed that Wesley did command the attention of his hearers and was known as much for his saintliness and "his holy walk as for his vast abilities, indefatigable and singular usefulness."[51]

As one attempts to analyze Mr. Wesley as a preacher, it would be in order to ask a question or two in conjunction with the above-stated observations of the professor and the historian: are not the characteristics which mark Wesley as a preacher more desirable than those which do not describe him? Is it not more important that a minister be known for his saintly life, commitment to study, zeal for God's glory, and clear speech than for eloquent oratory? For Wesley the manner of his preaching involved more than preference; it was a "moral issue."[52]

A Man of Organization

There is no question about Wesley's ability to organize and discipline his own life and also the lives of others. He had been trained well from his earliest years under the careful tutelage of his mother, Susanna. Wesley saw the necessity for organizing his converts into societies, classes, and bands for spiritual nurture and direction so that they might grow in the grace and knowledge of our Lord and not become spiritual castaways.

By contrast, those fellow evangelists who did not develop edifying communities, were building what Wesley called "ropes of sand."[53]

A Man with Spiritual Priorities

Nothing was more important to Wesley than taking time to be holy at the beginning of each day. Even a casual survey of his diary records will convince one that he placed a priority on his devotional time, often rising between 4:00 and 4:30 a.m. to read the Word and pray.

The Sermons on the Witness

It is of interest to note that Wesley penned his first sermon entitled "The Witness of the Spirit" in 1746, approximately eight years after his heart-warming experience when he first received the Spirit's witness to his conversion. The eight years subsequent to Aldersgate afforded Wesley ample time to reflect on his own experience as well as the experiences of many whom he had interviewed. It also gave him time for a careful study of the Scripture and church history in regard to this important doctrine.

The second sermon on the witness was penned and published in 1767, more than twenty years after the first. Critics often accused Wesley of being an enthusiast or a fanatic in his teaching on the Spirit's witness. As the Wesleyan Revival continued into the 1760's, there were indeed some cases of enthusiasm/fanaticism which precipitated justifiable criticism. Therefore it was an opportune time for Wesley to offer new comments on the doctrine and refutations to various objections which had been raised.[54]

According to Outler there is no evidence that either of these sermons was ever preached.[55] While this may be true, Wesley frequently referred to the witness of the Spirit, assurance, and the witness of one's own spirit in his preaching as is clearly revealed in his written sermons.

Similarities in the Sermons

Since the two sermons are on the same subject taken from the same text, one would naturally expect some overlap in content, but the fact is, there is little material that is identical or nearly so. Actually there are only two paragraphs in each sermon which are nearly identical (in Sermon I they appear back-to-back, but in Sermon II they are separated by ten paragraphs.[56]

In attempting to describe the testimony of God's Spirit and how He bears witness with one's spirit, Wesley penned these words in the 1746 sermon:

It is hard to find words in the language of men to explain "the deep things of God." Indeed there are none that will adequately express what the children of God experience. But perhaps one might say (desiring any who are taught of God to correct, to soften or strengthen the expression), the testimony of the Spirit is an inward impression on the soul, whereby the Spirit of God directly "witnesses to my spirit that I am a child of God"; that Jesus Christ hath loved me, and given himself for me; that all my sins are blotted out, and I, even I, am reconciled to God.[57]

When Wesley prepared his 1767 sermon on the witness, he inserted the above-quoted paragraph but added two words which are noted as underlined in this statement: "...whereby the Spirit of God <u>immediately and</u> directly witnesses to my spirit that I am a child of God."[58] The addition of these words does not change the essential meaning of Wesley's earlier statement, but it does give it a more detailed connotation.

It was not without careful thought and review that Wesley continued to embrace his definition of the witness in 1767 as he had understood it in 1746: "After twenty years' farther consideration I see no cause to retract any part of this. Neither do I conceive how any of these expressions may be altered so as to make them more intelligible."[59] Nevertheless, he was open to any revisions that would be clearer and more in alignment with Scripture: "I can only add, that if any of the children of God will point out any other expressions which are more clear, and more agreeable to the Word of God, I will readily lay these aside."[60]

There is one other paragraph found in each sermon wherein the wording is nearly identical albeit some statements are omitted in the 1767 sermon. The emphasis in these paragraphs is upon the sequence or the time element as regards the witness of God's Spirit and the witness of one's own spirit. Which witness comes first? Wesley argues that the witness of God's Spirit must precede the witness of one's own spirit for this reason: "We must be holy of heart and holy in life before we can be conscious that we are so."[61] This is good logic and easy to understand, since one's consciousness must relate to the reality of his state of being. For example, a sinner is conscious that he is a sinner because in reality he is a sinner in both heart and life.

However, Wesley's subsequent statement is difficult to follow: "But we must love God before we can be holy at all, this being the root of all holiness."[62] In stating this, Wesley is placing "doing" before "being." How can one love God until He first makes one's heart holy? Wesley goes on to say: "Now we cannot love God till we know he loves us: 'We love him, because he first loved us.' And we cannot know his love to us till his Spirit witnesses it to our spirit."[63] Since the Spirit cannot witness to a lie, as Wesley admits in his 1746 sermon,[64] it stands to reason that the Spirit cannot and will not witness to one's pardon (or initial sanctification) until one is, in fact, pardoned. Is not this the thrust of Paul's comment in Galatians 4:6, "And because ye are sons, God has sent forth the Spirit of his Son into your hearts, crying, Abba, Father." Not until one is first "made a son" does the Spirit bear witness. And to use Wesley's own argument, one cannot love God until he knows God loves him, and this one cannot know until His Spirit witnesses the same to him. Which means one must be holy (initially sanctified at conversion) before he can love God.[65]

While the two passages cited above are the only ones which are nearly identical in the two sermons, there is at least one other matter discussed in each sermon which bears overlapping similarity. At the outset of both sermons Wesley notes that there has been a tendency throughout church history for professors of religion to take extreme positions on the doctrine of the direct witness of the Spirit. One the one hand, those who have not understood the doctrine have often gone into enthusiasm or fanaticism.[66] On the other hand, those who have decried the way fanatics have abused the doctrine have rejected it, denied it, or tried to explain it away.[67]

In Sermon I Wesley states that some of the fanatics have "mistaken the voice of their own imagination for this 'witness of the Spirit' of God," and therefore falsely presumed "they were the children of God while they were doing the works of the devil."[68] It was Wesley's observation that it was nearly impossible to convince such that their witness was not of God.[69]

In Sermon II Wesley warned his readers of the dangers from either extreme. If the doctrine were denied, religion would tend to become formalistic; but if the doctrine were allowed but not understood, the tendency would be to enthusiasm/fanaticism.[70]

Wesley further stated that very little had been written on the subject in any clarity; however, some writings simply explained it away, no doubt as a reaction to the "crude, unscriptural, irrational explications of others."[71]

It is of interest to note that little had been written on the witness of the Spirit during the next two hundred years after Wesley had penned his two sermons. In 1952 Arthur Yates highlighted this fact in the Preface of his published dissertation for the Degree of Doctor of Philosophy as follows:

> "This is the first book, as far as I know, to offer a comprehensive survey of the Doctrine of Assurance. When I began this study, I inquired on both sides of the Atlantic for literature on the subject. The answer was that Assurance had been briefly treated in some books of theology and in pamphlets. That was all! Yet Assurance, or the 'Witness of the Spirit,' is one of the distinctive doctrines of Methodism—a doctrine which, as Dr. H. B. Workman says, is 'the fundamental contribution of Methodism to the life and thought of the church.'"[72]

One would have expected that much would have been written on the doctrine from the time of Wesley's death until Yates did the research for his dissertation. That it did not happen is rather shocking.

In light of the fact that little had been written on the subject prior to Wesley's day, he states in the introductory part of his 1767 sermon on the Witness these comments: "It more clearly concerns the Methodist, so called, clearly to understand, explain, and defend this doctrine, because it is one grand part of the testimony which God has given them to bear to all mankind. It is by his peculiar blessing upon them in searching the Scriptures, confirmed by the experience of his children, that this great evangelical truth has been recovered, which had been for many years wellnigh lost and forgotten."[73]

From the time Wesley penned his first sermon on the Witness in 1746 to the time of the second sermon in 1767 a shift in his thinking about the prominence of the doctrine appears to have evolved. For example, in a letter written to John Smith on December 30, 1745, Wesley calls assurance "the *main* doctrine of the Methodists,"[74] but in the 1767 sermon he calls it "one grand part of the testimony which God has given them..."[75] Further attention and discussion will be given to Wesley's emphasis and changing emphasis on the doctrine, particularly in the next two chapters which will deal with his letters.

Sermon I

Even after one has read Wesley's sermons on The Witness of the Spirit, I, and The Witness of the Spirit, II, numerous times it is not always easy to follow his train of thought or to experience as many eureka moments as one might desire.

Perhaps part of the difficulty relates to the writing style of two and a half centuries ago along with changes in word meanings.[76] Furthermore, when one endeavors to deal with the doctrine of the witness, he is, in the words of Dr. W. T. Stace, "trying to think non-sensuous objects in a sensuous way."[77]

Sometimes it is difficult to determine whether Wesley is stating his own position or that of another. One example is seen early in the first sermon where he notes that some manuscript copies on Romans 8:16 have a variant reading "which may be translated, 'The same Spirit beareth witness to our spirit, that we are the children of God' (the preposition σύν only denoting that he witnesses this *at the same time* that he enables us to cry, 'Abba, Father!'). But I contend not;..."[78]

Unfortunately, Wesley does not explicitly say that the parenthetical statement is another scholar's exegesis of σύν. Albert Outler interprets it as another person's explanation,[79] but Edward Sugden thinks Wesley is himself giving this position; yet he (Wesley) is not certain that this is a proper understanding when he adds these words: "But I contend not,..."[80] One can only wish Wesley had clarified his comments.

Wesley constructed Sermon I into two major divisions. In the first he raises three questions and in the second two questions.

The first division of the sermon puts forth these questions: "What is this 'witness (or testimony) of our spirit?' What is the 'testimony of God's Spirit?' And how does he 'bear witness with our spirit that we are the children of God?'"[81]

The Witness of One's Own Spirit

Throughout Sermon I references are made to the witness or testimony of one's own spirit. In the early part of the sermon Wesley devotes five paragraphs to a discussion of the witness of one's spirit. He notes that there are many Biblical texts that describe "the marks of the children of God," and when these Scriptural marks are applied, one may know whether he is God's child.[82] Wesley refers to these marks as "the infallible assurance of Holy Writ."[83]

Special attention is given to the "we know" or "ye know" passages in the First Epistle of John, among which are the following:

(1) Hereby we know that we do know him, if we keep his commandments [1 John 2:3].

(2) Whoso keepeth his word, in him verily is the love of God perfected; hereby know we that we are in him [1 John 2:5].

(3) If ye know that he is righteous, ye know that everyone that doeth righteousness is born of him [1 John 2:29].

(4) We know that we have passed from death unto life, because we love the brethren [1 John 3:14].

(5) Hereby know we that we dwell in him, ...because he hath given us of his (loving) Spirit [1 John 4:13].

(6) Hereby we know that he abideth in us, by the (obedient) spirit which he hath given us [1 John 3:24].

It is indeed strange that Wesley includes I John 4:13 and I John 3:24 in his treatment of the witness of one's own spirit. The most obvious meaning of I John 4:13 is that it points to the witness of God's Spirit, especially since the word "Spirit" has a capital S even in the way he presents it.

Wesley puts a peculiar twist on I John 3:24 when he inserts the word "obedient" in a parenthesis and then uses a small s for the word "spirit." Most versions use a capital S for "Spirit,"[84] thus pointing to the witness of God's Spirit.

By placing these two verses into his discussion of the witness of one's spirit, Wesley does not bring clarity but rather confusion.

However, he does clarify the basic idea of the witness of one's own spirit by using terminology which unfolds various shades of meaning. He identifies the witness of one's spirit as "rational evidence," the witness of "our reason or understanding," "the testimony of our conscience," and one's "inward consciousness."[85]

Wesley then asks a significant question in order to explain more clearly his understanding of spiritual knowledge. The question is simply this: "But how does it appear that we have these marks?" (that is, the above-mentioned Scriptural marks), by which he means, "How does it appear to *ourselves*—not to *others.*"[86]

Anticipating that such a question or questions would be raised by others, Wesley responds to the question by asking another: "How does it appear to you that you are alive? And that you are now in ease and not in pain?"[87] Which he then answers in simple, understandable language: "Are you not immediately conscious of it? By the same immediate consciousness you will know if your soul is alive to God; if you are saved from the pain of proud wrath, and have the ease of a meek and quiet spirit...And with regard to the outward mark of the children of God, which is (according to St. John) the keeping his commandments, you undoubtedly know in your own breast if, by the grace of God, it belongs to you."[88]

In assessing these comments Outler observes that this is "another instance of Wesley's direct intuitionism in spiritual knowledge" and further notes that "it presupposes self-awareness as self-evident."[89] Later in Sermon I he will add more details to his understanding of intuitive, spiritual knowledge.

Wesley concludes that this immediate perception or consciousness of one's spiritual state is "properly the 'testimony of our own spirit,' even the testimony of our own conscience, that God hath given us to be holy of heart, and holy in outward conversation."[90]

The Witness of God's Spirit

A careful reading and rereading of Sermon I will convince the reader that Wesley gives more attention to the witness of one's own spirit than to the witness of the Spirit, although the title of the sermon is "The Witness of the Spirit" (i.e. God's Spirit). This fact is noticeable, even in the six paragraphs Wesley devotes to answering the question, "What is the 'testimony of God's Spirit'"?

One must seriously question Wesley's exegesis of the main verb in Romans 8:16, συμμαρτυρεῖ, "bears witness with." Of course the verb μαρτυρέω means "to testify" or "to witness," and the preposition συμ or συν is normally translated "with" which, when coupled together to form a compound word in Romans 8:16, denotes a joint testimony of God's Spirit *with* man's spirit.

Unfortunately, Wesley does not consistently interpret συμμαρτυρεῖ as expressing a joint witness. He does do so at times,[91] but, on the other hand, in Sermon I he seems to stress the Spirit's witness more often in language which does not connote testimony conjointly given. This is seen in several instances where he speaks of the Holy Spirit bearing witness, not "with," but rather "to" one's spirit.[92]

Furthermore, the matter seems to be yet more confusing when he asks, "But what is that testimony of God's Spirit which is superadded to and conjoined with this?" ("this" clearly pointing to the testimony of one's own spirit as noted in the statement preceding the above question).[93] If the Spirit's witness is superadded and conjoined to the witness of one's spirit, would that not necessitate the latter witness being given first, then the former one added to and finally conjoined with the latter? If so, the opening statement in the next paragraph is even more confusing and inconsistent: "That this 'testimony of the Spirit of God' must needs, in the very nature of things, be antecedent to the 'testimony of our own spirit'..."[94] How can it be logically affirmed that one witness must precede another and at the same time hold to a witness given conjointly?

Does Wesley mean that the Holy Spirit always witnesses first and alone so that one will only be conscious of His witness in the unfolding of personal assurance; and then at some other point in time there will be a distinct consciousness of the witness of one's own spirit by itself; and then in yet some other time frame the two witnesses will be given together as the plain meaning of Romans 8:16 would declare?

One must also ask why Wesley defines the witness of God's Spirit as "an inward impression on the soul, whereby the Spirit of God directly witnesses *to my spirit* that I am a child of God..."[95] instead of "*with my spirit* that I am a child of God?" (emphasis mine). Why does Wesley not consistently treat the matter of assurance under a double witness as he is pressed to do when confronted by various objections?[96] This question deserves further discussion.

How God's Spirit Bears Witness with Man's Spirit

When Wesley comes to the third and last question in the first major division of Sermon I he expands the wording as follows: "Should it still be inquired, 'How does the Spirit of God "bear witness with our spirit that we are the children of God" so as to exclude all doubt, and evince the reality of our sonship?'—the answer is clear from what has been observed above."[97]

The answer Wesley offers is simply "the witness of our spirit" which entails intuitive knowledge, for "the soul as intimately and evidently perceives when it loves, delights, and rejoices in God, as when it loves and delights in anything on earth; and it can no more doubt whether it loves, delights, and rejoices, or no, than whether it exists, or no."[98]

To help explain this spiritual knowledge Wesley utilizes the logic of syllogism:

He that now loves God—that delights and rejoices in him with an humble joy,
    an holy joy, an holy delight, and an obedient love—is a child of God;
But I thus love, delight, and rejoice in God;
Therefore I am a child of God....[99]

Wesley does admit that he cannot explain "the *manner* how the divine testimony is manifested to the heart..." But he does affirm that "the fact we know: namely, that the Spirit of God does give a believer such a testimony of his adoption that while it is present to the soul he can no more doubt the reality of his sonship than he can doubt of the shining of the sun while he stands in the full blaze of his beams."[100]

Albert Outler sees Wesley's sermons on "the Witness of the Spirit" as his attempts to elucidate his understanding of the doctrine of assurance which his critics had "all too easily misconstrued as a one-sided subjectivism. Thus he had to clarify his distinction between the ways in which assurance might be felt ('the witness of our own spirit') and the objective ground of any such experience (viz., the prior and direct 'witness of the Holy Spirit')."[101]

Outler observes that the basic question which arose between the so-called "enthusiasts" and "rationalists" was this: "whether a believer's consciousness of justification and reconciliation was an inference from his religious and moral feelings or whether those feelings, if valid, were first prompted by a free and direct testimony of the Spirit to one's divine sonship, promptings to which faith had responded and in which hope and love would participate."[102]

In assessing Wesley's treatment of assurance Outler rightly concludes that Wesley "opts for a both/and solution, stressing the believer's own consciousness of God's favor but even more strongly the priority of the Spirit's prevenient and direct witness as the necessary precondition of any feelings of assurance."[103]

Also helpful to the discussion at hand are the comments by Outler regarding Charles Wesley's sermon, "Awake, Thou That Sleepest," where he asserts that the understanding of the Wesley brothers concerning religious knowledge was drawn from "Descartes and Malebranche through John Norris." Outler explains it thusly: "The human spirit is a 'spiritual sensorium,' analogous to our physical senses, and thus the capacity for intuitions of spiritual reality is comparable to sight and sound…Sin ('sleep,' 'death') deadens all spiritual stimuli ('inlets of spiritual knowledge'). Thus, conversion or awakening is, by analogy, the discovery of a new world."[104]

It may be beneficial to add one more quotation by Outler, since he appears to have had a deeper insight into Wesley's understanding of assurance than most scholars, particularly in regard to the direct witness being both "prevenient" and "objective." In expanding on this "spiritual sensorium" Outler asserts that "it is passive until acted upon by spiritual stimuli—e.g., divine light arouses our latent capacities for 'sight' and insight; revelation prompts us to insight and knowledge—always, however, as 'reactions' to initiatives beyond ourselves. Thus, no matter how intensely subjective our feelings may be in religious experiences, their source is prevenient, and in that sense, objective."[105]

Distinguishing the Genuine Witness from That of a Natural Mind

In the second main division of Sermon I Wesley gives his readers specific ways they will be able to distinguish the real witness from the spurious. This section is easier to understand since it is not as philosophical as the former.

The most explicit way one can discern genuine assurance is by carefully observing those Scriptural marks which precede, accompany, and follow the real witness of God's Spirit with that of one's own spirit. Wesley is so confident that a sincere seeker after God will note such a vast difference between the true and the false witness that "there will be no danger," he says, or "no possibility—of confounding the one with the other."[106]

Biblical Marks Preceding the Witness

The first mark to which Wesley points as going before the witness is that of "repentance or conviction of sin."[107] By connecting these marks together he seems to treat them as synonyms. Yet he only cites Scriptures about repentance and "a broken and a contrite heart." In the very nature of things conviction of sin would necessarily precede repentance, but it would not hold that the latter would always follow the former. Nevertheless, the Bible clearly reveals that without repentance there is no forgiveness, hence no assurance of conversion.

The second Biblical mark mentioned is the New Birth which is described as "passing from death unto life," and "from darkness to light."[108]

Biblical Marks Accompanying the Witness

The marks which fit into this category are essentially "the fruit of the Spirit" with special emphasis upon humility. Wesley identifies these marks as "an humble joy… meekness, patience, gentleness, long-suffering" and "a soft, yielding spirit, a mildness and sweetness, a tenderness of soul which words cannot express."[109]

Biblical Marks Following the Witness

Although Wesley refers to this third category at the outset of this part of the sermon, he does not specifically name this classification in his discussion as he does for the other two. It may be that he is pointing to this category when he speaks of "the sure mark" which he relates to I John 5:3, "This is the love of God, that we keep his commandments."[110]

Without question obedience to God's commandments is a mark which always identifies a child of God after his conversion.

Throughout his discussion of the Biblical marks supporting genuine assurance of salvation, Wesley notes that one who has a spurious witness is one who has never been broken over his sins and has never repented. Nor does he possess meekness and a humble joy. There is no carefulness to keep God's commandments. Rather that one is overbearing and does not engage in good works and self-denial.[111] Wesley rightly concludes: "He cannot be conscious of having those marks which he hath not, that lowliness, meekness, and obedience. Nor yet can the Spirit of the God of truth bear witness to a lie; or testify that he is a child of God when he is manifestly a child of the devil."[112]

Once again Wesley reverts to his theory of intuitive spiritual knowledge when he declares that one will have an immediate and direct perception which will enable him to distinguish the true witness from the false, provided one's "senses are rightly disposed."[113] It is quite obvious that if one is to obtain knowledge of physical matters his physical senses must be functioning properly. It is the same in the spiritual realm.

But how shall one know his spiritual "sensorium" or senses are rightly disposed? Wesley claims that one will know by the witness of his own spirit, by having a good conscience toward God.[114] This response is not very satisfactory. Both Sugden and Yates assess Wesley as returning to a cycle of circular reasoning in taking this position; but the confusion can be removed by giving a proper interpretation to συμμαρτυρεῖ, namely a joint testimony of God's Spirit with man's spirit.[115]

Distinguishing the Genuine Witness from the Delusion of the Devil

Wesley gives only brief attention to this matter. He points out that the devil does not humble and soften one's heart to seek after God, love one's neighbor, and put on gentleness, meekness, and the armor of God. When one has this kind of witness it is of God, not of Satan.[116]

Sermon II

That Wesley still regarded the Witness of the Spirit to be a significant doctrine more than twenty years after publishing his first sermon on this subject is seen in the opening words of his second sermon on the Witness: "None who believes the Scriptures to be the Word of God can doubt the *importance* of such a truth as this: a truth revealed therein not once only, not obscurely, not incidentally, but frequently, and that in express terms; but solemnly and of set purpose, as denoting one of the peculiar privileges of the children of God."[117]

By the time Sermon II was written (1767) the Revival had been in progress for more than a quarter of a century; consequently it is not strange that some cases of fanaticism erupted which naturally precipitated negative responses from critics. According to Howard Watkin-Jones, "the theological attitude of the Church of England in the eighteenth century was unfavorable" to teaching doctrines such as the direct witness of the Holy Spirit.[118] Lycurgus Starkey claims that any stress upon the work of the Holy Spirit in "religious experience was immediately suspected of being sectarian enthusiasm" among Anglicans in Wesley's day.[119]

Therefore, by 1767, it was fitting that Wesley should restate the doctrine of assurance, further explain it, and answer numerous objections which had arisen since Sermon I was published in 1746.

Although some endeavored to explain away the doctrine of assurance while others expressed it irrationally, Wesley laid out, in the introduction of Sermon II, one of the tasks of the Methodists as follows: "It more nearly concerns the Methodists, so called, clearly to understand, explain, and defend this doctrine which God has given them to bear to all mankind."[120] Furthermore, he observed that "it is by his peculiar blessing upon them in searching the Scriptures, confirmed by the experience of his children, that this great evangelical truth has been recovered, which had been for many years wellnigh lost and forgotten."[121]

The main part of Sermon II has three divisions: in the first he responds to the question, "What is the witness of the Spirit?"; in the next section he offers answers to this question: Is there such a phenomenon as the direct testimony of the Spirit?; and in the third division he deals with objections which have been raised concerning the doctrine.

The Witness of God's Spirit
In describing the witness of the Spirit, Wesley covers some of the same territory as he does in Sermon I, but he also adds new and helpful comments as well. As noted in the first sermon he sometimes refers to the witness of the Spirit being given "to" one's spirit and at other times "with" one's spirit. In the second sermon he couples both prepositions in one statement: "The testimony now under consideration is given by the Spirit of God *to* and *with* our spirit" (italics mine).[122] Perhaps Wesley utilizes the preposition "to" so that he can support another statement found in both sermons, namely that the Spirit's wit-

ness must "be antecedent to the testimony of our own spirit…"[123] But, if this is the case, he fails to present a convincing argument.

As Sugden sees it, Wesley has muddied the water "by regarding adoption and regeneration as two distinct operations of the Holy Spirit; whereas they are two aspects of the same thing, distinguishable in thought but not in fact."[124] Sugden quotes William Burton Pope who points out that "no terms are more strictly correlative than regeneration and adoption. They describe the same blessing under two aspects; …But they are not thus closely connected as cause and effect; they are coordinate, and the link between them is the common sonship."[125]

Sugden's position is more logical than Wesley's and is certainly in closer alignment with Romans 8:16, as is seen in these comments: "This witness is simultaneous, not, as Wesley tries to prove, successive. The Spirit bears witness *along with* our own spirit; and the testimony is joint and several. Neither is 'afore or after other.'"[126]

What the Witness Does Not Entail

It is helpful in studying any biblical doctrine if one can clearly explain what is not meant by various terminology. Wesley does an excellent job at this point and no doubt was thinking of those who charged him with enthusiasm/fanaticism when he discussed this matter.

First of all, Wesley declares that God's Spirit does not witness or testify by "any outward voice," by which he must mean an audible voice. But he continues by stating that the witness is not necessarily accompanied with "an inward voice, although he may do this sometimes." Nor does the witness mean that Scripture will necessarily be applied to one's heart, although God may often do so.[127]

What the Witness Does Entail

Wesley goes back to the Greek word for "witness," which is μαρτυρία, and notes that this term can also be translated "testimony" or "record." And what the Spirit testifies to in the witness is "that we are the children of God" as seen in Romans 8:16.[128]

In simple language Wesley explains the meaning of the witness until even a child can understand it: "He so works upon the soul by his immediate influence, and by a strong though inexplicable operation, that the stormy wind and troubled waves subside, and there is a sweet calm; the heart resting as in the arms of Jesus, and the sinner being clearly satisfied that God is reconciled, that all his 'iniquities are forgiven, and his sins covered.'"[129]

The Direct Witness of the Spirit

No one, even in Wesley's day, who studied the Scripture with an open mind would deny there is a witness of the Spirit or that in this witness the Spirit testifies with one's spirit that he is a child of God. "None can deny this without flatly contradicting the Scripture," Wesley wrote, and therefore "charging a lie upon the God of truth."[130]

Distinguishing the Direct Witness from the Indirect Witness

Wesley knew that religious people had no problem accepting "an *indirect* witness or testimony that we are the children of God," but too often this witness of one's own spirit was, for all practical purposes, the only witness accepted since the witness of God's Spirit tended to be interpreted in such a way as to be included under the witness of one's spirit.[131]

Although Wesley insisted that the witness of God's Spirit must precede the witness of one's own spirit (which involves a consciousness of possessing the fruit of the Spirit), he did hold to the fact that the two witnesses have a close relationship and an interconnectedness. "Nor do we assert that there can be any real testimony of the Spirit without the fruit of the Spirit. We assert, on the contrary, that the fruit of the Spirit immediately springs from this testimony." But one may not always be conscious of the fruit of the Spirit, as Wesley goes on to explain: "Not always, indeed, in the same degree, even when the testimony is first given, and much less afterwards. Neither joy nor peace are always at one stay; no, nor love;…"[132]

Earlier in the sermon Wesley declared that the Spirit's witness could not continue without the presence of the Spirit's fruit; but the witness will be destroyed by sins of commission or omission or by anything that will grieve the Spirit.[133] Yet he also admits that the witness of the Spirit is not "always equally strong and clear."[134] It would seem that the strength and clarity of one witness would have some bearing on the strength and clarity of the other. Nevertheless Wesley claims that "the direct witness may shine clear, even while the indirect one is under a cloud."[135]

By espousing a direct witness of the Holy Spirit, Wesley is on a solid biblical foundation, for as he states, this is "the plain, natural meaning of the text, 'The Spirit itself beareth witness with our spirit, that we are the children of God.'"[136]

Not only does Romans 8:16 affirm a direct witness of the Spirit, but Romans 8:15 and Galatians 4:6 are also supporting verses which Wesley marshals to strengthen his position. The Holy Spirit is identified in Romans 8:15 as "the Spirit of adoption" which a newborn child of God has received. Galatians 4:6 asserts, "Because ye are sons, God hath sent forth the Spirit of his Son into your hearts, crying Abba, Father." In conjunction with these verses Wesley asks, "Is not this something *immediate* and *direct*, not the result of reflection or argumentation?"[137]

Confirmation by Experience

The direct witness of the Spirit is further confirmed by the personal experiences of a great multitude (among which Wesley identifies himself) who never knew God's favor until "it was directly witnessed to them by his Spirit..."[138] Wesley interviewed vast numbers of converts which led him to conclude that those who are convicted of their sins and of God's wrath upon them "cannot be satisfied with anything less than a direct testimony from his Spirit that he is 'merciful to their unrighteousness, and remembers their sins and iniquities no more.'"[139]

Confirmation in Justification by Faith

One of the strongest supports for a direct witness is found in God's method for saving sinners, not justification by the law or good works, but by faith. Romans 4:5 reveals that God "justifieth the ungodly," who Wesley says "till the moment he is justified, is all ungodly, void of all true holiness;" consequently the Spirit's witness is "(not that they are good, or sincere, or conformable to the Scripture in heart or life, but) that God 'justifieth the ungodly.'"[140]

Since sinners are justified freely by God's grace and mercy, Wesley declares that those who deny the direct witness of the Spirit are also denying the doctrine of justification by faith.[141] In his response to objections put forth against the direct witness, Wesley writes: "I cannot but fear that a supposition of our being justified by works is at the root of all these objections."[142]

Objections to the Witness Refuted

Over the years Wesley heard a number of objections to the doctrine of the direct witness, which he classified under seven headings, although some of them included subdivisions. Some are irrelevant, while others misunderstand Wesley's position and are hardly worthy of notice.

Reference will be made to only three of them. One objection is stated this way: "The Scripture says, 'The tree is known by its fruits;' 'Prove all things;' 'Try the spirits;' 'Examine yourselves.'" To which Wesley agrees and responds thus: "Most true: therefore let every man who believes he 'hath the witness in himself' try whether it be of God. If the fruit follow, it is; otherwise it is not. For certainly 'the tree is known by its fruit.' Hereby we *prove* if it be of God."[143]

Another objection is this: "The direct witness is never referred to in the Book of God." Wesley's answer: "Not as standing alone, not as a single witness, but as connected with the other; as giving a *joint testimony*, testifying *with our spirit* that we are children of God."[144]

A third objection is more lengthy: "The direct witness of the Spirit does not secure us from the greatest delusions. And is that a witness fit to be trusted whose testimony cannot be depended on, that is forced to fly to something else to prove what it asserts?" In reply Wesley says, "To secure us from all delusion,

God gives us two witnesses that we are his children. And this they testify conjointly. Therefore 'what God hath joined together, let no man put asunder.' And while they are joined together we cannot be deluded: their testimony can be depended on. They are fit to be trusted in the highest degree, and need nothing else to prove what they assert."[145]

It is of interest to note that Wesley does lay strong emphasis upon the joint testimony of God's Spirit with man's spirit in refuting objections to the direct witness.

In the conclusion Wesley briefly summarizes the content of the sermon and then leaves two practical admonitions for his readers: (1) "let none ever presume to rest in any supposed testimony of the Spirit which is separate from the fruit of it;" and (2) "let none rest in any supposed fruit of the Spirit without the witness."[146]

Summary Statements

Although Wesley was not always clear and consistent in his presentation of the witness of the Spirit, he did strive for a balanced position based upon biblical foundations. It was by means of his sermons that Wesley chose to teach his theology of assurance.

1. Wesley admits that it is difficult, if not impossible, to explain spiritual matters by means of human language.

2. Perhaps the best one can do is to define the witness as "an inward impression on the soul, whereby the Spirit of God directly 'witnesses to my spirit that I am a child of God;' that Jesus Christ hath loved me and given himself for me; that all my sins are blotted out, and I, even I, am reconciled to God."[147]

3. Conviction of sin, repentance, and the new birth will precede the witness.

4. A humble joy, along with meekness, gentleness, and a tender, yielding spirit will accompany the witness.

5. The unmistakable mark that one has the witness will be manifest in one's obedience to God's commandments.

6. The witness may or may not involve an outward voice, an inward voice, or the application of Scripture.

7. It does entail the immediate operation of the Spirit, whereby the stormy wind in one's heart subsides, and a sweet peace follows, giving one a clear satisfaction that his sins are forgiven.

8. One should not rest in anything less than a clear witness of both God's Spirit and one's own spirit.

9. To avoid confusion, emphasis should always be placed on the dual-witness or joint-testimony of the Holy Spirit with one's human spirit.

10. Wesley's application of the Scripture, which is primarily related to a husband and wife, seems most fitting in a secondary application to the two witnesses: "What God hath joined together, let no man put asunder" (Mark 10:9).[148]

Endnotes

1. *Works,* 1:13.
2. Ibid., 21:118.
3. Students of Wesley are deeply indebted to Albert Outler for his excellent Introduction to Wesley's sermons in *Works,* 1:1-100, plus the specific introductory comments for each of the sermons. Outler's research will be incorporated repeatedly.
4. *Works,* 1:103.
5. Ibid., 1:40. Hereafter cited as *SOSO.*
6. Ibid.
7. Ibid., 1:38.
8. Ibid., 1:38, 62-63.
9. See comments in *Works,* 1:398.
10. Ibid., 1:103.
11. Ibid., 1:5.
12. Ibid., 1:55.
13. Ibid., 1:46.
14. Ibid., 1:86
15. Ibid., 1:40.
16. Ibid., 1:103
17. Quoted by Outler in *Works,* 1:25.
18. *Works,* 1:104.
19. Ibid.
20. Ibid.
21. Ibid., 1:26.
22. Ibid., 1:104.
23. Ibid., 1:XI, XII, 55-56.
24. Ibid., 1:XII.
25. Ibid., 1:105-6.
26. "Let me be a man of one book." See *Works,* 1:105.
27. Ibid., 1:57.
28. Ibid., 1:106.
29. Ibid., 1:13.
30. Ibid., 1:106.
31. Ibid., 1:56-57.
32. Ibid., 1:95.
33. Ibid., 1:XIII.
34. Ibid., 1:106.
35. Ibid.

36. Ibid., 1:107.
37. Ibid.
38. Ibid.
39. Ibid., 1:60-61.
40. Ibid. 1:57.
41. Ibid., 1:74.
42. Ibid., 1:74-75.
43. Ibid., 1:60.
44. bid., 1:71-89.
45. Ibid., 1:89.
46. Ibid., 1:XII.
47. Ibid., 1:66.
48. Ibid., 1:26.
49. Ibid., 1:103.
50. Ibid., 1:7, 8.
51. Ibid., 1:8.
52. Ibid., 1:25.
53. Ibid., 1:16.
54. Ibid., 1:268.
55. Ibid., 1:267.
56. Ibid., 1:274 and 1:286-87, 289-90.
57. Ibid., 1:274.
58. Ibid., 1:287.
59. Ibid.
60. Ibid.
61. Ibid., 1:290, 274.
62. Ibid.
63. Ibid.
64. Ibid., 1:281.
65. See Deuteronomy 30:6, where God circumcises one's heart before he can love Him.
66. *Works*, 1:269-70, 285.
67. Ibid., 1:270, 285.
68. Ibid., 1:269.
69. Ibid.
70. Ibid., 1:285.
71. Ibid.
72. Yates, IX.
73. *Works*, 1:285-86.
74. Ibid. 26:182.
75. Ibid., 1:285.
76. For example, the word "enthusiast" carried a different connotation in Wesley's day than it does today.

77. Quoted by Yates, 73.
78. *Works*, 1:270-71.
79. See Footnote 9 in *Works*, 1:271.
80. John Wesley, *Wesley's Standard Sermons*, ed. Edward H. Sugden, 6th ed., vol. 1 (London: The Epworth Press, 1966), 204. Hereafter cited as Sugden.
81. *Works*, 1:270.
82. Ibid., 1:271.
83. Ibid., 1:273.
84. The following versions use a capital *S*: King James, New King James, New American Standard, and New International Version.
85. *Works*, 1:272-75.
86. Ibid., 1:272-73.
87. Ibid., 1:273.
88. Ibid.
89. See Footnotes in *Works*, 1:273.
90. Ibid., 1:273.
91. Ibid., 1:270, 274.
92. Ibid., 1:271, 274-75.
93. Ibid., 1:274.
94. Ibid.
95. Ibid. If Wesley wanted to utilize another preposition besides "with," he would have presented a clearer argument if he would have used, not "to," but "in," as did his friend and contemporary Adam Clarke in *Christian Theology* (Salem, OH: Convention Book Store, 1967 repr.), 149-157. Furthermore, the lexicons are in uniform agreement on the meaning of συμμαρτυρέω and σύν. See Joseph Hnery Thayer, trans., A Greek-English Lexicon of the New Testament (Edinburgh: T. & T. Clarke, 1901; reprint, Grand Rapids: Baker Book House, 1977), 596, where the verb is defined as "to bear witness with, bear joint witness." See also Arndt and Gingrich, 786, where the verb is defined as "testify or bear witness with ...confirm, testify in support of someone or someth." Likewise in Liddell and Scott, 1459, the definition is "to bear witness with or in support of another." Strong agreement is also seen in the meaning of the preposition σύν: Thayer, 598-99, gives these possible meanings: "to be with one, to accompany one;" "to associate with one;" "to be on one's side;" "to assist one;" "In composition σύν denotes ...association, community, fellowship, participation." Liddell and Scott, 1470, affirm that the preposition means "along with, in company with, together with;" "furnished with, endued with;" "together, at once, jointly;" in composition it means "with, along with, together, at the same time." Arndt and Gingrich point out that σύν can also mean "besides" or "in addition to." Clearly then, the overwhelming thrust of συμμαρτυρέω in its various shades of meaning is that of a joint testimony.
96. This will show up in Sermon II; see *Works*, 1:295.
97. Ibid., 1:275.
98. Ibid., 1:275-76.
99. Ibid., 1:276.

100. Ibid.
101. See an "Introductory Comment" by Outler in *Works*, 1:267-68.
102. Ibid., 1:267.
103. Ibid., 1:267-68.
104. See Footnote 52 in *Works*, 1:146.
105. See Footnote 46 in *Works*, 1:276.
106. *Works*, 1:278.
107. Ibid.
108. Ibid., 1:279.   •
109. Ibid.
110. Ibid., 1:280.
111. Ibid., 1:278-80.
112. Ibid., 1:281.
113. Ibid., 1:282.
114. Ibid., 1:283.
115. See Sugden, 213, and Yates, 77.
116. *Works*, 1:283-84.
117. Ibid., 1:285.
118. Howard Watkin-Jones, *The Holy Spirit form Arminius to Wesley* (London: The Epworth Press, 1929), 313.
119. Lycurgus M. Starkey, Jr., *The Work of the Holy Spirit: A Study in Wesleyan Theology* (Nashville: Abingdon Press, 1962), 74.
120. *Works*, 1:285.
121. Ibid., 1:285-86.
122. Ibid., 1:286.
123. Ibid., 1:274, 289-90.
124. Sugden, 208, 213.
125. Ibid., 208.
126. Ibid., 209.
127. *Works.*, 1:287.
128. Ibid., 1:286.
129. Ibid., 1:287.
130. Ibid.
131. Ibid., see 287ff.
132. Ibid., 1:288.
133. Ibid., 1:286.
134. Ibid., 1:288.
135. Ibid., 1:294.
136. Ibid., 1:288.
137. Ibid., 1:289.
138. Ibid., 1:290-91.
139. Ibid., 1:291.
140. Ibid.

141. Ibid., 1:291-92.

142. Ibid., 1:294.

143. Ibid., 1:295.

144. Ibid.

145. Ibid.

146. Ibid., 1:297-98.

147. Ibid., 1:274.

148. For further insights regarding Wesley's sermon on the Witness of the Spirit, see John Wesley, *DOCTRINAL STANDARDS: The Sermons, with Introductions, Analysis, and Notes,* ed. N. Burwash (the only reference to place and date in the original printing is: Canada, 1881; repr., Salem, OH: Convention Book Store, H. E. Schmul, 1967), 90-93.

Chapter Six

The Witness in Wesley's Letters: Part I

Communicating one with another by means of letter-writing is an ancient practice. There are numerous references to letters and copies of letters in the Old Testament, while most of the books in the New Testament are letters, written either to individuals or to churches.

According to renowned Wesley scholar, Frank Baker, "the full flowering of letter-writing as a literary form came during Wesley's lifetime," and of particular significance is the fact that "the letter is one of the most enduring literary forms, as well as the most intimate and revealing."[1]

A Voluminous Writer

It is doubtful if anyone in the eighteenth century wrote more letters than Voltaire whose "published correspondence comprises twenty thousand letters to and from some seventeen hundred correspondents..."[2] Horace Walpole, contemporary with Wesley, is considered to have been England's greatest letter-writer, having written more than "four thousand letters to approximately two hundred correspondents."[3]

Walpole claimed that one should write in the same way as he talks, since letters are "nothing but extempore conversations on paper."[4] Wesley certainly fit into this pattern. His friend Alexander Knox affirmed that Wesley "wrote as he spoke...He...literally talks upon paper."[5]

Wesley probably wrote more letters than Walpole; his correspondents were eight times as many as Walpole's, numbering some sixteen hundred. It appears that approximately ten thousand letters passed between Wesley and these correspondents.[6]

The Oxford/Bicentennial Edition of *The Works of John Wesley* plans to publish about 3,500 letters that Wesley wrote, which is about one-third more than those included in Telford's edition.[7] In preparing the new edition "well over two thousand Wesley holographs have been traced and utilized."[8]

For more than two centuries Wesley's letters have been published. It is quite amazing that the collection of letters has grown over the years. Telford gives a brief overview of the ongoing collection of published letters from 1791 (the year Wesley died) to 1931 (the year Telford published his eight volumes of letters).[9] In 1791 Dr. Priestly published 12 letters written by Wesley. By the time Joseph Benson published the second edition of Wesley's *Works* (1809-13), 400 letters were included. When Thomas Jackson published another edition of Wesley's *Works* (1829-31), the number of letters more than doubled to 900. A later edition expanded the count to 955. In 1906 Rev. Richard Green, one of the founders of the Wesley Historical Society, had collected 1,600 letters for publication. By 1915 the collection was enlarged to 2,120 letters. When Telford published his eight volumes of letters in 1931 the number had increased to 2,670.

In his Preface remarks Telford stated that "the way in which letters have recently come in from all parts of the world makes it probable that others may yet be added."[10] What an understatement! About a half century later as Frank Baker was preparing to publish the first volume of letters for the Oxford/Bicentennial Edition, he echoed words similar to Telford's: "...for letters hitherto unknown ... will surely continue to surface even after the last volume has added its quota of those coming to hand too late to be included in their chronological setting."[11]

To write such a vast number of letters, it was necessary for Wesley to give "many hours of correspondence almost every week from the beginning of organized Methodism in 1739 until within a week or two of his death on March 2, 1791."[12] Pressed into a busy schedule, he would often pen a letter hastily, as seen in a comment to Mary Cooke in a letter dated March 31, 1787: "...considering that I am usually obliged to write in haste, I often doubt whether my correspondence is worth having."[13] Such a statement confirms the fact Wesley often sandwiched his letter-writing into a schedule that was already full.

Double Letters and Enclosures

Due to the vast number of his correspondents Wesley soon learned how he could save both money and time. In some cases he would write to two different people in the same letter, requesting that the portion written to the other person be forwarded by the one receiving the letter. An example of this kind is seen in a letter dated June 28, 1738, sent to his brother Charles, with this opening statement: "You will send my mother, wherever she is, her letter, by the first opportunity."[14]

In yet other cases Wesley would simply add a postscript to his letter in which he asked the recipient to verbally communicate a message to someone else. An example of this sort is found in a letter addressed to Thomas Rankin, dated January 13, 1765, and stated thus: "Pray give my love to Brother Mallon, or Mary Week Society. I thank him for his letter, and exhort him to stand fast in the liberty wherewith Christ has made him free."[15]

Amanuenses and Secretaries

In order to redeem time Wesley often secured the services of an amanuensis, or transcriber, who would take the original draft and write out a copy of it, which would be sent to the recipient so that he (Wesley) could retain his own copy as a reference.[16] There were also occasions when, because of a physical problem or some other difficulty, Wesley would dictate a letter to his amanuensis, who would then transcribe it. In such cases Wesley would simply add his own signature to the transcription.[17]

Furthermore, Wesley sometimes utilized the services of secretaries. These individuals wrote their own letters and signed their own names but made it clear that their letters were written for and in behalf of Mr. Wesley.[18]

One can readily see how errors could arise in the copies that were made, either because Wesley failed to proofread some of them or because he did not find the error(s) after he had read them. And, as copies were made, it was inevitable that errors would ensue, particularly in misreading dates. Baker claims that hundreds of errors occurred in Telford's edition, but he also admits it is not humanly possible to produce an error-free edition.[19]

A Neat Writer

As one studies Wesley's life, he is soon convinced that Wesley was a perfectionist, a detailed person who demanded much from both himself and others. In commenting upon his letters Baker notes that "Wesley was neat and methodical in all his ways, and this reveals itself neatly in his letters. Every page was set out carefully, with a square left margin, and lines so straight and equidistant from each other that one might wonder whether he used a ruler guide."[20] Wesley did not leave a margin on the right side and only ¼ to ½ inch on the left side.[21]

Writing Materials

Eighteenth century writing materials were, as one would expect, different from those of the twenty-first century. Although writing paper has been in use for a long, long time, the kind used by Wesley was not the same as is normally used in the current century. "All Wesley's publications, and all his letters, were produced on handmade 'laid' paper, prepared by dipping a rectangular mould or sieve into a porridge made of rotted rags soaked in water."[22] It sounds like it was a cumbersome task, but apparently the result was a rather good quality of paper for letter-writing.

Nor did Wesley have access to the kinds of writing instruments that are now so common. Experiments with fountain pens were taking place in his day, but the quill-pen was the normal writing instrument for his century and into the next, as well. It is probable that Wesley wrote his letters with goose-quill pens.[23]

Writing ink is also a product of antiquity, dating back several millennia. Wesley's early and middle letters reveal the use of brown ink. In the last couple decades of his life the ink he used tended to get gradually darker until approximately ten percent of the letters penned in his final years were in "pure black ink."[24]

Wesley did not use envelopes, since they had not yet been invented. The paper sheets he used were folded into two parts, thus making four nearly equal-sized pages, three of which could be used for writing the letter, while the fourth is left open for the name and address of the recipient, as well as the date. By means of a simple folding scheme the written letter would be concealed and kept intact by using sealing wax or wafers to hold the flap to the body of the letter.[25]

Letter Form

Brief reference should be given to the forms Wesley utilized in the letter itself. He used a wide variety of terms in the salutation, which Baker lists "in ascending order of intimacy," as follows: "Sir/Madam; Dear sir/Dear Madam; My dear Mr. — Mrs. — Miss X; My dear brother/sister; Dear James/Jane, etc.; Dear Jemmy/Jenny, etc."[26]

Even when writing to family members Wesley normally employed formal address. His father was addressed as "Dear sir," his mother as "Dear mother," and each of his brothers as "Dear brother." Since he had several sisters, he tended to relax the formality somewhat in letters to them.[27]

Wesley saw no need to ornament his letters or fill in all the available space. Indeed he wrote as he spoke. His shortest letter was comprised of just three words, namely these, "All is well;" sent to James Chubb on August 13, 1774.[28]

In closing a letter Wesley often repeated the kind of address he used in the salutation and then concluded with a variety of expressions. A search through Telford's eight volumes of letters reveals that the closure most often used by Wesley was "Your affectionate brother," which was sometimes shortened to "Yours affectionately" or lengthened to "Your affectionate friend and brother" (used extensively in his last few years). The term "servant" was used from time to time in various formulas, such as "Your affectionate servant," "Your affectionate brother and servant," or "Your humble servant." It is quite obvious that Wesley was fond of the terms "affectionate" and "affectionately."

Regardless of the length of a letter, he ordinarily closed "on a pastoral note, with a challenge, a promise, a blessing, a prayer or a request for prayer, frequently in scriptural language."[29]

Personal Revelation

As noted in the previous chapter, Wesley chose the medium of sermons to communicate his theology. Although he sometimes discloses theology in his letters, "their major importance is as a revelation of him as a man.... They furnish us, in fact, with a portrait through seventy years both more revealing in detail and fuller in coverage than any other source."[30]

Many of Wesley's published works reveal what he thought and did, with little attention given to his feelings. His letters address this aspect of his life most convincingly. Baker sums it up in these words: "The fullest personal revelation ...undoubtedly comes in his letters. Here he expresses emotion more frequently and more fully. Here only can we meet the John Wesley known personally to his friends and followers, when he was writing to and for one person alone, whom instinctively he visualized, and to whom he wrote, as it were, face to face."[31]

Purpose of the Letters

Students of Wesley know that if one wants to become acquainted with the activities and events of his life, one must read his *Journals and Diaries*; if one desires to study his theology, he must study Wesley's *Sermons*; but if one wants to see him as a spiritual guide, as a soul-friend, he must read Wesley's *Letters*. In summarizing the underlying theme of Wesley's letters Baker asserts that "to some extent they were all pastoral, all variations upon one all-pervading theme— personal religion, 'the life of God in the soul.'"[32] At the very heart of personal religion is the matter of personal assurance or the witness of the Spirit, which is one of the major ingredients in Wesley's theology.

Wesley soon learned that bringing sinners to the Savior was only a part, and a small part at that, of helping people land safely on heaven's shore. Only a few month's prior to his death Wesley wrote to Adam Clarke, stating that "to retain the grace of God is much more than to gain it: hardly one in three does this."[33] What solemn words!

George Whitefield was a strong evangelist, probably more gifted than Wesley in evangelistic preaching. However, Whitefield failed to do the necessary follow-up in nurturing his converts and helping them get rooted and grounded in establishing grace. Whitefield was aware of his failure in this area of ministry; thus when he compared the results of his labors with those of Wesley's, he lamented, "This I neglected and my people are a rope of sand."[34]

Wesley's genius is seen in his ability to structure societies, classes, and bands for his converts (or those who wanted to flee the wrath to come) and to delegate leadership roles to others so that the initial work in saving souls would not be in vain. But it may well be that Wesley's greatest gift as a soul-friend is revealed in the spiritual guidance he gave to others by means of his written letters.

In his insightful study of Wesley's way of providing spiritual direction through his letters, Wes Tracy lists several characteristics of Mr. Wesley's spiritual leadership as follows: "affection;" "reciprocal openness;" "commendation and encouragement;" "accountability;" and "discernment."[35] As one reads Wesley's letters, it will be obvious that these characteristics occur again and again.

The remaining part of this chapter will deal with the letters sent to and from Wesley which discuss the assurance of salvation, particularly the witness of God's Spirit with man's spirit. Special attention will be given to Wesley's understanding of the witness, his emphasis upon the witness, any shift in emphasis, and his counsel to others regarding the witness.

Since Wesley was a prolific letter-writer throughout his adult life, the ensuing study will follow the time frames which are marked by dates covered in each of the available volumes of his letters.[36]

1721-1739

Wesley's heart-warming experience at Aldersgate took place on May 24, 1738. Consequently, one would not expect to see as many references to the witness of God's Spirit in Wesley's letters prior to 1738 as after that date. Indeed this is exactly what transpired. The Oxford Edition of Wesley's *Works*, Volume 25, lists letters to and from Wesley for the years 1721-1739. The Holy Spirit is mentioned at least 115 times in these letters, but there are only 13 or 14 references to the witness of God's Spirit with man's spirit that he is a child of God. Interestingly enough, Wesley's first clear reference to the direct witness took place in a letter to Rev. William Law, dated May 14, 1738, just two weeks prior to Aldersgate.[37]

Letters To and From Family Members

The above-stated statistics and facts do not tell the whole story. Various terms are used in the letters which deal with assurance of salvation other than the witness of the Spirit. From September 23, 1723 (second letter in Oxford Edition), to the mid 1730's most of Wesley's letters are to or from his immediate family: mother, father, sisters, and brothers. Particularly helpful to the spiritual well-being of Wesley were the letters he received from his mother.

Letters To and From Susanna Wesley

In a letter from her dated February 23, 1724 [/5], Mrs. Susanna Wesley admonished John (then in his early twenties when he was contemplating the entrance into Holy Orders) to "make religion the business of your life;" to which she added these comments: "I heartily wish you would now enter upon a serious examination of yourself, that you may *know* whether you have a reasonable hope of salvation by Jesus Christ, that is, whether you are in a state of faith and repentance or not, which you know are the conditions of the gospel covenant on our part."[38]

John Wesley had a close and loving relationship with his mother, whom he considered to be a valuable and trusted counselor. This is seen, in part, by the size and number of letters to and from her. The approximate number of letters to and from family members during the decade of Wesley's young adulthood are as follows (for the period of September 23, 1723-February 28, 1729/30): his mother: 35; his father: 23; his older brother Samuel: 7; his younger brother Charles: 3; his sister Emily: 1; and his sister Martha: 1.

No doubt Mrs. Wesley's admonition to her son, to "make religion the business of your life," helped spark his serious pursuit for assurance of salvation over the next thirteen years of his life, culminating in a crisis experience on May 24, 1738.

Bishop Jeremy Taylor on Assurance. In a letter to his mother dated June 18, 1725, he questions the validity of some of Bishop Jeremy Taylor's comments regarding both humility and knowledge of sins forgiven.[39] He shares a quotation from Taylor concerning assurance; actually it involves a lack of assurance: "A true penitent must all the days of his life pray for pardon, and never think the work completed till he dies. Whether God has forgiven us or no, we know not; therefore still be sorrowful for ever having sinned."[40]

Responding to this statement, John correctly concludes that "if we can never have any certainty of our being in a state of salvation, good reason it is that every moment should be spent, not in joy, but in fear and trembling, and then undoubtedly in this life we are of all men most miserable."[41]

When Mrs. Wesley responded in a letter dated July 21[1725], she stated that she knew "little or nothing of Dr. Taylor's Living and Dying" and therefore was not able to comment intelligently concerning his rules which John thought to be "impracticable."[42] She does express her thoughts on humility, but not on assurance, at least not in the letters extant in the Oxford Edition.[43]

In his follow-up letter to his mother dated July 29, 1725, John returned to the matter of assurance of salvation: "That we can never be so certain of the pardon of our sins as to be assured they will never rise up against us I firmly believe. We know that they will infallibly do so if ever we apostatize, and I am not satisfied what evidence there can be of our final perseverance, till we have finished our course. But I am persuaded we may know if we are *now* in a state of salvation, since that is expressly promised in the Holy Scriptures to our sincere endeavors, and we are surely able to judge of our own sincerity."[44]

Dialogue on Faith. In this same letter he told his mother that he understood faith "to be an assent to any truth upon rational grounds," apart from which he did not think he could believe anything.[45]

Mrs. Wesley endeavored to correct John's "notion of faith" in her next letter: "All faith," she asserted, "is an assent, but all assent is not faith." She pointed out that there are truths to which one may give assent, but these "are not properly faith but science," since these truths are reached by a "formal process of reason." She further declared that "divine faith is an assent to whatever God has revealed to us, because he has revealed it."[46] Since faith plays a vital part in bringing one to a knowledge of sins forgiven, John's understanding of faith at different junctions in his spiritual pursuit of assurance will be a crucial matter to observe in subsequent letters.

In her letter to John dated August 18, 1725, Mrs. Wesley continued to express her concern about his understanding of faith: "I wish you had …a better notion of that faith which is proposed to us as a condition of salvation," to which she added her own perspective regarding which she had no doubt: "I insist upon it that the virtue of faith, by which through the merits of our Redeemer we must be saved, is an assent to the truth of whatever God hath been pleased to reveal, because he hath revealed it, and not because we understood it."[47]

Several months later, in her letter dated March 30, 1725, Mrs. Wesley penned these words to John: "I am much more pleased and thankful because I have observed sometime that the Holy Jesus …seems to have taken the conduct of your soul into his own hand, in that he has given you a true notion of saving faith, and, I hope, an experimental knowledge of repentance."[48]

Over the next few years the letters to and from John do not particularly highlight the subjects of faith and assurance. However, in a letter to his mother dated February 28, 1729/30, he talks about the distinctions Bishop Taylor draws between faith and hope, and then assesses Taylor's position on assurance: "In all this he appears to steer "in the middle road exactly: to give assurance of pardon to the penitent, but to no one else."[49]

Letters To and From Literary Circle of Ladies

From August of 1730 through December of 1731 most of the letters to and from Wesley in the Oxford Edition involve "the literary circle into which Wesley found himself drawn through his friendship with Robin Griffiths, Sally Kirkham being 'Varanese', Ann Granville 'Selima', Mary

Pendarves 'Aspasia', and he himself 'Cyrus'...."[50] There are only three references to the Holy Spirit in Wesley's correspondence with these ladies, but none of them deal with the witness of the Spirit; rather they discuss the blasphemy against the Spirit.[51]

Since the decade of the 1730s is the crucial period in which Wesley's long pursuit for assurance of sins forgiven is finally climaxed at Aldersgate Street in May of 1738, one would expect to see signs of advancement in his spiritual journey as he progressed toward this important milestone. In the good providences of God his correspondence with the so-called "literary circle" of ladies began to dwindle.[52]

Personal Concern for Assurance

From early 1732 into the first months of 1738 there are no helpful comments on the witness of the Spirit/assurance in the letters to or from Wesley. It does appear that he was deeply concerned about his spiritual state in the Spring of 1734, as may be inferred from his mother's admonitions to him in a letter dated March 30 of that year: "As your course of life is austere, and your diet low, so the passions, as far as they depend on the body, will be low, too. Therefore you must not judge of your interior state by your not feeling great fervours of spirit and extraordinary agitations, as plentiful weeping, etc., but rather by the firm adherence of your will to God."[53]

When they received word that their father's death was imminent, John and Charles Wesley made their way to Epworth. As he listened to the persuasive affirmation from his dying father, "The inward witness, son; the inward witness! That is the strongest proof of Christianity,"[54] John's personal pursuit for assurance must have been greatly intensified. Nevertheless, it would be more than three years before he received the witness of the Spirit.[55]

Continued Search Through Missionary Labors

The fact that Wesley lacked assurance motivated him to serve as a missionary to American Indians in Georgia for about two years. In a letter to Rev. John Burton dated October 10, 1735, he gave this reason for going to Georgia: "My chief motive ...is the hope of saving my own soul," which he further described as obtaining "faith and love and joy in the Holy Ghost."[56]

Pre-Aldersgate Providences

Far from finding assurance in America, Wesley met with numerous frustrations which eventually forced him to leave in December of 1737. Arriving back in England on February 1, 1738, events in God's gracious providence would soon bring him to a point in time when he would know his sins were forgiven, because an assurance would be given to him by the Spirit of God.

The human instrument God chose to be a spiritual guide to Wesley was

Peter Böhler, a Moravian minister passing through Britain on his way to America. It was Böhler who convinced Wesley of unbelief, of lacking that faith whereby alone one is saved. Böhler saw that Wesley was trying to obtain righteousness by the works of the law and not by faith. Wesley asked him if he should stop preaching until he obtained this faith, to which Böhler responded: "By no means. Preach faith *till* you have it, and then, *because* you have it, you *will* preach faith."[57]

When Wesley penned a letter to James Hutton on April 28, 1738, he had not yet come to saving faith, but he was preaching it, as is seen in the opening part of the letter: "This thing I do: I still follow after, if haply I may attain faith. I preach it to all, that at length I might feel it. Only may I never be content with any other portion!"[58]

End of Search

Little did Wesley know that in less than a month he would "break the faith barrier." Oh, how near he was, just a few hours from receiving that "blessed assurance" when he wrote these words to Rev. John Gambold on May 24, 1738: "Do we already feel 'peace with God', and 'joy in the Holy Ghost'? Does his 'Spirit bear witness with our spirit, that we are the children of God'? Alas with *mine* he does not. Nor, I fear, with yours. O thou Savior of men, save us from trusting in anything but *thee*!"[59] That evening, about 8:45 p.m. (as noted in chapter four) while he listened to a man at a society meeting reading from Luther's Preface to his commentary on Romans and describing "the change which God works in the heart through faith in Christ," Wesley said, "I felt my heart strangely warmed. I felt I did trust in Christ, Christ alone for salvation, and an assurance was given me that he had taken away *my* sins, even *mine*, and saved *me* from the law of sin and death."[60] What an unforgettable milestone in his spiritual journey!

Visit and Interaction with Moravians

About three weeks after his heart-warming experience Wesley traveled to Germany in order to interview Count Zinzendorf and other Moravians that he might learn more about faith and assurance of salvation. While yet visiting with the Moravians, John wrote to his brother Charles on June 28, 1738. In the letter he stated that some of the Moravians made clear-cut distinctions between (1) faith, (2) justifying faith, (3) the assurance of faith, and (4) the new birth (the latter, they said, often came at a later time, distant from the three kinds of faith.) Furthermore, the Moravians taught that "a man may have, and frequently has, justifying faith before he has the assurance that he is justified."[61] Among other things Wesley discovered that religious experiences were not stereotyped, but varied in some respects one from another.

Letters To and From Various People

From September of 1738 through December of 1739 there are only a dozen or so letters to or from Wesley which discuss assurance or the witness of the Spirit. Half or more of these are letters to or from his brother Samuel, which leaves only a small amount of correspondence with others on this subject.

To Revd. Arthur Bedford

When Wesley wrote to Arthur Bedford on September 28, 1738, the letter was basically a response to Bedford's sermon entitled *The Doctrine of Assurance*, which had allegedly been written against Wesley.

Wesley stated that he could agree with some of Bedford's comments concerning assurance; however, the phrase "assurance of salvation" was understood in totally different ways by the two men. For Bedford it meant "an assurance that we shall persevere in a state of salvation," whereas for Wesley the term simply meant "an assurance that we are in such a state."[62]

As far as terminology is concerned, Wesley admitted that "that assurance of which alone I speak I should not choose to call an assurance of salvation, but rather (with the Scriptures), the assurance of faith."[63] Wesley went on to explain what he understood by "assurance of faith," giving Bedford the following detailed description:

> This πληροφορία πίστεως, however we translate it, I believe is neither more nor less than hope; or a conviction, wrought in us by the Holy Ghost, that we have a measure of the true faith in Christ, and that as he is already made justification unto us, so *if* we continue to watch and strive and pray, he will gradually become "our sanctification here and our full redemption hereafter." This assurance, I believe, is given to some in a smaller, to others in a larger degree; to some also sooner, to others later, according to the counsels of his will. But since it is promised to all, I cannot doubt but it will be given to all that diligently seek it. I cannot doubt but all "who truly believe in Christ Jesus, and endeavor to walk in all good conscience before him", will in due time "be assured that they are in a state of grace, and may persevere therein unto salvation", by the Holy Spirit enabling them to discern in themselves those graces to which the promises of life are made, and "bearing witness with their spirits that they are the children of God."[64]

These comments may be Wesley's clearest description of assurance after Aldersgate, since they were written about four months later.

From William Delamotte

In a letter to Wesley dated October 10, 1738, William Delamotte asked this question: "Can a man properly be said to be born of God till he has an assurance of faith?"[65] Delamotte continued by saying, "St. John makes the test of our new birth *our* victory over the world and sin; if so, I fear, I am still unregenerate, for sin works powerfully in me, and seems to be frequently proclaiming its conquests over me. And yet my soul is in a sweet peace, nay, sometimes overwhelmed with joy, and always pants for a closer union, a fuller manifestation of the Son of God. How is this consistent with the true justifying faith?"[66] Unfortunately, there is no response to Delamotte in the extant collection of letters; nonetheless answers to these kinds of questions will be forthcoming in subsequent letters.

To Benjamin Ingham and James Hutton

When he wrote to his friends Ingham and Hutton (Nov. 16, 1738), Wesley is obviously concerned about accurate theology regarding assurance. While he had the utmost confidence in Charles Kinchin as a genuine man of God, Wesley was not pleased with some of his teaching. Wesley told these brethren that Kinchin along with Brother Hutchings "mightily insists both in conversation and preaching that no one can be justified without knowing it, and that none is born again, or has saving faith, till he has the full assurance of faith, continual joy in the Holy Ghost, and the immediate witness of the Spirit with his spirit," and then Wesley asked: "O when will our Lord give us to be of one mind and one soul, to speak and think the same thing!"[67]

To Revd. George Whitefield

In this letter dated March 16, 1739, Wesley continues to express his disagreement with the teaching of Kinchin and Hutchings by telling Whitefield that Miss Molly Kinchin (sister of Revd. Charles Kinchin) "has forgiveness, but not the witness of the Spirit." Rather humorously, Wesley suggests the reason might be "the conviction of our dear brother Hutchings, who seemed to think them inseparable."[68]

Letters To and From Samuel Wesley, Jr

The most significant exchange of letters on the subject of assurance/witness of the Spirit in 1738 and 1739 took place between Wesley and his older brother Samuel. They took radically different positions as is seen in their candid responses one to another. John highlighted their underlying differences in his April 4, 1739 letter: "Your 'assurance' and mine are as different as light and darkness. I mean an assurance that I am *now* in a state of salvation, you an assurance that I shall *persevere* therein."[69]

In what was apparently the last letter John wrote to Samuel in which he expounded on assurance, John referred to their previous correspondence as "an unprofitable dispute" and once again affirmed that the witness of the Spirit is "an assurance of *present* salvation only. Therefore, not necessarily perpetual, neither irreversible."[70]

Several months earlier in his letter to Samuel on October 30, 1738, John initiated the series of letters between him and Samuel, which especially focused on assurance. Herein he described a Christian as "one who so believes in Christ ...that sin hath no more dominion over him." By way of personal testimony John then said: "And in this obvious sense of the word I was not a Christian till May 24 last past."[71]

John did confess that he had been set free by faith and did at the present time have at least a small measure of faith. But then he went on to make this rather shocking confession: "'the seal of the Spirit', 'the love of God shed abroad in my heart', and producing joy in the Holy Ghost, 'joy which no man taketh away', 'joy unspeakable, and full of glory'—this witness of the Spirit I have not, but I patiently wait for it."[72] What may be even more shocking is the fact that John is making this confession a little more than five months after Aldersgate!

John endeavored to further explain the witness by saying: "Those who have not yet received joy in the Holy Ghost, the love of God, and the *plerophory* of faith (any or all of which I take to be the witness of the Spirit with our spirit that we are the sons of God), I believe to be Christians in that imperfect sense wherein I call myself such."[73] If this is, in fact, what he understood to be the witness, it seems strange that he was not conscious of at least one of these evidences.

In response to this letter Samuel wrote to John on November 15, 1738, and among other comments said this: "Such doctrine as encourages and abets spiritual fireballs, apparitions of the Father, etc., etc., is delusive and dangerous."[74]

When John replied a couple of weeks later, he admitted that weak-minded people might distort the doctrine, but they could easily do such to any biblical teaching. In forceful language John wrote these words: "...I believe every Christian who has not yet received it ought to pray for 'the witness of God's Spirit with his spirit, that he is a child of God!' Moreover he went so far as to say, "This witness, I believe, is necessary for my salvation. How far invincible ignorance may excuse others, I know not."[75] His position will be softened and modified somewhat in his later and more mature understanding. Indeed, Samuel could not bring himself to believe John was not a Christian prior to May 24, 1738.[76] It does not appear that either was able to change the thinking of the other. Apparently John's last letter to his brother was penned less than two weeks before Samuel's death. One can only wonder if Samuel received the witness of the Spirit before he died.

Overemphasis on Feelings

Before concluding this study of Wesley's letters written from 1721-1739, it may be helpful to observe the heavy emphasis he placed on feelings, especially in the period following Aldersgate. For example, in a letter written on July 25, 1739, to a learned Anglican minister, Dr. Henry Stebbing, to whom Wesley wrote: "You charge me with 'vain and confident boastings ...damning all who do not *feel* what I *feel*'"[77]

In this letter Wesley denies Stebbing's charge but does justify emphasis upon feelings by declaring that "joy in the Holy Ghost" is "joy, though not *unfelt*, yet *unspeakable* and full of glory." The fruit of the Spirit, Wesley insists, "must be *felt*." Then, in a direct address, he says, "I beseech you, sir, by the mercies of God, that if as yet you 'know nothing of such inward feelings', if you do not 'feel in yourself these mighty workings of the Spirit of Christ', at least you would not contradict and blaspheme." Driving his point home with his usually good logic, Wesley wrote: "As you 'hear the wind, and feel it, too,' while it 'strikes upon your bodily organs', you will know you are under the guidance of God's Spirit the same way, namely, by *feeling it in your soul*; by the present peace and joy which you feel within..."[78]

Without question Wesley's rationale for embracing heart-felt religion is convincing. But one must ask, "How could Wesley describe joy in the Holy Ghost if he had not personally experienced it?" Just ten months earlier, in his letter to his brother Samuel (Oct. 30, 1738) he clearly stated that he did not have the witness of the Spirit (which, said he, included joy in the Holy Ghost).

So, what happened in Wesley's personal experience? Surely he received the witness at Aldersgate on May 24, 1738. Did he then lose it by October of the same year and then regain it by the time he wrote to Dr. Stebbing in July of 1739? Or, is it possible, when he claimed to have no witness, that he simply meant the witness was not shining clear or that it was temporarily withdrawn? Or could it be that he was referring to what he had once experienced?

As one endeavors to analyze Wesley's life at this period of time, it appears that he placed an undue emphasis upon his own feelings as an evidence of assurance or a lack thereof. For instance, in his *Journal* entry for January 4, 1739, he wrote these strange words: "My friends affirm *I am mad*, because I said 'I was not a Christian a year ago.' I affirm, I am not a Christian now. Indeed, what I might have been I know not, had I been faithful to the grace then given, when, expecting nothing less, I received such a sense of the forgiveness of my sins as till then I never knew. But that I am not a Christian at this day I as assuredly know as that Jesus is the Christ."[79]

But, one must further ask, "How did Wesley know 'assuredly' that he was not a Christian in January of 1739?" The indications are that he was basing his knowledge upon his feelings. No doubt one of Wesley's biographers, C. T. Winchester, is correct in noting that "it was the one most unfortunate result of the Moravian influence that Wesley for a time tended to confuse ...assurance with the evidence of fluctuating personal feeling."[80] According to Winchester there are no negative notes sounded by Wesley in his *Journal* after 1739.[81] If that is, in fact, an accurate statement regarding Wesley's *Journal* entries, it does not apply to his letters, as will be observed at a later period in his life.

A great deal of space has been given to Wesley's understanding and personal experiences concerning assurance in this important, formative period of his life, since what he learned and experienced at this time will play an important role in his subsequent work as a soul friend, giving guidance by means of his letters.

1740-1755

The remaining part of this chapter will deal with the witness of the Spirit/ assurance as found in Wesley's letters dated from 1740-1755.[82]

As one would expect, there is a significant increase in the references to the witness of the Spirit in this period of time versus those dating from 1721-1739. While the Holy Spirit is mentioned by name approximately 115 times in the first period (1721-1739), the number increases to more than 175 times in the second period (1740-1755). But the greatest increase is seen in the references to the direct witness of the Spirit, from about 14 in the former period to more than 65 in the latter. All the references to the Spirit's witness in Volume 25 occurred in 1738 and 1739; in Volume 26 most of the citations are clustered around two time frames: (1) 1745-1748; and (2) 1755.

Letter to John Bennet

In a short letter dated June 1, 1744, to one of his itinerant preachers, John Bennet, Wesley began with words of warning: "You are in great danger of running from one extreme to the other, from Calvinism to Pelagianism."[83] Apparently he was trying to give this young preacher some guidance in practical theology, especially as then understood by Methodists, some three and one-half weeks before the convening of the first Methodist Conference (June 25, 1744).

Wesley continues his letter by identifying vital Christianity: "If the Bible be true, then none is a Christian who has not the marks of [a] Christian there laid down. One of these is, the love of God, which must be felt, if it is in the soul, as much as fire upon the body. Another is, the witness of God's Spirit with my spirit that I am a child of God."[84]

To these comments Wesley added this one: "Till I have these marks I am not a Christian."[85] These words were penned more than six years after Aldersgate. By insisting that God's love "must be felt," does he mean that *feeling* must always be accompanied with *possessing?* He does not clarify his affirmation, but a few more years of observation and dialogue would cause him to make some concessions. It is also difficult to correlate these comments with those in his letter to Benjamin Ingham and James Hutton on November 16, 1738 (as noted earlier in this chapter).

Letters To and From "John Smith"
The most intensive discussions on the witness of the Spirit in Volume 26 took place from 1745-1748 and consisted of a series of twelve letters which passed between Wesley and a man who identified himself as "John Smith." The Oxford Edition presents all twelve letters in their total content.

No one knows for certain who "John Smith" was. Some think he might have been Thomas Secker (1693-1768) who served as Bishop of Oxford at the time the letters were being exchanged; and then at a later date he served as Archbishop of Canterbury. However, some characteristics of "Smith" do not seem to fit Secker. Hence Smith's true identity remains a mystery.

However, this much is known about the pseudonymous writer: he "was a devout and scholarly churchman who challenged Wesley's beliefs that his doctrine and Methodist practices were in line with the teaching of the Bible and the Church of England, and a genuine demonstration of the operation of the Holy Spirit."[86]

It was Smith who initiated the correspondence. He claimed to be "a contender for truth and not for victory" and therefore would be glad to convince Wesley of any errors he might find in him, but he also would even be "abundantly more glad to be convinced of errors in himself." Smith chose to limit his discussion to matters of doctrine, phraseology, and fact.[87]

Long Letters
There are approximately 85 pages in the twelve letters, about 34 pages for Smith's and 50 for Wesley's. Since the publisher used a smaller print for Smith's letters, it may be that they are virtually the same in length as Wesley's. Since both writers were well educated and of strong philosophical mind-set, it is challenging to follow their arguments, affirmations, and denials back and forth through the twelve letters.

Congenial but Candid
Most of the letters begin and end on kind and congenial notes. However, as the correspondence continues, the letters become more candid and even

border on sarcasm at times. In his fifth letter Smith writes: "If this debate is to go any further, I must insist upon your keeping your temper, and upon your bearing with patience your adversary's supposing himself in the right, and you in the wrong..."[88] What a spirit!

In his fifth letter to Smith, Wesley said this: "It appears to me that you show more eagerness of spirit, more warmth and resentment, in your last than you ever have from the beginning."[89]

In spite of these statements both men could agree on some points and even apologize for misunderstandings and oversights which had arisen.

Repetitious and Circular

Each writer repeats himself over and over again, sometimes restating and sometimes enlarging his comments. But, since each has a difficult time accepting the position of the other, the arguments seem to go around and around without reaching a clear and satisfying closure.

Key Issue

At the heart of the debate are the doctrines of the witness of the Spirit and faith. Smith chose to use his own words to express what he understood Wesley to teach, so that the latter could more readily see whether the former was mistaken. Smith laid out his understanding of Wesley's position as follows:

> ...faith (instead of being rational assent and moral virtue for the attainment of which men ought to yield the utmost attention and industry) is altogether a divine and supernatural illapse from heaven, the immediate gift of God, the mere work of Omnipotence, given instantaneously and arbitrarily, not with any regard to the fitness of the recipient, but the absolute will of the Donor. That the moment this faith is received, the recipient's pardon is signed in heaven, or he is justified. This pardon or justification is immediately notified to him by the Holy Ghost, and that (not by his imperceptibly working a godly assurance, but) by such a perceptible, such a glaring attestation as is as easily discernible from the dictates of reason or suggestions of fancy as light is discernible from darkness. Upon this perceptible and infallible notification the recipient is saved...."[90]

Obviously Smith misunderstood and misinterpreted Wesley in more ways than one. Too often when one is debating an issue it is easy to set up false choices by structuring an either/or situation, directly or indirectly. Most often accurate theological positions involve *both/and* rather than *either/or* formulas.

On nearly every matter which Smith discusses Wesley will agree with him that his positions do bear segments of truth, but not the whole scope of truth, certainly not biblical truth. For instance, Wesley will admit that "God imperceptibly works in some a gradually increasing assurance of his love," but on the other hand he will also insist that God "works in other a full assurance thereof in one moment."[91] As one carefully reads all of Smith's letters, it becomes exceedingly clear that it is this aspect of Wesley's teaching on direct and instantaneous assurance which he cannot (or *will* not) accept.

Wesley correctly asserts that Smith is defining faith in a general sense with emphasis on growth or progress, whereas he (Wesley) is referring to Christian faith in the sense of "the first rise of faith," which he also calls "saving faith;" and then he describes it as "a divine conviction of invisible things, a supernatural conviction of the things of God, with a filial confidence in his love."[92]

When he explains "perceptible inspiration," Wesley uses nearly identical language in both his second and third letters: "We mean that inspiration of God's Holy Spirit whereby he fills us with righteousness, peace, and joy, with love to him and all mankind. And we believe it cannot be, in the nature of things, that a man should be filled with this peace and joy and love by the inspiration of the Holy Ghost without perceiving it, as clearly as he does the light of the sun."[93]

In his second letter he immediately adds these words: "This is (so far as I understand them) *the main doctrine of the Methodists.* This the *substance* of what we all preach."[94] Wesley further expounds his position in strong language: "No man can be a *true Christian* without such an inspiration of the Holy Ghost as fills his heart with peace and joy and love; which he who perceives not, has it not. This is the point for which alone I contend. And this I take to be the very foundation of Christianity."[95]

It is possible that his correspondence with Smith caused Wesley to rethink some of his viewpoints. For example, in 1745 he refers to assurance as "the main doctrine of the Methodists, but twenty-two years later, in 1767, he calls the doctrine "*one grand part* of the testimony which God has given them..."[96]

One can understand why Smith would accuse Wesley of being inconsistent and contradictory at times. Although Wesley would say that no one could be a "true Christian" without the Spirit's witness, he would also make exceptions for cases of "invincible ignorance," by which he meant those "who never heard of these doctrines."[97]

The fact that God's Spirit bears witness with man's spirit, Smith could not deny, since Romans 8:16 clearly states the same. However, Smith contends that Wesley distorted Romans 8:16 and that neither it nor any other scripture taught the "doctrine of a direct, perceptible inspiration..."[98] Rather, Smith says, the Spirit bears witness with man's spirit "by his attestation in the Holy Scriptures."[99]

Wesley counters Smith's position by declaring that "imperceptible assurance is no assurance at all..."[100] In two of his letters Wesley expounds Romans 8:16 in such a manner that an uneducated person should be able to understand it:

> You allow there is a testimony of the Spirit with our spirit that we are the
> children of God. But you say it is not a *perceptible* one. How is this? Let us
> examine it thoroughly. It is allowed, (1) The Spirit of God, (2) bears testi-
> mony to my spirit, (3) that I am a child of God. But I am not to perceive it.
> Not to perceive what? The first, second, or third particular? Am I not to
> perceive *what is testified*—"that I am a child of God"? Then it is not testified
> at all. This is saying and unsaying in the same breath. Or am I not to perceive
> *that it is testified to my spirit*? Yea, but I must perceive what passes in my
> own soul. Or, lastly, am I to perceive that I am a child of God, and that this
> is testified to my spirit, but not to perceive *who it is that testifies?* Not to
> know it is the Spirit of God? O sir, if there be really a man in the world who
> hath this *testimony* in himself, can it be supposed that he does not know who
> it is that testified? Who it is that speaks to his heart?[101]

It is difficult to imagine how any Bible scholar could unfold the plain
statement of Romans 8:16 more clearly than Wesley does in the comments
given above. Nevertheless, in his last letter Smith declares that Wesley's "new
notions of inspiration... can no more be supported by the Eighth of Romans
than by the First of Genesis."[102] Perhaps Smith's preconceived ideas and theological biases produced mental barriers which made it nearly impossible for
him to accept Wesley's logic and interpretation. In his fifth letter to Smith,
Wesley confessed that he did not expect his friend to change his thinking, "touching points wherein we differed."[103]

No doubt Wesley's strongest argument for the direct witness of the
Spirit (in his last letter to Smith) is not provided in marshaling facts and
expositions by skillful logic, but rather in an illustration regarding his father's
experience at the end of his life. Wesley noted that during his father's last
illness, which lasted for eight months, he "enjoyed a clear sense of his acceptance with God. I heard him express it more than once, although at that
time I understood him not. 'The inward witness, son, the inward witness,'
said he to me, 'that is the proof, the strongest proof, of Christianity.'"[104]
Wesley then concluded with these words concerning his father: "I cannot
therefore doubt but the Spirit of God bore an inward witness with his spirit
that he was a child of God."[105]

Letter to the Revd. Charles Wesley

On July 31, 1747, Wesley wrote a letter to his brother Charles concerning
two significant doctrines, namely justifying faith and assurance. At the outset
of the letter John asks this question: "Is justifying faith a sense of pardon?" to
which he answers, *"Negatur*—it is denied."[106]

Frank Baker notes that during the first four Methodist conferences

(1744-1747), several theological matters were discussed, one of which was the relationship of justifying faith to assurance of salvation. In the 1747 conference this question was raised: "Is justifying faith a divine assurance that Christ loved me, and gave himself for me?" which was answered as follows: "We believe it is."[107] Baker suggests that Wesley's series of letters to and from "John Smith" may well have had some bearing on the doubt being raised as to the answer given above in the July 31, 1747 letter to Charles.[108]

In his correspondence with Charles, John defines "justifying faith" as "that faith which whosoever hath is not under the wrath and the curse of God." He then defines "a sense of pardon" as "a distinct, explicit assurance that my sins are forgiven."[109]

While John did affirm that such assurance is "the common privilege of real Christians," he denied that justifying faith is "such an assurance, or necessarily connected therewith" for the following reason: "If justifying faith necessarily implies such an explicit sense of pardon, then everyone who has it not, and everyone so long as he has it not, is under the wrath and the curse of God. But this is a supposition contrary to Scripture as well as to experience."[110]

The Scripture citations to which he refers are Isaiah 50:10 and Acts 10:34, the latter stating this: "Of a truth I perceive that God is no respecter of persons; but in every nation he that feareth God and worketh righteousness is accepted with him."

In dealing with experience John observes that "J[onathan] R[eeves], etc., etc., had peace with God, no fear, no doubt, before they had that sense of pardon." At this point in the letter John adds this personal testimony: "And so have I frequently had."[111] This is an interesting admission on John's part.

The strongest support favoring his position follows: "The assertion that justifying faith is a sense of pardon is contrary to reason: it is flatly absurd. For how can a sense of our having received pardon be the condition of our receiving it?"[112] Once again Wesley's logic is sharpened into a clear focus which would be difficult to dispute. At this junction in his spiritual journey one can detect a shift in Wesley's understanding as regards faith and assurance.

The closing paragraph in his letter to Charles, dealing with objections and responses, gives further evidence that John was expressing an evolution in his thinking about assurance at this time:

> If you object: (1). "J. R., St. Paul, etc. had this sense," I grant they had; but they were justified before they had it. (2). "We know fifteen hundred persons who have this assurance." Perhaps so; but this does not prove that they were not justified till they received it. (3). "We have been exceedingly blessed in preach-

ing this doctrine." We have been blessed in preaching the great truths of the gospel, although we tacked to them, in the simplicity of our hearts, a proposition which was not true. (4). "But does not our church give this account of justifying faith?" I am sure she does of saving or Christian faith; I think she does of justifying faith too. But to the law and to the testimony. All men may err: but the word of the Lord shall stand for ever.[113]

It is to Wesley's credit that he places Scripture above traditions, reason and experience. It should also be noted that Wesley is, at this point in time, making a distinction between "justifying faith" and "saving faith" (the latter he apparently considers to be synonymous with "Christian faith").

The last correspondence of import in Volume 26, regarding assurance/the witness of the Spirit, took place in ten letters which passed between Richard Tompson and John Wesley. Since only four of these letters appear in Volume 26, the discussion of these will appear in the next chapter, which will deal with Wesley's letters, dated 1755-1791, in Telford's edition.

Endnotes

1. See *Works*, 25:12. Preparatory to Wesley's *Letters*, as is the case with his *Journals* and *Sermons*, an excellent introduction with background materials is presented. A great deal of the content in the early part of this chapter has been distilled from Baker's insightful research.

2. Ibid., 25:13.

3. Ibid.

4. Quoted by Baker in *Works*, 25:12.

5. Quoted by Baker in *Works*, 25:7.

6. *Works*, 25:82.

7. Ibid., 25:18. Unfortunately, only two volumes of letters in the new edition have been published thus far. Consequently, it will be necessary to use Telford's edition for the letters written in 1755-1791.

8. Ibid., 25:107.

9. John Wesley, *The Letters of the Reverend John Wesley, A.M.*, 8 vols., ed. John Telford (London: Epworth Press, 1960 repr.) 1:VII-VIII (hereafter cited as *Letters)*.

10. *Letters*, 1:VII.

11. *Works*, 25:124. If the collection keeps growing, it may be necessary to add an additional volume to those already planned.

12. Ibid., 25:88.

13. *Letters*, 7:377.

14. *Works*, 25:554. Mrs. Wesley's portion was probably written on pages 1 and 2 of the folded letter which Charles would doubtless cut off from the part addressed to him and then forward her part sent in a letter from himself.

15. *Letters*, 4:288.

16. *Works*, 25:44-45.

17. Ibid., 25:45.
18. Ibid.
19. Ibid., 25:110-111.
20. Ibid., 25:53.
21. See Ibid., 25:58-59.
22. Ibid., 25:15.
23. Ibid., 25:17.
24. Ibid., 25:18.
25. Ibid., 25:68-71. See Appendix C for a picture of both sides of a letter.
26. Ibid., 25:48.
27. Ibid., 25:49.
28. Ibid., 25:51-52.
29. Ibid., 25:58.
30. Ibid., 25:IX.
31. Ibid., 25:1.
32. Ibid., 25:96.
33. *Letters*, 8:249.
34. Quoted by Wesley Tracy, 44.
35. Ibid., 61-69.
36. As noted earlier, only two volumes are now available in the Oxford/Bicentennial Edition of *Wesley's Works*. Therefore it will be necessary to use Telford's edition for subsequent letters.
37. *Works*, 25:542.
38. Ibid., 25:160 (italics mine).
39. Taylor's devotional classics to which Wesley refers are *Rule and Exercise of Holy Living* (1650) and *Rule and Exercise of Holy Dying* (1651).
40. Quoted by Wesley in *Works*, 25:169.
41. Ibid., 25:170.
42. Ibid., 25:172.
43. See *Works*, 25:173, where Outler says a few pages of this letter are missing. See also W. H. Fitchett, *Wesley and His Century* (New York: Abingdon Press, 1929 repr.), 69, where he quotes Mrs. Wesley as stating to John: "An absolute certainty that God has forgiven us you can never have until you come to heaven." Fitchett does not cite his source, but it may be that Mrs. Wesley had penned these words in the part of the letter that is now missing. Or perhaps she passed the message to him through another channel.
44. *Works*, 25:175.
45. Ibid.
46. Ibid., 25:179. This letter is dated Aug. 18, 1725.
47. Ibid., 25:183.
48. Ibid., 25:193.
49. Ibid., 25:245.
50. See Footnote 2 in *Works*, 25:246.

51. Ibid., 25:316, 318.
52. See Footnote 1 in *Works*, 25:389.
53. Ibid., 25:385.
54. Fitchett, 93.
55. Samuel Wesley's death occurred on April 25, 1735.
56. *Works*, 25:439-40.
57. *Works*, 18:228.
58. Ibid., 25:537.
59. Ibid., 25:551.
60. Ibid., 18:249-50.
61. Ibid., 25:554.
62. Ibid., 25:563.
63. Ibid.
64. Ibid., 25:564.
65. Ibid., 25:567.
66. Ibid., 567-68.
67. Ibid., 579-80. Is recent Moravian influence expressed here?
68. Ibid., 25:608.
69. Ibid., 25:622.
70. Ibid., 25:645. This letter is dated May 10, 1739. Samuel died on Nov. 6, the same year.
71. Ibid., 25:575.
72. Ibid., 25:576-77.
73. Ibid., 25:577.
74. Ibid., 25:579.
75. Ibid., 25:594.
76. Ibid., 25:598.
77. Ibid., 25:669.
78. Ibid., 25:671-72.
79. Ibid., 19:29.
80. C. T. Winchester, *The Life of John Wesley* (New York: The Macmillan Company, 1916 repr.), 61.
81. Ibid.
82. These are the letters which appear in Volume 26 of the Oxford Edition of Wesley's *Works*. This is the last volume of letters in the new edition that is available at the time of this writing.
83. *Works*, 26:107.
84. Ibid., 26:108.
85. Ibid.
86. Ibid., 26:138. See Footnote 18 for further details concerning "John Smith."
87. Ibid., 26:139.
88. Ibid., 26:238.
89. Ibid., 26:245.

90. Ibid., 26:139.
91. Ibid., 26:157.
92. Ibid., 26:159.
93. Ibid., 26:181-82, 202.
94. Ibid., 26:182 (italics mine).
95. Ibid.
96. Ibid., 1:285 (italics mine).
97. Ibid., 26:182.
98. Ibid., 26:246, 259.
99. Ibid., 26:168.
100. Ibid., 26:291.
101. Ibid., 26:247.
102. Ibid., 26:259.
103. Ibid., 26:252.
104. Ibid., 26:288-89.
105. Ibid., 26:289.
106. Ibid., 26:254.
107. Ibid. See Footnote 6.
108. Ibid.
109. Ibid., 26:254.
110. Ibid., 26:254-55.
111. Ibid., 26:255.
112. Ibid.
113. Ibid.

Chapter Seven

The Witness in Wesley's Letters: Part II

As noted in the previous chapter, Frank Baker claims that the basic thrust in Wesley's letters are "to some extent …variations upon one all-pervading theme—personal religion, 'the life of God in the soul.'"[1] Wesley was concerned about helping people get into the kingdom of God, but an even greater concern was to help them continue in the kingdom. One of the ways he was able to aid others in getting rooted in the establishing grace of God was through his letters.

The purpose of this final chapter is to continue the exploration of Wesley's letters (from 1755 until the close of his life in 1791) as he deals with the witness of the Spirit/assurance, faith and closely related matters. Since the time period of these letters involves the maturing years of his ministry and life, special attention will be given to Wesley's understanding of the witness as his study of Scripture and his experiences unfolded. Particular interest will center on any change in emphasis or teaching.

All but four letters in this chapter are taken from Telford's edition, Volumes III-VIII. In the letters to and from Richard Tompson two sent by him and two sent by Wesley are taken from Volume 26 of the Oxford Edition (the last volume of letters available at the time of this writing).

1755-1758

Since this period of time is relatively short (due to the fact that it is necessary to begin on page 158 in Volume III of Telford's edition in order to connect with the last letters presented in Volume 26 of the Oxford Edition), one would not expect to find as many references to the witness of the Spirit as in other volumes which cover more years. But the fact is, the doctrine of the witness appears more often in Volume III of Telford's edition than in each of his last three volumes. The letters dated from August of 1755 to January of 1758 refer to the person of the Holy Spirit at least fifty-five times, while there are about fifteen references to the witness[2] There are also several discussions on assurance.

Letters To and From Richard Tompson

Richard Tompson initiated the correspondence which eventually involved ten letters passing between him and John Wesley. Tompson only identified himself as "P.V." until his fifth letter when he disclosed his name. He withheld his real identity early on because he knew Wesley had referred to him in a journal entry dated June 17, 1739, which read thus: "In the afternoon I saw poor R—d T—n, who had left our Society and the Church. We did not dispute, but pray; and in a short space the scales fell off from his eyes. He gladly returned to the Church, and was in the evening readmitted into our Society."[3] Frank Baker describes Tompson as one who was "self-taught, intelligent, and thoughtful, with a strong strain of scepticism …agreeing with most of Wesley's teaching, but entertaining doubts about assurance and perfection."[4]

Wesley's First Letter

In his first letter to Tompson (known at that time only as "P.V.") Wesley welcomed his correspondent to critique his writings: "If you have observed anything in any of the tracts I have published which you think is not agreeable to Scripture or reason, you will oblige me by pointing [it] out, and by communicating to me any remarks you have occasionally made."[5]

Tompson's Second Letter

In response to Wesley's challenge Tompson noted that he differed from him regarding "*assurance* being essential to *justifying faith*."[6] Especially did Tompson have a problem with this position of Wesley's: "that no person is a *true believer in Christ* but he who either certainly *knows*, or has known, by the *immediate revelation of the Holy Ghost*, that his sins are forgiven."[7]

Tompson insisted that "*assurance* is neither of the *essence* of *faith*, neither is it essentially connected with it." Which he then explains in the following statement: "I must believe *antecedently* to the act of justification, and that act must pass before God can reveal to me that he has passed such an act."[8]

Tompson then expressed his frustration to reconcile two of Wesley's statements, namely these: (1) "that a person may be a believer who is not freed from doubt and fear;" and (2) "that a man cannot be justified without knowing that he is so."[9]

Furthermore, Tompson could not understand how Wesley could equate "a sure trust or confidence in God, that my sins are forgiven" with an assurance that they are forgiven "by immediate revelation from him."[10]

Wesley's Second Letter

Wesley's second letter opens with a compliment to his correspondent: "Of all the disputants I have known, you are the most likely to convince me of any mistakes I may be in; because you have found out the great secret, of speaking the truth in love."[11]

Since the Methodists had already made some concessions concerning assurance, Wesley thought it best to send Tompson conference minutes from the previous few years so that areas of agreement and disagreement would be readily seen. "And if you can show me," Wesley wrote, "that any farther concessions are needful, I shall make them with great pleasure."[12]

It was also Wesley's belief that in the early centuries of church history "the whole Christian Church ...enjoyed" what he called "the assurance of faith." As he saw it, no one who would carefully read the writings of the Ante-Nicene Fathers could doubt whether they possessed this assurance.[13]

Although he is not dogmatic in his position, Wesley says this about Christian faith: "I think *a divine conviction* of pardon is directly implied in *the evidence* or *conviction* of things unseen. But if not, it is no absurdity to suppose that when God pardons a mourning broken-hearted sinner his mercy *necessarily obliges* him to another act, to witness to his spirit that he has pardoned him."[14]

At this point in his letter Wesley adds a personal testimony: "I know that I am accepted; and yet that knowledge is sometimes shaken, though not destroyed, by doubt or fear. If that knowledge were destroyed, or wholly *withdrawn*, I could not then say I had Christian faith."[15] For Wesley, there is no difference in saying, "I *know* God has accepted me" or "I have a *sure trust* that God has accepted me."[16] As will be noted later, all these statements will shock and astonish Tompson.

Before closing the letter Wesley points out areas of agreement with Tompson: "That justifying faith cannot be a conviction that I am justified; and that a man who is not assured that his sins are forgiven may yet have a kind or degree of faith which distinguishes him not only from a devil, but from an heathen; and on which I may admit him to the Lord's Supper."[17]

Notwithstanding these admissions, Wesley could still hold that "the proper Christian faith which purifies the heart implies such a conviction."[18]

Tompson's Third Letter

At the close of Tompson's third letter he states that he had written hastily and would like to have had more time to "put it in better order."[19] Similarly, when he penned his second letter to Tompson, Wesley lamented that he had less time to write than he desired.[20] In the first five letters which passed between them, it is quite obvious that Tompson put far more thought and time into his writing than did Wesley. No doubt his schedule was less hectic than Wesley's.

In the opening part of his third letter Tompson notes that Wesley sent to him, not the conference minutes of the past few years which he had intended to send, but other materials which did not reveal concessions on assurance which the Methodists had made.

It is indeed unfortunate that Tompson had not received the intended conference minutes, for it would doubtless have affected at least part of the content in his third letter.

In response to Wesley's second letter Tompson expresses strong disagreement with Wesley's opinion that "the whole Christian church in the first centuries enjoyed *the assurance of faith.*" Nor does Tompson believe that the Ante- and the Post-Nicene Church believed that "no person is a true believer in Christ till he knows that his sins are forgiven;" for had they held to this, Tompson reasons, how could they "have been entirely silent in an article of such importance?"[21]

Tompson does think that Clemens Romanus, Ignatius, Polycarp and many in the Ante- and Post-Nicene Church experienced and enjoyed the assurance of faith. "But," said he, "that every true believer therein was possessed of a clear assurance that his sins were forgiven I must take the liberty to deny till I see it proved..."[22]

Asserting that he had read the epistles of Romanus, Ignatius, and Polycarp again and again, he declares that he could not "find the least intimation either that the writer himself, or any of those to whom he writes, was possessed of an assurance of faith or anything like it."[23]

Tompson also asks Wesley if he can name any Reformers "who have taught clearly and plainly that no person is a true believer in Christ till he knows by *immediate revelation* that his sons are forgiven?" In dogmatic tones Tompson insists that this doctrine had never been taught in the Christian Church until "the Moravians invented it a few years ago."[24]

Since several of Tompson's other disagreements with Wesley will be treated in his next letter, no further reference to Tompson's critique will be noted at this time. That he often misunderstood Wesley will be evident in the unfolding of future dialogue.

Wesley's Third Letter

Early in this letter Wesley confesses that he is at a disadvantage in his correspondence with "P.V." for at least two reasons: (1) he does not know to whom he is writing, whereas his correspondent knows him; and (2) his busy schedule prohibits him from writing as much or as accurately as he would like. "All, therefore, which you can expect from me is," Wesley affirms, "not a close-wrought chain of connected arguments, but a short sketch of what I should deduce more at large if I had the leisure."[25]

This is Wesley's longest and most detailed letter to Tompson. One can only wish Wesley would have had more time to buttress his positions with more accurate and detailed arguments. Nonetheless, as Telford observes, "Wesley's patience and courtesy amid his crowd of engagements with the leisured correspondent are striking."[26]

Wesley continues to assert that "Christian faith ...implies a divine evidence or conviction or our acceptance," which Tompson does not accept.[27] Yet, Wesley will agree with Tompson that "the Spirit's witnessing that we are accepted cannot be the faith whereby we are accepted," for, as Wesley will admit, "A conviction that we are justified cannot be implied in justifying faith."[28]

It is unfortunate that Wesley did not distinguish more clearly between "Christian faith" and "justifying faith," as he used the terms. If he had sent Tompson a copy of the letter written to Charles Wesley on July 31, 1747, it would have brought more clarity to the discussion.

While Wesley claims "the ancient Fathers are far from being silent on our question," he then weakens his position by this admission: "None that I know have treated it professedly." To which he adds: "But I have not leisure to wade through that sea."[29]

In a similar vein Wesley says he knows many of the Reformers were conscious of being accepted by God; yet he does not cite any clear example, simply excusing himself with this further confession: "Neither have I leisure to re-examine this cloud of witnesses."[30]

For these omissions Wesley deserves constructive criticism. If he did not have the time to find the necessary supporting citations to affirm the assertions he made regarding the Church Fathers and the Reformers, he should never have mentioned them. But, on the other hand, to leave such a long period of Church history unsubstantiated with clear witnesses is not desirable either. But he did justice to neither.

Wesley points out that Tompson had completely misunderstood him by thinking that "I allow no degrees in grace, and that I make no distinction between the full assurance of faith and a low or common measure of it."[31]

Tompson took issue with Wesley regarding his statement that God's "mercy necessarily obliges him..."[32] Tompson claims that obligation is no part of mercy, for "mercy is a mere voluntary thing."[33] No doubt, as Telford suggests, Wesley was impressed with the careful articulation of his correspondent;[34] nevertheless, Wesley responded with skillful logic:

Certainly, as His own nature obliges Him (in a very clear and sound sense) to act according to truth and justice in all things; so in some sense His love obliged Him to give His only Son, that whosoever believeth in Him might not perish. So much for the phrase. My meaning is, The same compassion which moves God to pardon a mourning, broken-hearted sinner moves Him to comfort that mourner by witnessing to his spirit that his sins are pardoned.[35]

Would it not be difficult for Tompson or anyone else to refute these facts in light of God's personal attributes?

An area of agreement for both men is that "full assurance excludes all doubt," but Wesley alone will also allow for other degrees of faith where doubts are sometimes mingled with faith. As noted earlier, Wesley made this confession: "I know that I am accepted; and yet that knowledge is sometimes shaken, though not destroyed, by doubt or fear. If that knowledge were destroyed, or wholly *withdrawn*, I could not then say I had Christian faith."[36] Tompson claimed there was no difference at all in faith being shaken, withdrawn, or destroyed.[37] The shallowness of his thinking is revealed in Wesley's simple but logical response: "The wind rises: the house *shakes*, but it is not *overthrown*; it *totters*, *but* it is not *destroyed*."[38]

Wesley's Fourth Letter

Tompson's fourth letter was dated February 12, 1756. He indicated that his true identity would probably be revealed soon. In less than a week Wesley responded with answers to the questions his correspondent had raised. The letter is short and is as follows:

Sir, — You ask,

1. "Can a man who has not a clear assurance that his sins are forgiven be in a state of justification?"
   I believe there are some instances of it.

2. "Can a person be in a state of justification who, being asked, 'Do you know your sins are forgiven?' answers, 'I am not certainly sure; but I do not entertain the least doubt of it'?"
   I believe he may.

3. "Can he who answers, 'I trust they are'?"
   It is very possible he may be in that state.

4. "Can any one know that his sins are forgiven while he doubts thereof?"
   Not at that instant when he doubts of it. But he may generally know it, though he doubts at some particular time.

I answer as plainly and simply as I can, that, if I am in a mistake, I may the more easily be convinced of it.[39]

Wesley's Fifth Letter

Tompson responded to Wesley's fourth letter on February 25, 1756, in which he stated: "I had the pleasure of yours, which gave me a great satisfaction, as I think your concessions are abundantly sufficient to put a stop to any farther dispute between us concerning this Article."[40]

Prior to this letter Wesley's correspondent had only identified himself as "P.V." He then made known his true identity and his reasons for concealing it.[41]

Wesley responded on March 16, 1756, and told Tompson his reasons for concealment were appropriate. Wesley summarized his understanding of assurance thus: "My belief in general is this—that every Christian believer has a divine conviction of his reconciliation with God. The sum of those concessions is, 'I am inclined to think there may be some exceptions.'"[42]

The words in his summary statements are carefully chosen. Wesley never relinquished his belief that a true believer does have a conscious awareness of being accepted by God. Yet he would not insist there are no exceptions.

Assurance and Faith

Wesley often writes about one having experiential knowledge of salvation with terminology other than the witness of the Spirit. For example, in a letter to Dorthy Furly on May 18, 1757, Wesley tells her that her spiritual strength "will either increase or decrease in the same proportion with your *sense of His love.*"[43]

Writing to Samuel Walker on September 19, 1757, Wesley said: "Assurance is a word I do not use because it is not scriptural." He then went on to use language with which he felt more comfortable in describing justifying faith: "I hold a divine evidence or conviction that Christ loved *me* and gave Himself for *me* is essential to if not the very essence of justifying faith."[44] Wesley's emphasis upon Christ loving *me* and giving Himself for *me* reminds one of his Aldersgate testimony.

In an extremely long letter comprised of some thirty-seven pages to Dr. Lavington, Bishop of Exeter, in December of 1751, Wesley stated that he did not use the expression, "Assurance of pardon and salvation." Rather, he preferred to use biblical terminology, especially that of faith. He explained the various degrees of faith as follows:

> (1) That faith is one thing, the full assurance of faith another. (2) That even the full assurance of faith does not imply the full assurance of perseverance: this bears another name, being styled by St. Paul "the full assurance of hope." (3) Some Christians have only the first of these; they have faith but mixed with doubts and fears. Some have also the full assurance of faith, a full conviction of present pardon; and yet not the full assurance of hope, not a full conviction of

their future perseverance. (4) The faith which we preach as necessary to all Christians is the first of these, and no other. Therefore, (5) It is no evasion at all to say, "This (the faith which we preach as necessary to all Christians) is not properly an assurance of what is future."[45]

1758-1766

In Telford's fourth volume, spanning more than eight years, there are more references to the Holy Spirit than appear in the remaining four volumes collectively. The Spirit of God is mentioned approximately two hundred times and out of these are about thirty references to the witness of the Spirit.

Dislike of the Term *Assurance*

Wesley continues to express his disfavor of the word "assurance," even as he had done more than three years earlier. However, in his letter to the Editor of "Lloyd's Evening Post" on December 20, 1760, he responded to this statement made by the Editor: "No Protestant divine ever taught your doctrine of Assurance." In his reply Wesley is quite forceful: "I hope you know no better; but it is strange you should not. Did you never see Bishop Halls Works? Was not he a Protestant divine? Was not Mr. Perkins, Bolton, Dr. Sibbs, Dr. Preston, Archbishop Leighton?"[46]

Although Wesley frowns on the use of the term "assurance," he can not totally avoid the use of it if for no other reason than to refute charges made against him. Thus he goes on to give this definition: "By assurance (if we must use the expression) I mean 'a confidence which a man hath in God that by the merits of Christ his sins are forgiven and he reconciled to the favour of God!'"[47]

Emphasis on Faith

Wesley prefers to talk about faith when he discusses the matter of knowing one is justified or born again. He never seems to tire of defining faith as "a divine evidence or conviction that Christ loved *me* and gave Himself for *me*."[48] This is a low degree of faith which can blossom into a high degree as affirmed by Wesley: "When this evidence is heightened to exclude all doubt, it is the *plerophory or full assurance of faith*."[49]

It is not always easy to follow Wesley in his admonitions to others about faith. In reading his letters to those who are struggling to be certain that they are clear before God, one is greatly impressed with the fact that Wesley patiently and continuously encourages his readers to look up, believe God and trust His promises. It is obvious that Wesley strives to arrive at a balanced position regarding the part a person must play in cooperation with God's work, as noted in a letter to Richard Hart dated July 11, 1763: "God gives me the power to believe. But does He believe for me? He works faith in me. But still is it not I that believe? And, if so, is not believing an inward act performed by me?"[50]

Wesley knew that Satan would labor vigorously in tempting one who had been justified to cast away his confidence before obtaining entire sanctification. Therefore when he wrote to Dorthy Furly on December 15, 1763, Wesley reminded her: "God gave you His Spirit that you might know the things which He had freely given you. Hold fast the beginning of your confidence stedfast unto the end." To which he added this needful word of caution: "You are continually apt to throw away what you have for what you want."[51] What a fitting message for one of little faith.

Wesley as a Spiritual Guide

Only eternity will reveal the full measure of Wesley's influence upon hundreds of correspondents to whom he wrote. Space will permit reference to only a few letters for this time period.

Letters to Miss March

In this, the seventh of many letters to Miss J. C. March, dated January 30, 1762, Wesley dealt with the matter of not always having a clear witness of the Spirit and a suggestion as to why it may not always be given: "When you was justified, you had a direct witness that your sins was forgiven; afterward this witness was frequently intermitted, and yet you did not doubt of it. In like manner, you have had a direct witness that you are saved from sin; and this witness is frequently intermitted, and yet even then you do not doubt of it. But I much doubt if God withdraws either the one witness or the other without some occasion on our part."[52]

Unfortunately, he does not specify what the occasion(s) might be in this particular letter. In subsequent letters one may be able to observe possible occasions which could precipitate these intermissions.

When he wrote to her on May 13, 1762, Wesley asked, "Is your mind always stayed on God…Do no vain thoughts (useless, trifling, unedifying) lodge within you?" Before closing the letter he kindly warned, "Beware of sins of omission."[53]

In an April 7, 1763 letter he reminded her that she lived in "a poor, shattered house of clay, which presses down the immortal spirit."[54]

More than a year later Wesley urged her to "give no place to evil reasoning," but rather to "be as a little child." He does not specifically state what "evil reasoning" entails, but the context would at least suggest the end result of such involves the casting away of one's confidence in what God had done for her.[55]

In his October 13, 1764 letter, Wesley told Miss March that ofttimes God's people have a wilderness experience of darkness or distress following both justification and sanctification. The cause of this state, he thinks, is often that of "evil reasoning." How then can one be delivered from such a condition? Simply "by resuming your confidence ...by more grace...Dare to believe! Look up and see thy Savior near!"[56]

About a year later Wesley wrote to Miss March in these words: "If you have not yet uninterrupted communion with Him, why not this moment, and from this moment? If you have not, I incline to think it is occasioned by reasoning or by some inward or outward omission."[57]

Letter to Mrs. Bennis

This is Wesley's first of twenty-seven letters to Mrs. Elizabeth Bennis. It is the only letter appearing in volume 4 of Telford's edition. Several will be noted later from volume 5.

In his August 23, 1763 letter, Wesley mentioned "the abiding witness of the Spirit," concerning which he then said, "And this you may boldly claim on the warrant of that word, 'We have received the Spirit that is of God; that we may know the things which are freely given to us of God.'"[58]

Letters to Lady Maxwell

Seven of Wesley's letters to Lady Maxwell appear in volume 4 (Telford). Since Mrs. Maxwell was not a Christian, Wesley kindly admonished her not to rest "before His Spirit witnesses with your spirit that you are a child of God."[59]

In another letter to her, dated July 10, 1764, knowing she suffered physically as well as emotionally (with the loss of her husband and somewhat later her only child), Wesley, with consummate skill and tenderness, passionately penned these words:

> Do not stop, my dear Lady, one moment "because you have not felt sorrow enough." Your Friend above has felt enough of it for you... Look, look unto Him, and be thou saved! He is not a God afar off; He is now hovering over you with eyes of tenderness and love! Only believe! Then He turns your heaviness into joy. Do not think you are not humble enough, not contrite enough, not earnest enough. You are nothing; but Christ is all, and He is yours. The Lord God write it upon your heart, and take you for an habitation of God through the Spirit.[60]

When he wrote to Mrs. Maxwell on August 17, 1764, he endeavored to encourage her with these words: "You shall witness the kingdom of God within you, even righteousness, peace, and joy in the Holy Ghost."[61]

In his May 25, 1765 letter he told her he was afraid she was seeking salvation, not by faith, but by the works of the law or by her own righteousness. "O let it all go! None but Christ! None but Christ! ...Do not wait for this or that preparation! for something to bring to God! Bring Christ! Rather let Him bring you, bring you home to God!"[62] One can feel the pathos of Wesley's own heart as he endeavors to cheer her on to put all her hopes and confidence in Christ alone.

Especially insightful are Wesley's words to Mrs. Maxwell in his July 5, 1765 letter. While he expresses a desire to see her "experience ...an instantaneous work," he wants her to know that God works differently in each individual, and therefore she may not have a striking instantaneous experience as some have had.

> It may be He that does all things well has wise reasons, though not apparent to us, for working more gradually in you than He has done of late years in most others. It may please Him to give you the consciousness of His favour, the conviction that you are accepted through the Beloved, by almost insensible degrees, like the dawning of the day. And it is all one how it began, so you do but walk in the light. *Be this given in an instant or by degrees, hold it fast.* Christ is yours; He hath loved you; He hath given Himself for you.[63]

Is this counsel not further evidence that Wesley is continually learning that God is not limited to certain stereotypes in bringing saving grace to a sincere seeker?

In his last letter to Mrs. Maxwell in volume 4 (Telford's edition) Wesley urges her to press beyond her wavering faith that has doubtless already "received a gleam of light from above." Therefore, Wesley goes beyond any of his admonitions thus far and says, "'Fear not; only believe! Woman, thy sins are forgiven thee! Go in peace; thy faith hath made thee whole.'"[64]

Perhaps Wesley felt clear at this point to say, only what Christ can say, in order to help Mrs. Maxwell break through to a sure confidence in a pardoning God.

1766-1772

Many years have now passed since Aldersgate. As stated to Samuel Furly in a letter dated July 9, 1766, Wesley gave himself to "much searching of the Scriptures and mature deliberation" before writing his first sermon on "the witness of God's Spirit" and also his sermon on "the witness of our own spirit." About twenty years later, and prior to writing his second sermon on the witness, he asserts: "I have not yet seen any reason to change my judgement on either of these subjects; rather I am confirmed therein more and more both by the living and dying children of God." As further confirmation Wesley had found many in Britain, Ireland, Germany, Holland and America who "enjoyed that immediate witness before they had any sort of connexion with the Methodists or any knowledge either of their persons or writings."[65]

Telford's fifth volume of letters has at least seventy references to the Holy Spirit and twenty or more notations regarding the witness.

In a brief letter to Peggy Dale on June 18, 1767, Wesley declared that "the witness of sanctification as well as of justification is the privilege of God's children."[66]

Specificity is given to this matter of assurance being the privilege of God's people in a letter to Dr. Thomas Rutherforth, dated March 8, 1768. In response to certain objections, Wesley gives, in a descending order, what may be his clearest statements on various stages of assurance.

> I come now to your particular objections. I begin with the subject of your third charge—assurances; because what I have to say upon this head will be comprised in few words. Some are fond of the expression: I am not; I hardly ever use it. But I will simply declare (having neither leisure nor inclination to draw the saw of controversy concerning it) what are my present sentiments with regard to the thing which is usually meant thereby.
>
> I believe a few, but very few, Christians have an assurance from God of everlasting salvation; and that is the thing which the Apostle terms the plerophory on full assurance of hope.
>
> I believe more have such an assurance of being now in the favour of God as excludes all doubt and fear. And this, if I do not mistake, the Apostle means by the plerophory or full assurance of faith.
>
> I believe a consciousness of being in the favour of God (which I do not term plerophory, or full assurance, since it is frequently weakened, nay perhaps interrupted, by returns of doubt or fear) is the common privilege of Christians fearing God and working righteousness.
>
> Yet I do not affirm there are no exceptions to this general rule. Possibly some may be in the favour of God, and yet go mourning all the day long. But I believe this is usually owing either to disorder of body or ignorance of the gospel promises.[67]

Another interesting comment regarding the witness appears in a January 2, 1770 letter to Mary Bosanquet. Wesley points out that when folk are justified they become "babes in Christ, little children," apparently coupling these two classifications into one stage in the Christian journey. However, at the next stage, that of "young men," Wesley asserts that "they have the abiding witness of pardon."[68]

Significant Letters

In the remaining discussion of this time period (1766-1772) the letters of John Wesley will be limited to two of his correspondents.

Letter to Charles Wesley

One of the strangest letters Wesley ever penned was to his brother Charles, to whom he knew he could pour out his heart without reservation.

From various comments made in his *Journal* and *Letters* it would appear that John Wesley knew what it was to struggle with his own feelings from time to time. No doubt the many frustrations he endured with his estranged wife had some impact upon him. Nevertheless, it will be noted that he writes as one would expect, in the third paragraph below:

> In one of my last I was saying I do not feel the wrath of God abiding on me; nor can I believe he does. And yet (this is the mystery) [I do not love God. I never did]. Therefore [I never] believed in the Christian sense of the word. Therefore [I am only an] honest heathen, a proselyte of the Temple, one of the φοβούμενοι τὸν Θεόν (those that fear the Lord). And yet to be so employed of God! and so hedged in that I can neither get forward nor backward! Surely there never was such an instance before, from the beginning of the world! If I [ever have had] *that faith*, it would not be so strange. But [I never had any] other ἔλεγχος (proof or conviction) of the eternal or invisible world than [I have] now; and that is [none at all], unless such as fairly shines from reason's glimmering ray. [I have no] direct witness, I do not say that [I am a child of God], but of anything invisible or eternal.
>
> And yet I dare not preach otherwise than I do, either concerning faith, or love, or justification, or perfection. And yet I find rather an increase than a decrease of zeal for the whole work of God and every part of it. I am φερόμενος (borne along), I know not how, that I can't stand still. I want all the world to come to ὃν οὐκ οἶδα (what I do not know). Neither am I impelled to this by fear of any kind. I have no more fear than love. Or if I have [any fear, it is not that of falling] into hell but of falling into nothing.
>
> I hope you are with Billy Evans. If there is an Israelite indeed, I think he is one. O insist everywhere on *full* redemption, receivable by *faith alone!* Consequently to be looked for *now*. You are *made*, as it were, for this very thing. Just here you are in your element. In connexion I beat you; but in strong, pointed *sentences* you beat me. Go on, in your *own way*, what God has peculiarly called you to. Press the *instantaneous* blessing: then I shall have more time for my peculiar calling, enforcing the *gradual* work.[69]

Letters to Mrs. Bennis

The first letter Wesley sent to Mrs. Bennis appeared in Telford's fourth volume. There are seventeen letters in the fifth volume. Several of these are relevant to the doctrine of the witness.

Apparently Mrs. Bennis indicated to Wesley that she had experienced a direct witness of the Spirit. For in a letter dated March 29, 1766, he wrote: If I understand you right, you find a direct testimony that you are a child of God."[70]

When Mrs. Bennis responded to Wesley's letter, she expressed the fact that along with a "consciousness that I was changed ...I also found doubts, fears, and questionings" (which would fit Wesley's description of the baby/childhood stage). But when she cried for the witness of God's Spirit, her prayer was answered "in such a manner as was very clear to me."[71]

In his August 14, 1766 letter Wesley gave her this helpful message: "What you say concerning the witness of the Spirit is agreeable to all sound experience. We may in some measure be satisfied without it in the time of broad sunshine: but it is absolutely necessary in the time of clouds and heaviness and temptation; otherwise it would be hardly possible to hold fast your confidence."[72]

No doubt Mrs. Bennis had an analytical mind that liked to figure out phenomena in life, both physical and spiritual. Such a mindset has notable qualities, but it can be harmful, at times, to the exercise of faith. In at least three letters, separated by as much as five years, Wesley pleads with her not to rationalize;[73] in two other letters he pinpoints her problem as "evil reasoning," which he calls "one of your constant enemies, ...the most dangerous of all" and "a bad disease" which often brings sickness and "hinders both your holiness and happiness."[74]

If reasoning is not the proper course to take, what advice does Wesley give to her? "Believe, and feel Him near."[75] "Pray for and expect the continual and direct witness of the Spirit."[76] "Draw near to the fountain by simple faith, and take all you want."[77] "It is your part simply to spread all your wants before Him who loves you."[78] "All that God has already given you hold fast."[79] How privileged indeed was Mrs. Elizabeth Bennis to have John Wesley as her soul-friend!

1772-1780

The sixth volume of Telford's edition of Wesley's letters covers a time period of less than seven and one-half years. It is of interest to note that the number of references to the Holy Spirit, including those of the Spirit's witness, are practically half the number in the preceding volume, which covered a slightly shorter period (1766-1772). For this time frame the Holy Spirit is mentioned approximately thirty-five times, while the witness of the Spirit is found about ten times.

Emphasis on the Witness

As one would expect, Wesley in his more mature years continues to stress the importance of the witness, even if it is less frequently. In a March 22, 1775 letter to John Fletcher, Wesley writes in a confident tone: "It is certain every babe in Christ has received the Holy Ghost, and the Spirit witnesses with his spirit that he is a child of God."[80]

In writing to Mrs. William Smith on October 15, 1777, Wesley agreed with her own admission when he said: "You are in the right not to rest satisfied without the *present* witness that you are a child of God." To which he then added these words: "The bare remembrance of *past things* will neither make you holy nor happy."[81]

Helpful Letters

Once again it will be necessary to limit the ensuing discussions to letters sent to three of Wesley's correspondents.

Letters to Mrs. Bennis

The sixth volume of Telford's edition includes nine letters from Wesley to Mrs. Bennis. That she is still struggling with her reason is evident from his letter to her on December 16, 1772, where he states: "I think you make most of your trials by unbelief and giving too much way to reasoning. Do not stoop to reason with the adversary, but flee to the Strong for more strength, which, by asking, you will receive."[82]

More than a year later Wesley gave Mrs. Bennis insight that might help her understand her condition: "A will steadily and uniformly devoted to God is essential to a state of sanctification, but not an uniformity of joy or peace or happy communion with God. These may rise and fall in various degrees; nay, and may be affected either by the body or by diabolical agency, in a manner which all our wisdom can neither understand nor prevent." In her present state she should "go straight to God as a little child, and tell Him all your troubles and hindrances and doubts, and desire Him to turn them all to good."[83]

Perhaps Wesley's most helpful letter to Mrs. Bennis was penned on December 21, 1776, when he again diagnosed her problem and then followed up with the remedy: "You are a great deal less happy than you would be if you did not reason too much. This frequently gives that subtle adversary an advantage against you. You have need to be continually as a little child, simply looking up for whatever you want."[84]

Letter to Hannah Ball

In a letter to Miss Hannah Ball dated December 2, 1778, Wesley explained that the work of the Holy Spirit goes far beyond human comprehension. The fact is, man does not need to know about God's reasons for His manner of operation: "Undoubtedly, He has wise reasons for pouring out His Spirit at one time rather than another; but they lie abundantly too deep for human understanding to fathom."[85]

Letters to Alexander Knox

Sixteen letters passed from Wesley to Alexander Knox from January of 1776 to January of 1780. Mr. Knox was a young man who suffered with both physical and spiritual needs. Wesley was very warm and tender in his letters to Knox, encouraging him to expect both inward and outward healing.

In an August 29, 1777 letter Wesley described the state of Mr. Knox as being that which is "between a child of God and a child of the devil—namely, a servant of God." he went on to say, "You are not yet a son, but you are a servant; and you are waiting for the Spirit of adoption, which will cry in your heart, 'Abba, Father.'" Wesley continued, "Without being pained for what you have not, you have cause to bless God for what you have, and to wait patiently till He gives the rest by revealing His Son in your heart."[86]

Wesley may have shocked Knox in the July 11, 1778 letter by telling him that he was not "void of every degree of saving faith." For Wesley went on to tell him that he was saved "from many outward sins ...and also "in a degree from inward sin..." In closing he urged Knox to look to the Lord: "O praise God for all you have, and trust Him for all you want!"[87]

It may be that Wesley's best advice to Knox is found in the letter dated September 27, 1778, which doubtless was surprising, if not overwhelming: "Some time since, I was reading an account of a person in France, whom his confessor absolutely forbade (for such a time) to think of his sins, and ordered him 'to think only of the mercies of God in Christ.' It had an admirable effect on that desponding man. I know not but it might have the same upon you." Then Wesley gave this admonition: "Do not look down, but look up... God has not forsaken you."[88]

1780-1787

Like the preceding volume of Telford's letters, this one covers the same approximate time period and contains about the same number of references to the Holy Spirit (about thirty-five) and to the witness of the Spirit (about ten).

Vigorous Health

It is amazing how Wesley continued to keep active in every aspect of his ministry, including that of letter-writing. At age seventy-nine he could write: "It pleases God to give me much better health in general than I had at five-and-twenty. For many years also I was frequently weary; but I know not now what weariness means. I have just strength enough for what I am called to do; and at the end of my work I feel just the same as at the beginning."[89]

Emphasis on the Witness Continued

That Wesley continued to stress the importance of one possessing the witness is obvious in various letters during this late period of his life.

In a May 3, 1783 letter to Thomas Tattershall, Wesley expresses himself thus: "I hope you still find a witness in yourself, not only of your acceptance, but of your salvation from inbred sin and of your loving God with all your heart." He follows on with this admonition to exercise present-tense faith: "And you should constantly and explicitly exhort all believers to aspire after this, and encourage them to expect it *now*."[90]

When he wrote to his nephew, Samuel, Wesley encouraged the young man to "let the Spirit of God bear witness with your spirit that you are a child of God, and let the love of God be shed abroad in your heart by the Holy Ghost which is given unto you…"[91] The implication is clear: God cannot bear witness or shed abroad His love without the seeker's consent.

A key word for Wesley in defining the witness in both of his sermons entitled "The Witness of the Spirit" is the term "impression:" The testimony of the Spirit is an inward *impression* on the soul."[92] But when he wrote to Joseph Benson on May 1, 1781, Wesley was willing to make a concession regarding terminology if a better term could be found. " …I do not insist on the term 'impression.' I say again, I will thank anyone that will find a better; be it 'discovery,' 'manifestation,' 'deep sense,' or whatever it may." But Wesley will hold fast to other related matters: "That some consciousness of our being in favour with God is joined with Christian faith I cannot doubt; but it is not the essence of it. A consciousness of pardon cannot be the condition of pardon."[93] These latter statements echo what Wesley had said nearly thirty-four years earlier in a letter to his brother Charles."[94]

It would appear that Wesley takes a stronger position than he did in his earlier ministry, of coupling the two witnesses, that of God's Spirit and that of man's spirit. For, in a May 11, 1780 letter to Mrs. Crosby, he makes this emphatic statement: "Neither must the *witness* supersede the fruits, nor the fruits the witness of the Spirit."[95]

About seven years later Wesley told Mary Cooke that "there can be no stronger proof that we are of God than "when the witness and the fruit of the Spirit meet together." However, Wesley warns that there is an ever-present danger of losing the witness by rationalizing: "…you may relapse into painful doubts if you do not steadily watch against evil reasonings; and were you to substitute the deductions of reason for the witness of the Spirit you never would be established."[96]

What profound insight and needful warnings that would save many sincere Christians from "painful doubts" and a lack of the Spirit's witness. Could it be that Wesley's personal confessions to his brother Charles (noted earlier in this chapter) about not loving God and not having the direct witness were the results of his own rationalizing?[97] Certainly his brilliant mind possessed all the needed characteristics to give himself to undue reasoning, if he chose to do so.

Edifying Letters

Wesley's God-given abilities to discern spiritual deficiencies and offer proper prescriptions gave him the necessary qualifications to be an effective soul-guide. Letters to three individuals affording them scriptural and sensible advice will now be presented.

Letter to Alexander Knox
     It may well be that Wesley's letter to Alexander Knox dated December 23, 1780, is the most helpful and instructive one ever sent to a man who seemed to be unable to obtain a consciousness of acceptance with God. Observe Wesley's simple yet subtle approach:

> You are very ingenious in finding out arguments against yourself; and if you set your wit to it, they will never be wanting. Besides, there is an old sophister, who has been puzzling causes for these six thousand years that will always be ready to supply you with reasons for every kind of unbelief. But 'God will not give faith to the double minded, to him who asks what he does not desire to receive.' No, not while he is double-minded; but He will first take away your double-mindedness (perhaps while you are reading this!), and then give you the faith to which all things are possible. 'Yes, to-morrow, or at some other time.' No time like the time present! 'To-day, if you will hear His voice,' He says, 'I am thy salvation.' Why not to-day? Is not one day with Him as a thousand years? And whatever He could do in a thousand years can He not do in one day? That this cannot be done without a miracle is absolutely certain. But why should not you expect that miracle? This is no presumption: it is an expectation that the God of truth will not be worse than His word. He will not, Alleck! He will not! Do not imagine He will. He knows your simpleness. All your faults are before Him; and it may be the word is just now gone forth, 'I will heal him, for My own name's sake.' Do not reason, look up! Let your heart (dull and cold as it is) cry out, 'Be it unto me according to Thy word!'[98]

Letter to John Atlay
     In a May 26, 1781 letter to John Atlay, Wesley gives detailed comment regarding faith and assurance which would doubtless help any struggling seeker after God:

> I think the 'Instructions of comforting Afflicted Consciences' in the eighth volume of the [*Christian*] *Library* are excellent. I believe Robert Bolton [see letter of Oct. 14, 1757] there answers all your questions: (1) None have a right to say their sins are forgiven if they have not faith in Christ; and (2) None that has faith in Christ *need* doubt of this. But they *will* doubt if they have but *little faith*. In these faith is but a glimmering light; yet we must not discourage them. Perhaps it is to them especially St. John says, '*These things have I written unto you, that ye may know* (most assuredly) *that ye* have eternal life,' without all doubt and fear. (3) Faith may subsist for a time with very little joy, especially if there was little sorrow before. (4) It is very possible to mistake joy for faith, and then certainly we shall trust in joy instead of Christ. (5) The promises are the most strengthening and comforting truths in all the oracles of God; particularly to (believers in Christ) the promises of full sanctification.[99]

Letter to Mary Cooke

When Wesley wrote to Mary Cooke on October 30, 1785, he told her that he had once been like her in that he said he had no faith, but a spiritual guide rightly informed him, "You have faith, but it is weak." Wesley then affirmed the same to Mrs. Cooke, along with an admonition: "You have faith, but it is only as a grain of mustard-seed. Hold fast what you have, and ask for what you want."[100]

In kind and passionate words Wesley affirms that the Spirit operates differently in different people, and He may therefore work in her in a way unlike that in others.

> There is an irreconcilable variability in the operations of the Holy Spirit on the souls of men, more especially as to the manner of justification. Many find Him rushing upon them like a torrent, while they experience
>
> The o'erwhelming power of saving grace.
>
> This has been the experience of many; perhaps of more in this late visitation than in any other age since the times of the Apostles. But in others He works in a very different way:
>
> He deigns His influence to infuse,
> Sweet, refreshing, as the silent dews.
>
> It has pleased Him to work the latter way in you from the beginning; and it is not improbable He will continue (as He has begun) to work in a gentle and almost insensible manner. Let Him take His own way: He is wiser than you; He will do all things well. Do not reason against Him; but let the prayer of your heart be,
>
> Mould as Thou wilt Thy passive clay![101]

1787-1791

Retirement never seemed to enter Wesley's mind. How blessed he was to have a strong and healthy body, mind, and spirit. When he was nearly eighty-five years of age he penned these words to his brother Charles: "I have not one hour to spare from four in the morning till nine at night." He did, however, make some room for Charles to meet with him: "But you may see me on Thursday at Mr. Griffith's, who will come in his coach to fetch you."[102]

The eighth and last volume of Telford's edition contains letters which span approximately the last four years of his life.

Although the total references to the Holy Spirit only number fifteen or so, including a few references to the witness, there is no question about Wesley's emphasis upon and adherence to the doctrine of the direct witness/assurance to the very end of his life.

Questions Wesley Asked

Often Wesley would ask questions about his correspondent's consciousness of acceptance with God. For example, in a letter to Jane Bisson dated December 17, 1787, Wesley asked: "Do you always find a clear sense of the presence of the ever-blessed Trinity?"[103]

When he wrote to Elizabeth Baker a few months later, one of the questions he asked her was this: "Have you a constant witness of the pardoning love of God?"[104]

Then, in another letter to Miss Baker some three weeks later, on September 16, 1788, Wesley asked: "In what sense do you see God? Are you always sensible of His loving presence?"[105]

Wesley's last letter to Miss Baker was written about fourteen months prior to his death. His concern that she possess the witness of the Spirit, in this case to a second definite work of grace, is evident in the question he posed for her: "Have you ever received a clear, direct witness that you are saved from inbred sin? At what time? In what manner? And do you find it as clear as it was at first?"[106]

Desire that Others Have the Witness

Charles Wesley died on March 29, 1788. About three weeks later Wesley wrote to his niece, Sarah Wesley, Charles' daughter. In the closing lines of the letter he expressed his deepest desire for her: "...you have not yet received the Spirit of adoption, crying in your heart, Abba, Father! See that you do not stop short of all the promises for you! If you feel your want, it will soon be supplied; and God will seal that word upon your heart, 'I am merciful to thy unrighteousness, and they [sic] sins and iniquities I remember no more.'"[107]

Last Letter

Wesley preached his last sermon on February 23, 1901, one week before his death. On February 24, he wrote his last letter. Consequently, as Telford puts it, "His work was done. The following day found him back at City Road, and on March 2, 1791, a week after he had preached at Leatherhead, he died as he wished, 'without a lingering groan.'"[108]

Summary Statements

Eternity will doubtless reveal the full measure of Wesley's ministry through his letters. Nevertheless, several things may be noted regarding this significant area of his labors.

1. In no other part of his ministry do we see so clearly Wesley as a fellow human.

2. His own struggles and confessions are unveiled from time to time in

his letters, which must have afforded some encouragement to his correspondents who would have experienced similar struggles.

3. Both his passion and his patience for guiding his correspondents to spiritual victories are constantly revealed.

4. He endeavors to fan every little spark of faith he detects in his correspondents.

5. If one mistakes joy for faith, he will "trust in joy instead of Christ."[109]

6. Wesley prefers to talk about faith of assurance rather than assurance of salvation.

7. He always encourages his correspondents to press on from little faith to full assurance of faith, to pray for and expect the witness of the Spirit.

8. The greatest enemies to the witness are doubtless evil reasonings, deductions, or rationalizations; unbelief; and inward or outward omissions.

9. Wesley's continual admonitions to sincere seekers are to look up, trust God, wait patiently, and expect His victory now!

10. "Dare to believe! Look up and see thy Savior near!"[110]

11. "...be continually as a little child, simply looking up for whatever you want."[111]

12. "Do not look down, but look up... God has not forsaken you."[112]

Endnotes

1. The *Letters*, 4:221. In writing to Mrs. Elizabeth Bennis on Aug. 23, 1763, Wesley penned these words: "You did well to write. This is one of the means which God generally uses to convey either light or comfort. Even while you are writing, you will often find relief; frequently while we propose a doubt it is removed."

2. It should be noted that a lengthy letter of some thirty-seven pages to Dr. Lavington, written in December of 1751, is included in this tabulation.

3. Quoted by Telford in *Letters*, 3:174.

4. See Footnote 7 in *Works*, 26:566.

5. *Works*, 26:567.

6. Ibid.

7. Ibid., 26:568.

8. Ibid.

9. Ibid., 26:568-69.

10. Ibid., 26:569.

11. Ibid., 26:574.

12. Ibid.

13. Ibid., 26:575.

14. Ibid.

15. Ibid.

16. Ibid.

17. Ibid.

18. Ibid.

19. Ibid., 26:580.

20. Ibid., 26:574.

21. Ibid., 26:576.

22. Ibid. One will search nearly in vain throughout the indices of the massive set of thirty-eight volumes of the Ante-Nicene, Nicene and Post-Nicene Fathers to find references to *assurance* (found only once and even then it deals with the impossibility of being assured of one's salvation) or the witness of the Spirit (not found in any of the indices). Romans 8:16 and Galatians 4:6 are quoted at least once, but there are no comments on them. See Alexander Roberts and James Donaldson, eds., *Ante-Nicene Fathers*, 10 vols. (Peabody, MA: Hendrickson Publishers, Inc., 1994). See also Philip Schaff, ed., *Nicene and Post-Nicene Fathers*, First Series, 14 vols. (Peabody, MA: Hendrickson Publishers, Inc., 1994). See also Philip Schaff and Henry Wace, eds., *Nicene and Post-Nicene Fathers*, Second Series, 14 vols. (Peabody, MA: Hendrickson Publishers, Inc., 1994). There are no clear statements regarding the witness of the Spirit in David W. Bercot, ed., *A Dictionary of Early Christian Beliefs: A Reference Guide to More Than 700 Topics Discussed by the Early Church Fathers* (Peabody, MA: Hendrickson Publishers, Inc., 2000). Brief comments by Origen, Diodore, and Ambrosiaster on Rom. 8:16 appear in Gerald Bray, ed., and Thomas C. Oden, gen. ed., *Romans, Ancient Christian Commentary on Scripture*, VI (Downers Grove, IL: InterVarsity Press, 1998), 219. However, these comments are not particularly insightful; they are essentially restatements of Scripture. Another helpful resource for the doctrines of assurance/witness of the Spirit among the Church Fathers is Thomas C. Oden, *Life in the Spirit: Systematic Theology*, vol. 3 (Peabody, MA: Print Press, an imprint of Hendrickson Publishers, 1998).

23. *Works*, 26:577.

24. Ibid. That Luther had an experience similar to Wesley is clear from his own testimony: "I grasped that the justice of God is that righteousness by which through grace and sheer mercy God justifies us through faith. Thereupon I felt myself to be reborn and to have gone through open doors into paradise. The whole of Scripture took on a new meaning, and whereas before the 'justice of God' had filled me with hate, now it became to me inexpressibly sweet in greater love." Quoted by Roland H. Bainton, *Here I Stand: A Life of Martin Luther* (Nashville: Abingdon Press, n.d.; New York: Mentor, First Printing, 1955), 49-50.

25. *Letters*, 3:158-59.

26. See Telford's comments prior to Wesley's letter to Tompson dated Feb. 5, 1756, in *Letters*, 3:158.

27. *Letters*, 3:158.

28. Ibid., 3:161-62.

29. Ibid., 3:159.

30. Ibid.

31. Ibid. See Appendix D for answers John and Charles Wesley gave to numerous questions which had been raised concerning faith and assurance. Wesley incorporated these in his third letter to Tompson.

32. *Works*, 26:575.

33. Ibid., 26:578.

34. *Letters*, 3:158.

35. Ibid., 3:161.

36. *Works*, 26:575.

37. Ibid., 26:578.

38. *Letters*, 3:161

39. Ibid., 3:163-64.

40. Ibid., 3:174.

41. I bid.

42. Ibid.

43. Ibid., 3:215 (italics mine).

44. Ibid., 3:222.

45. Ibid., 3:295, 305.

46. Ibid. 4:126.

47. Ibid.

48. Iid., 4:34, 116, 117.

49. Ibid., 4:116.

50. Ibid., 4:220.

51. Ibid., 4:225.

52. Ibid., 4:170.

53. Ibid., 4:181.

54. Ibid., 4:208.

55. Ibid., 4:251.

56. Ibid., 4:270.

57. Ibid., 4:311.

58. Ibid., 4:250. The Scripture quotation is 1 Corinthians 2:12.

59. Ibid., 4:250.

60. Ibid., 4:252-53.

61. Ibid., 4:260-61.

62. Ibid., 4:301.

63. Ibid., 4:308-9 (italics mine).

64. Ibid., 4:317.

65. Ibid., 5:21.

66. Ibid., 5:56.

67. Ibid., 5:358.

68. Ibid., 5:175. For an interesting treatment of Wesley's states and stages in his own journey, see David L. Cubie, "Placing Aldersgate in John Wesley's Order of Salvation," Wesleyan Theological Journal 24 (1989):41-47.

69. *Letters*, 5:16. The insertion of Greek translations in parentheses are mine.

70. Ibid., 5:6.
71. Ibid., 5:24, Telford's note.
72. Ibid., 5:24.
73. Ibid., 5:56, 269, 284, 337.
74. Ibid., 5:152, 193.
75. Ibid., 5:56.
76. Ibid., 5:142.
77. Ibid., 5:194.
78. Ibid., 5:269.
79. Ibid., 5:291.
80. Ibid., 6:146.
81. Ibid., 6:283.
82. Ibid., 6:6.
83. Ibid., 6:68.
84. Ibid., 6:243.
85. Ibid., 6:331.
86. Ibid., 6:272-73.
87. Ibid., 6:315.
88. Ibid., 6:320.
89. Ibid., 7:132.
90. Ibid., 7:178
91. Ibid., 7:231.
92. *Works*, 1:274, 287 (italics mine).
93. Ibid., 7:61.
94. *Works*, 26:254-55.
95. *Letters*, 7:18.
96. Ibid., 7:377-78.
97. See *Letters*, 5:16.
98. Ibid., 7:44.
99. Ibid., 7:64.
100. Ibid., 7:298.
101. Ibid.
102. Ibid., 8:39.
103. Ibid., 8:27.
104. Ibid., 8:85.
105. Ibid., 8:89.
106. Ibid., 8:181.
107. Ibid., 8:56.
108. Ibid., 8:266.
109. *Letters*, 8:64.
110. Ibid., 4:270.
111. Ibid., 6:243.
112. Ibid., 6:320.

Chapter Eight

Conclusion

We have just concluded our journey in Scripture and through the life of John Wesley concerning one of the most comforting as well as important doctrines in the entire Bible: that we may possess a personal, present knowledge that "we are the children of God" by means of a dual witness, namely the Holy Spirit bearing witness with our spirits (Rom. 8:16).

I cannot think of a better spiritual director than Mr. Wesley to guide us in both becoming and being Christian in the fullest biblical sense, even though he has been dead for over two hundred years; for "he being dead, yet speaketh." How much Wesley has taught us from his biblical expositions, his personal experiences, and the lessons he learned from others.

Perhaps the most valuable insight we glean from Wesleyan theology is that it is a theology of hope. God is working behind the scenes and in ways not observable to the human eye, for he is "not willing that any should perish, but that all should come to repentance (2 Peter 3:9). That God's redemptive plan is not founded on a limited atonement is clear from Paul's declaration in Titus 2:11 NKJ), that "the grace of God that bringeth salvation has appeared to all men."

What a glorious message we have to proclaim! While it is the responsibility of every Christian to share this good news, I want to especially put forth a passionate plea to my fellow ministers that we be faithful to proclaim the full message of the Gospel: repentance and faith, justification, regeneration, adoption, the witness of the Spirit, entire sanctification, and the abiding witness.

Like Wesley, we need to press the instantaneous blessing, receivable now by faith alone in Christ. Let us encourage and help our converts "grow in grace and in the knowledge of our Lord and Savior Jesus Christ" (2 Peter 3:18), so that they may pass from spiritual babyhood into childhood and then still onward into mature adulthood (1 John 2:12-14).

We live in a world marked by uncertainty: no one is certain about health or wealth, relationships, or what will transpire tomorrow. What a sharp contrast, then, to have an inward certitude that my sins are all forgiven, as attested by the witness and the fruits of the Spirit.

Since many in the religious world of Wesley's day did not believe it possible to obtain a definite assurance of sins forgiven, at least not until the end of life, much criticism was often brought against his teaching on the witness.

Wesley's strongest arguments were drawn particularly from the Pauline and Johannine epistles. Wesley also built upon Christian antiquity, reason, and personal experience.

Surely the lives and lips of numerous saints throughout church history have given testimony to conscious acceptance by God. If the Holy Spirit awakens the sinner and convicts him of his sins, would it not be strange if the Spirit never notified him of pardon upon his "repentance toward God, and faith toward our Lord Jesus Christ" (Acts 20:21b, c)? If God's Spirit is at work in pre-conversion, would He not also work in conversion and post-conversion experiences ? Most assuredly, and for this we have the strong support of Scripture, antiquity, reason, and personal experience.

How often do we labor among some who are predisposed to doubt, fear, and worry. These are prone to be introspective, to look within, and to gauge their spiritual progress by their fluctuating feelings. Let us not tire of admonishing them to "have faith in God" (Mark 11:22) and to look up to the One who is mighty to save and strong to deliver, until they can say with the Apostle Paul, "I know whom I have believed, and am persuaded that he is able to keep that which I have committed unto him against that day" (1 Tim. 1:12).

Perhaps we need to learn the old Methodist hymn which describes so well this inward religion that entails the dual witness of God's Spirit with our spirits:

> *How can a sinner know*
> *His sins on earth forgiven?*
> *How can my gracious Saviour show*
> *My name inscribed in heaven?*
> *What we have felt and seen,*
> *With confidence we tell;*
> *And publish to the sons of men*
> *The signs infallible.*

> *We who in Christ believe*
> *That he for us hath died,*
> *We all his unknown peace receive,*
> *And feel his blood applied;*
> *Exults our rising soul,*
> *Disburden'd of her load,*
> *And swells unutterably full*
> *Of glory and of God.*

His love, surpassing far
  The love of all beneath,
We find within our hearts, and dare
  The pointless darts of death.
Stronger than death and hell,
  The mystic power we prove;
And, conquerors of the world, we dwell
  In heaven, who dwell in Love.

We by his Spirit prove
  And know the things of God,
The things which freely of his love
  He hath on us bestow'd:
His Spirit to us he gave,
  And dwells in us, we know:
The witness in ourselves we have,
  And all its fruits we show.

The meek and lowly heart
  That in our Saviour was,
To us his Spirit doth impart,
  And signs us with his cross:
Our nature's turn'd, our mind
  Transform'd in all its powers;
And both the Witnesses are join'd,
  The Spirit of God with ours.

Whate'er our pardoning Lord
  Commands, we gladly do;
And, guided by his sacred Word,
  We all his steps pursue:
His glory our design,
  We live our God to please:
And rise, with filial fear divine,
  To perfect holiness.[1]

Endnotes

1. Wesley, John. *A Collection of Hymns for the Use of the People Called Methodists* London: Wesleyan Conference Office, n.d.; repr. Salem, OH: Allegheny Publications, 984), 95-97.

Appendix A

Roman Method of Adoption

The following comments on Roman adoption are those of William Barclay in
The Letter to the Romans (Philadelphia: The Westminster Press, 1957), p. 110:

Roman adoption was always rendered more serious and more difficult by the
Roman *patria potestas*. The *patria potestas* was the father's power over his
family; that power was absolute; it was actually the power of absolute disposal
and control, and in the early days it was actually the power of life and death. In
regard to his father a Roman son never came of age. No matter how old he was,
he was still under the *patria potestas*, in the absolute possession, and under the
absolute control, of his father. Obviously this made adoption into another family
a very difficult and a very serious step. In adoption a person had to pass from one
patria potestas to another. He had to pass out of the possession and control of
one father into the equally absolute possession and control of another. There
were two steps. The first was known as *mancipatio*, and it was carried out by a
symbolic sale, in which copper and scales were symbolically used. Three times
the symbolism of sale was carried out. Twice the father symbolically sold his
son, and twice he bought him back; and the third time he did not buy him back,
and thus the *patria potestas* was held to be broken. After the sale there followed
a ceremony called *vindicatio*. The adopting father went to the *praetor*, one of the
Roman magistrates, and presented a legal case for the transference of the person
to be adopted into his *patria potestas*. When all this was completed then the
adoption was complete.

Appendix B

Conversion Experience of Charles Wesley

Charles Wesley reveals his own conversion experience in *The Journal of Charles Wesley*, ed. Thomas Jackson, vol. 1 (London: John Mason, publisher, 1849; repr., Grand Rapids: Baker Book House, 1980), 90-92:

Sun., May 21st, 1738. I waked in hope and expectation of His coming. At nine my brother and some friends came, and sang an hymn to the Holy Ghost. My comfort and hope were hereby increased. In about half-an-hour they went: I betook myself to prayer; the substance as follows: — "O Jesus, thou hast said, 'I will come unto you;' thou hast said, 'I will send the Comforter unto you;' thou hast said, 'My Father and I will come unto you, and make our abode with you.' Thou art God who canst not lie; I wholly rely upon thy most true promise: accomplish it in thy time and manner." Having said this, I was composing myself to sleep, in quietness and peace, when I heard one come in (Mrs. Musgrave, I thought, by the voice) and say, "In the name of Jesus of Nazareth, arise, and believe, and thou shalt be healed of all thy infirmities." I wondered how it should enter into her head to speak in that manner. The words struck me to the heart. I sighed, and said within myself, "O that Christ would but speak thus to me!" I lay musing and trembling: then thought, "But what if it should be Him? I will send at least to see." I rang, and, Mrs. Turner coming, I desired her to send up Mrs. Musgrave. She went down, and, returning, said, "Mrs. Musgrave had not been here." My heart sunk within me at the word, and I hoped it might be Christ indeed. However, I sent her down again to inquire, and felt in the meantime a strange palpitation of heart. I said, yet feared to say, "I believe, I believe!" She came up again and said, "It was I, a weak, sinful creature, spoke; but the words were Christ's: he commanded me to say them, and so constrained me that I could not forbear."

I sent for Mr. Bray, and asked him whether I believed. He answered, I ought not to doubt of it: it was Christ spoke to me. He knew it; and willed us to pray together: "But first," said he, "I will read what I have casually opened upon: 'Blessed is the man whose unrighteousness is forgiven, and whose sin is covered: blessed is the man to whom the Lord imputeth no sin, and in whose spirit is no guile.'" Still I felt a violent opposition and reluctance to believe; yet still the Spirit of God strove with my own and the evil spirit, till by degrees he chased away the darkness of my unbelief. I found myself convinced, I knew not how, nor when; and immediately fell to intercession.

Mr. Bray then told me, his sister had been ordered by Christ to come and say those words to me. This she afterwards confirmed, and related to me more at large the manner of her believing. At night, and nearly the moment I was taken ill, she dreamt she heard one knock at the door: she went down, and opened it; saw a person in white; caught hold of and asked him who he was; was answered, "I am Jesus Christ," and cried out, with great vehemence, "Come in, come in!" She waked in a fright. It was immediately suggested to her, "You must not mind this: it is all a dream, an illusion." She continued wavering and uneasy all Friday till evening prayers. No sooner were they begun than she found herself full of the power of faith, so that she could scarce contain herself, and almost doubted whether she was sober. At the same time she was enlarged in love and prayer for all mankind, and commanded to go and assure me from Christ of my recovery, soul and body. She returned home repeating with all joy and triumph, "I believe, I believe:" yet her heart failed her, and she durst not say the words to me that night.

On Sunday morning she took Mr. Bray aside, burst into tears, and informed him of the matter; objecting she was a poor weak sinful creature, and should she go to a Minister? She could not do it; nor rest till she did. He asked whether she had ever found herself so before. "No, never." "Why, then," said he, "go. Remember Jonah. You declare promises, not threatenings. Go in the name of the Lord. Fear not your own weakness. Speak you the words: Christ will do the work. Out of the mouth of babes and sucklings hath he ordained strength."

They prayed together, and she then went up, but durst not come in till she had prayed again by herself. About six minutes after she had left him, he found and felt, while she was speaking the words, that Christ was with us. I never heard words uttered with like solemnity. The sound of her voice was entirely changed into that of Mrs. Musgrave. (If I can be sure of anything sensible.) I rose and looked into the Scripture. The words that first presented were, "And now, Lord, what is my hope? truly my hope is even in thee." I then cast down my eye, and met, "He hath put a new song in my mouth, even a thanksgiving unto our God. Many shall see it, and fear, and shall put their trust in the Lord." Afterwards I opened upon Isaiah xl:1 "Comfort ye, comfort ye, my people, saith your God: speak ye comfortably to Jerusalem, and cry unto her, that her warfare is accomplished, that her iniquity is pardoned; for she hath received of the Lord's hand double for all her sin."

I now found myself at peace with God, and rejoiced in the hope of loving Christ. My temper for the rest of the day was, mistrust of my own great, but before unknown, weakness. I saw that by faith I stood; by the continual support of faith, which kept me from falling, though of myself I am ever sinking into sin. I went to bed still sensible of my own weakness, (I humbly hope to be more and more so,) yet confident of Christ's protection.

Appendix C

Copy of One of John Wesley's Letters

Appendix D

Questions Submitted to John and Charles Wesley Regarding Faith and Assurance

The following excerpts are taken from John Wesley's lengthy letter, dated February 5, 1756, to Richard Tompson (*Letters* 3:159-160).

Several years ago some clergymen and other gentlemen with whom we had a free conversation proposed the following questions to my brother and me, to which we gave the answer subjoined:—

'June 25, 1744.

'QUESTION. What is faith?

'ANSWER. Faith in general is a divine, supernatural ἔλεγχος [evidence or conviction]¹ of things not seen—that is, of past, future, or spiritual. It is a spiritual sight of God and the things of god. Justifying faith is a divine ἔλεγχος that Christ loved *me* and gave Himself for *me*.

'Q. Have all Christians this faith? And may not a man have it and not know it?

'A. That all Christians have such a faith as implies a consciousness of God's love appears from Rom. viii.15; Eph. iv.32; 2 Cor. xiii.5; Heb. viii. 10; 1 John iv.10, v.1, &c. And that no man can have it and not know that he has appears from the nature of the thing. For faith after repentance is ease after pain, rest after toil, light after darkness. It appears also from its immediate fruits, which are peace, joy, love, and power over sin.

'Q. Does any one believe any longer than he sees, loves, obeys God?

'A. We apprehend not; "seeing God" being the very essence of faith, love and obedience the inseparable properties of it.'

'August 2, 1745.

'QUESTION. Is an assurance of God's pardoning love absolutely necessary to our being in His favour? Or may there possibly be some exempt cases?

'ANSWER. We dare not positively say there are not.

'Q. Is it necessary to final salvation in those (as Papists) who never heard it preached?

'A. We know not how far invincible ignorance may excuse. 'Love beareth all things.'

'Q. But what if one who does hear it preached should die without it?

'A. We determine nothing. We leave his soul in the hands of Him that made it.

'Q. Does a man believe any longer than he sees a reconciled God?

'A. We conceive not. But we allow there may be very many degrees of seeing God, even as many as are between seeing the sun with the eyelids closed and with the eyes open.'

Endnotes

1. The inclusion of the English translation of the Greek word is mine.

Selected Bibliography

A. Primary Sources

1. Greek Texts

The Greek New Testament, eds. Barbara Aland, Kurt Aland, Johannes Karavidopoulos, Carlo M. Martini, and Bruce M. Metzger. Stuttgart: Deutsche Bibelgesellschaft, 1994.

The Greek New Testament According to the Majority Texts, eds. Zane C. Hodges and Arthur L. Farstad. Nashville: Thomas Nelson Publishers, 1985.

The Greek Text of Stephens 1550, 3rd ed. London: Samuel Bagster and Sons, Limited, 1896.

The New Testament in the Original Greek, eds. B. F. Westcott and F. J. A. Hort. New York: The Macmillan Company, 1928.

Novum Testamentum Graece, eds. D. Eberhard Nestle, D. Erwin Nestle, and D. Kurt Aland. Stuttgart: Privileg. Wurtt. Bibelanstalt, 1956.

2. Literature of the Church Fathers

Ante-Nicene Fathers, 10 vols., eds. Alexander Roberts and James Donaldson. Peabody, MA: Hendrickson Publishers, Inc., 1994.

Nicene and Post-Nicene Fathers, 14 vols., First Series, ed. Philip Schaff. Peabody, MA: Hendrickson Publishers, Inc., 1994.

Nicene and Post-Nicene Fathers, 14 vols., Second Series, eds. Phillip Schaff and Henry Wace. Peabody, MA: Hendrickson Publishers, 1994.

3. Puritan Literature

Baxter, Richard. *The Saints' Everlasting Rest*. Edited by Benjamin Fawcett. Grand Rapids: Baker Book House, 1978 reprint.

Bolton, Robert. *General Directions for a Comfortable Walking with God*. First published in 1626; reprint, Ligonier, PA: Soli Deo Gloria Publications, 1991

Marshall, Walter. *The Gospel-Mystery of Sanctification*. First published in 1692. Grand Rapids: Zondervan Publishing House, 1954.

Owen, John. *The Works of John Owen*, vol. 2, *On Communion with God the Father, Son, and Holy Ghost*, ed. William H. Goold. London: The Banner of Truth Trust, 1966 reprint.

Preston, John. *The Breast-Plate of Faith and Love*, 5th ed. London: Imprinted by R.Y. for Nicholas Bourne, 1634; reprint, Carlisle, PA: The Banner of Truth Trust, 1979.

Sibbes, Richard. *Works of Richard Sibbes*, ed. Alexander B. Grossart. Reprint, Carlisle, PA: The Banner of Truth Trust, 1977.

4. The Writings of Wesley and Others

Ambrose, Isaac. *Directions to a Man in the Act of the New Birth. A Christian Library*. Vol. VII. Edited by John Wesley. London: T. Cordeux for T. Blanchard, 1819.[1]

Bercot, David W., ed. *A Dictionary of Early Christian Beliefs: A Reference Guide to More than 700 Topic Discussed by the Church Fathers*. Peabody, MA: Hendrickson Publishers, Inc., 2000.

Bolton, Robert. *General Directions for a Comfortable Walking with God. A Christian Library*. Vol. IV. Edited by John Wesley. London: T. Cordeux for T. Blanchard, 1819.

Bray, Gerald, and Thomas C. Oden, eds. *Romans, Ancient Christian Commentary on Scripture*. Vol. 6. Downers Grove, IL: Intervarsity Press, 1998.

Edwards, Jonathan. *A Treatise on Religious Affections. A Christian Library*. Vol. XXX. Edited by John Wesley. London: T. Cordeux for T. Blanchard, 1819.

Wesley, Charles. *The Journal of Charles Wesley*. Vol. I. London: Published by John Mason, 1849; reprint, Grand Rapids: Baker Book House, 1980.

Wesley, John. *A Christian Library*, 30 vols., 3rd. ed. London. Printed by T. Cordeaux, for T. Blanchard, 1819.

___. *Extracts form the Works of Dr. Robert Leighton. A Christian Library*. Vol. XX. London: T. Cordeux for T. Blanchard, 1819.

___. *Extracts from the Works of Rev. Richard Allein. A Christian Library*. Vol. XVIII. London: T. Cordeux for T. Blanchard, 1819.

___. *The Preface* (entails Wesley's reasons for putting together the *Christian Library*). *A Christian Library*. Vol. I. London: T. Cordeux for T. Blanchard, 1819.

___. *The Preface* (entails Wesley's critique of the Puritan writers). *A Christian Library*. Vol. IV. London: T. Cordeux for T. Blanchard, 1819.

___. *Extracts from the Works of the Rev. John Preston; Extracts from the Works of the Rev. Richard Sibs; and Extracts from the Works of the Rev. Thomas Goodwin. A Christian Library*. Vol. VI. London: T. Cordeux for T. Blanchard, 1819.

___. *Extracts from the Works of Mr. Isaac Ambrose. A Christian Library*. Vol. IX. London: T. Cordeux for T. Blanchard, 1819.

___. *The Lives of Various Eminent Persons, Chiefly Extracted from Mr. Samuel Clark: The Life of John Row. A Christian Library*. Vol. XV. London: T. Cordeux for T. Blanchard, 1819.

___. *Christian Letters, by Joseph Alleine. A Christian Library*. Vol. XXIX. London: T. Cordeux for T. Blanchard, 1819.

___. *Extracts from the Works of Mr. Flavel. A Christian Library*. Vol. XXVII. London: T. Cordeux for T. Blanchard, 1819.

___. *Extracts from the Works of the Rev. Richard Baxter. A Christian Library*. Vol. XXII. London: T. Cordeux for T. Blanchard, 1819.

___. *Extracts from the Works of the Rev. John Preston. A Christian Library*. Vol. V. London: T. Cordeux for T. Blanchard, 1819.

___. *A Collection of Hymns for the Use of the People Called Methodists*. London:

___.Wesleyan Conference Office, n.d.; reprint, Salem, OH: Allegheny Publications, 1984.

___. *Wesley's Doctrinal Standards: The Sermons with Introductions, Analysis, and Notes,* ed. N. Burwash. No publisher listed, 1881; reprint, Salem, OH: Convention Book Store, 1967.

___. *Explanatory Notes Upon the New Testament.* San Francisco: Carlton & Lanahan, n.d.; reprint, Salem, OH: Schmul Publishers, 1976.

___. *The Letters of the Rev. John Wesley, A.M.,* vol. 1, 1721-1741, ed. John Telford. First published in 1931; reprint, London: Epworth Press, 1960.

___. *The Letters of the Rev. John Wesley, A.M.,* vol. 2, 1742-1749, ed. John Telford. First published in 1931; reprint, London: Epworth Press, 1960.

___. *The Letters of the Rev. John Wesley, A.M.,* vol. 3, 1749-1758, ed. John Telford. First published in 1931; reprint, London: Epworth Press, 1960.

___. *The Letters of the Rev. John Wesley, A.M.,* vol. 4, 1758-1766, ed. John Telford. First published in 1931; reprint, London: Epworth Press, 1960.

___. *The Letters of the Rev. John Wesley, A.M.,* vol. 5, 1766-1772, ed. John Telford. First published in 1931; reprint, London: Epworth Press, 1960.

___. *The Letters of the Rev. John Wesley, A.M.,* vol. 6, 1772-1780, ed. John Telford. First published in 1931; reprint, London: Epworth Press, 1960.

___. *The Letters of the Rev. John Wesley, A.M.,* vol. 7, 1780-1787, ed. John Telford. First published in 1931; reprint, London: Epworth Press, 1960.

___. *The Letters of the Rev. John Wesley, A.M.,* vol. 8, 1787-1791, ed. John Telford. First published in 1931; reprint, London: Epworth Press, 1960.

___. *Wesley's Standard Sermons,* ed. Edward H. Sugden. 6th Edition, vol. 1. London: The Epworth Press, 1966.

___. *The Works of John Wesley,* vol. 25, Oxford Edition, *Letters I (1721-1739),* ed. Frank Baker. Oxford: Clarendon Press, 1980.

___. *The Works of John Wesley,* vol. 26, Oxford Edition, *Letters II (1740-1755),* ed. Frank Baker: Oxford: Clarendon Press, 1982.

___. *The Works of John Wesley,* vol. 1, Bicentennial Edition, *Sermons I, 1-33,*ed. Albert C. Outler. Nashville: Abingdon Press, 1984.

___. *The Works of John Wesley,* vol. 18, Bicentennial Edition, *Journal and Diaries I (1735-1738),* eds. W. Reginald Ward and Richard P. Heitzenrater. Nashville: Abingdon Press, 1988.

___. *The Works of John Wesley,* vol. 19, Bicentennial Edition, *Journal and Diaries II (1738-1743),* eds. W. Reginald Ward and Richard P. Heitzenrater. Nashville: Abingdon Press, 1990.

___. *The Works of John Wesley,* vol. 20, Bicentennial Edition, *Journal and Diaries III (1743-1754),* eds. W. Reginald Ward and Richard P. Heitzenrater. Nashville: Abingdon Press, 1991.

___. *The Works of John Wesley,* vol. 21, Bicentennial Edition, *Journal and Diaries IV (1755-1765),* eds. W. Reginald Ward and Richard P. Heitzenrater. Nashville: Abingdon Press, 1992.

___. *The Works of John Wesley*, vol. 22, Bicentennial Edition, *Journal and Diaries V (1765-1775)*, eds. W. Reginald Ward and Richard P. Heitzenrater. Nashville: Abingdon Press, 1993.

___. *The Works of John Wesley*, vol. 23, Bicentennial Edition, *Journal and Diaries VI (1776-1786)*, eds. W. Reginald Ward and Richard P. Heitzenrater. Nashville: Abingdon Press, 1995.

___. *The Works of John Wesley*, 14 vols., ed. Thomas Jackson. Grand Rapids: Baker Book House, 1978.

Endnotes

1. In listing various works in *A Christian Library* two forms are used. If the name of the original writer is part of the title in Wesley's abridgment, that particular writing is listed with Wesley as the author. If, however, the original writer's name is not part of the title in Wesley's abridgment, the writing is placed under the original author's name with Wesley listed as the editor.

B. Secondary Sources

1. New Testament Greek Resources

Arndt, W. F. and F. W. Gingrich. *A Greek-English Lexicon of the New Testament and Other Early Christian Literature.* Chicago: The University of Chicago Press, 1957.

Cremer, Hermann. *Biblico-Theological Lexicon of New Testament Greek.* 4th edition, 1895; reprint, Edinburgh: T. & T. Clark, 1954.

Liddell, Henry George and Robert Scott. *A Greek-English Lexicon.* New York: Harper & Brothers, 1897; reprint, New York: Oxford University Press, 1983.

Machen, J. Gresham. *New Testament Greek for Beginners.* New York: The Macmillan Company, 1965.

Moulton, James Hope and George Milligan. *The Vocabulary of the Greek Testament: Illustrated from the Papyri and Other Non-Literary Sources.* First published in 1930; reprint, Grand Rapids: Wm. B. Eerdmans Publishing Company, 1985.

Moulton, W. F., A. S. Geden and H. K. Moulton. *A Concordance to the Greek Testament.* Edinburgh: T. & T. Clark, 1984.

Strathmann, Herman. συμμαρτυρέω, vol. 4, *Theological Dictionary of the New Testament*, ed. Gerhard Kittel. Grand Rapids: Wm. B. Eerdmans Publishing Co., 1983.

Trites, A. A. *Witness, Testimony*, vol. 3, *The New International Dictionary of New Testament Theology*, ed. Colin Brown. Grand Rapids: Zondervan Publishing House, 1978.

2. Books

Bainton, Roland H. *Here I Stand: A Life of Martin Luther.* Nashville: Abingdon Press, n.d.; New York: Mentor, First Printing, 1955.

Barclay, William. *The Letter to the Romans,* 2nd ed., The Daily Study Bible Series. Philadelphia: The Westminster Press, 1957.

____. *The Letters to the Galatians and Ephesians,* 2nd ed., The Daily Study Bible Series. Philadelphia: The Westminster Press, 1954.

____. *The Letters of John and Jude.* Edinburgh: The Saint Andrews Press, 1958; reprint, Philadelphia: The Westminster Press, 1960.

Beet, Joseph Agar. *A Commentary on St. Paul's Epistle to the Galatians.* No city or publisher listed, 1897; reprint, Salem, OH: Schmul Publishers, 1981.

____. *A Commentary on St. Paul's Epistle to the Romans.* London: Hodder and Stoughton, 1902; reprint, Salem, OH: Allegheny Publications, 1982.

Bruce, F. F. *The Gospel of John.* Grand Rapids: William B. Eerdmans Publishing Company, 1983.

Calamy, Edmund. *The Nonconformist's Memorial,* 2nd ed., 3 vols. London: Printed for Button and Son, and T. Hurst, Paternoster-Row, 1802-3.

Carter, Charles W. *The First Epistle of Paul to the Corinthians,* vol. 5, *The Wesleyan Bible Commentary.* Grand Rapids: Baker Book House, 1966.

Clarke, Adam. *Clarke's Commentaries,* vol. 6. Nashville: Abingdon Press, n.d.

____. *Christian Theology: Selected from His Published and Unpublished Writings and Systematically Arranged.* 2nd ed. published in 1835; reprint, Salem, OH: Convention Book Store, 1967.

Cole, Alan. *The Epistle of Paul to the Galatians,* vol. 9, *Tyndale New Testament Commentaries,*ed. R. V. G. Tasker. Grand Rapids: Wm. B. Eerdmans Publishing Company, 1965.

Collins, Kenneth J. and John H. Tyson, eds. *Conversion in the Wesleyan Tradition.* Nashville: Abingdon Press, 2001.

Crosby, Fanny. *Worship in Song.* Kansas City, MO: Lillenas Publishing Company, 1972.

Dayton, Wilber T. *The Epistle of Paul to the Romans,* vol. 5, *The Wesleyan Bible Commentary.* Grand Rapids: Baker Book House, 1966.

Dunning, H. Ray. *Grace, Faith, and Holiness: A Wesleyan Systematic Theology.* Kansas City: Beacon Hill Press of Kansas City, 1988.

Findlay, G. G. *The Epistle to the Galatians, The Expositor's Bible.* New York: George H. Doran Company, n.d.

Fitchett, W. H. *Wesley and His Century.* New York: Abingdon Press, 1929 reprint.

Godbey, W. B. *Acts-Romans,* vol. 5, *Commentary on the New Testament.* Cincinnati: Revivalist Office, 1899.

Greathouse, William M. *The Epistle to the Romans,* vol. 8, *Beacon Bible Commentary.* Kansas City: Beacon Hill Press of Kansas City, 1968.

Grider, J. Kenneth. *A Wesleyan-Holiness Theology.* Kansas City: Beacon Hill Press of Kansas City, 1994.

Henry, Matthew A. *Acts to Revelation,* vol. 6, *A Commentary on the Whole Bible.* Old Tappan: Fleming H. Revell Company, n.d.

Howard, Richard E. *Newness of Life: A Study in the Thought of Paul.* Kansas City:

Beacon Hill Press, 1975.

Huxtable, E. *Galatians,* vol. 2, *The Pulpit Commentary,* eds. H. D. M. Spence and Joseph S. Excell. Grand Rapids: Wm. B. Eerdmans Publishing Company, 1953 reprint.

James, William. *The Varieties of Religious Experience: A Study in Human Nature.* First published in 1902; reprint, New York: The Modern Library, 1929.

Maddox, Randy L. *Aldersgate Reconsidered.* Nashville: Kingswood Books, 1990.

Monk, Robert C. *John Wesley: His Puritan Heritage.* Nashville: Abingdon Press, 1966.

Nuttall, Geoffrey F. *The Holy Spirit in Puritan Faith and Experience.* Oxford: Basil Blackwell, 1947.

Oden, Thomas. *Life in the Spirit: Systematic Theology,* vol. 3. Peabody, MA: Prince Press, an imprint of Hendrickson Publishers, 1998.

Packer, J. I. *A Quest for Godliness: The Puritan Vision of the Christian Life.* Wheaton, IL: Crossway Books, 1990.

Pope, William Burt. *A Compendium of Christian Theology: Being Analytical Outlines of a Course of Theological Study, Biblical, Dogmatic, Historical.* New York: Phillips & Hunt, n.d.

Ralston, Thomas N. *Elements of Divinity,* ed. T. O. Summers. First published by Lamar & Barton, 1924; reprint, Salem, OH: Convention Book Store, 1971.

Sanday, William and Arthur C. Headlam. *The Epistle to the Romans, International Critical Commentary.* Edinburgh: T. & T. Clark, 1930.

Smith, William M. *Bible Doctrines.* Westfield, IN: Union Bible Seminary, 1970 reprint.

Starkey, Lycurgus M., Jr. *The Work of the Holy Spirit: A Study in Wesleyan Theology.* Nashville: Abingdon Press, 1962.

Tenney, Merrill C. *Galatians, The Charter of Christian Liberty.* Grand Rapids: Wm. B. Eerdmans Publishing Company, 1950.

Thomas, W. H. Griffith. *St. Paul's Epistle to the Romans.* Grand Rapids: Wm. B. Eerdmans Publishing Company, 1947.

Turner, George Allen. *A Vision Which Transforms.* Kansas City: Beacon Hill Press of Kansas City, 1964.

Turner, George Allen and Julius R. Mantey. *The Gospel According to John,* vol. 4., *The Evangelical Commentary on the Bible.* Grand Rapids: Wm. B. Eerdmans Publishing Company, n.d.

Tuttle, Robert G., Jr. *John Wesley: His Life and Theology.* Grand Rapids: Zondervan Publishing House, 1978

Wakefield, Samuel. *A Complete System of Christian Theology,* vol. 2. New York: Carlton & Porter, 1862; reprint, Salem, OH: Schmul Publishing Co., Inc., 1985.

Watkin-Jones, Howard. *The Holy Spirit from Arminius to Wesley.* London: The Epworth Press, 1929.

Whedon, D. D. *Acts-Romans,* vol. 3, *Commentary on the New Testament.* New York: Nelson & Phillips, 1871; reprint, Salem, OH: Schmul Publishers, 1977.

___. *1 Corinthians-2 Timothy*, vol. 4, *Commentary on the New Testament*. New York: Nelson & Phillips, 1875; reprint, Salem, OH: Schmul Publishers, 1977.

___. *Titus-Revelation*, vol. 5, *Commentary on the New Testament*. New York: Phillips & Hunt, 1880; reprint, Salem, OH: Schmul Publishers, 1978.

Wiley, H. Orton. *Christian Theology*, vol. 2. Kansas City: Beacon Hill Press, 1960 (seventh printing).

Williams, Colin W. *John Wesley's Theology Today*. Nashville: Abingdon Press, 1960.

Winchester,C. T. *The Life of John Wesley*. New York: The Macmillan Company, 1916 reprint.

Yates, Arthur. *The Doctrine of Assurance: With Special Reference to John Wesley*. London: The Epworth Press, 1952.

C. Journals

Collins, Kenneth J. "Twentieth-Century Interpretations of John Wesley's Aldersgate Experience: Coherence or Confusion?" *Wesleyan Theological Journal* 24 (1989).

Cubie, David L. "Placing Aldersgate in John Wesley's Order of Salvation." *Wesleyan Theological Journal* 24 (1989).

Gunter, W. Stephen. "Personal and Spiritual Knowledge: Kindred Spirits in Polanyian and Wesleyan Epistemology." *Wesleyan Theological Journal* 35, No. 1 (Spring 2000).

Hahn, Roger. "Pneumatology in Romans 8: Its Historical and Theological Context." *Wesleyan Theological Journal* 21, Nos. 1 and 2 (Spring-Fall 1986).

Kisker, Scott. "Justified but Unregenerate? The Relationship of Assurance to Justification and Regeneration in the Thought of John Wesley." *Wesleyan Theological Journal* 28, Nos. 1 and 2 (Spring-Fall 1993).

Staples, Rob L. "John Wesley's Doctrine of the Holy Spirit." *Wesleyan Theological Journal* 21, Nos. 1 and 2 (Spring-Fall 1986).

D. Unpublished Works

Benner, Forest T. *The Immediate Antecedents of the Wesleyan Doctrine of the Witness of the Spirit*. Ph.D. dissertation, Temple University, 1966.

Tracy, Wesley D. *The Wesleyan Way to Spiritual Formation: Christian Spirituality in the Letters of John Wesley*. Ph.D. dissertation, San Francisco Theological Seminary, 1987.